Introduction to Networks
of Networks

Introduction to Networks of Networks

Jianxi Gao
Computer Science Department, Rensselaer Polytechnic Institute, Troy, New York, USA

Amir Bashan
Department of Physics, Bar-Ilan University, Ramat-Gan, Israel

Louis Shekhtman
Department of Physics, Bar-Ilan University, Ramat-Gan, Israel

Shlomo Havlin
Department of Physics, Bar-Ilan University, Ramat-Gan, Israel

IOP Publishing, Bristol, UK

© IOP Publishing Ltd 2022

ISBN   978-0-7503-1046-8 (ebook)
ISBN   978-0-7503-1047-5 (print)
ISBN   978-0-7503-1820-4 (myPrint)
ISBN   978-0-7503-1116-8 (mobi)

DOI   10.1088/978-0-7503-1046-8

Version: 20220901

IOP ebooks

British Library Cataloguing-in-Publication Data: A catalogue record for this book is available from the British Library.

Published by IOP Publishing, wholly owned by The Institute of Physics, London

IOP Publishing, Temple Circus, Temple Way, Bristol, BS1 6HG, UK

US Office: IOP Publishing, Inc., 190 North Independence Mall West, Suite 601, Philadelphia, PA 19106, USA

Shlomo Havlin dedicates the book to his dear wife Hava.

Contents

Preface

The essence of network science is the realization that the behavior of many complex systems in nature and technology cannot be understood only by analyzing their components. Rather, the interactions between the components, considered as a network usually, play a critical role in the functioning of the system. Network science, initiated around the year 2000, has successfully formulated methodological frameworks and scientific tools to study complex systems composed of many interacting elements, leading to a deep and detailed understanding of their structural and functional fundamental features. A decade later, in 2010, scientists from diverse fields started to develop mathematical frameworks and study more complex scenarios where the networks themselves are interconnected and dependent on each other, forming *networks of networks*. These systems have also been referred to as interdependent networks, multilayer networks, multiplex networks or multi-dimensional networks.

In this book, we introduce the basic concepts and tools in the developing field of *networks of networks*, reviewing their fundamental features and new properties, while focusing especially on interdependent networks, which are unique since the interactions between the networks (dependency links) are different from the interactions within the networks (connectivity links). The book is intended both for readers who want a broad overview of the field as well as to those who are interested in a deeper exploration of the methods and applications of this new paradigm. To enable readers to dive deeper into the material, we have chosen to maintain the notation in equations from the original manuscripts where the results were published even though this may lead to differing notation throughout the book. We still believe that this supports further delving into the material through the original sources and have made sure to define variables clearly in each section they are used so that confusion will be avoided.

Ramat-Gan, Israel
Boston, MA, USA
January, 2022

Jianxi Gao
Amir Bashan
Louis Shekhtman
Shlomo Havlin

Acknowledgements

We would like to acknowledge all of the researchers who have contributed to the study of networks of networks including Ginestra Bianconi, Jose Mendes, Sergey Dorogovtsev, Gareth Baxter, Stefano Boccaletti, Vito Latora, Yamir Moreno, Jesus Gomez Gardenes, Alex Arenas, Jurgen Kurths, Mason Porter, James Gleeson, Mikko Kivela, Marc Barthelemy, Kwang Il-Goh, Byungnam Kahng, Peter Mucha, Raissa Dsouza, Janos Kertesz, and many others. We further thank our numerous collaborators in this field including Ivan Bonamassa, Michael Danziger, Yehiel Berezin, Sergey Buldyrev, Bnaya Gross, Dana Vaknin, Lidia Braunstein, Roni Parshani, Ronny Bartsch, Plamen Ivanov, Orr Levy, Alex Smolyak, Stefano Boccaletti, Yanqung Hu, Dror Kenett, Nadav Shnerb, Gene Stanley, Dong Zhou, Gaogao Dong, Reuven Cohen, Xin Yuan, Jingfang Fan, Lucas Valdez, Daqing Li, Xueming Liu, Xuqing Huang and many more.

Author biographies

Jianxi Gao

Dr Jianxi Gao has been an assistant professor in the Computer Science Department at Rensselaer Polytechnic Institute since 2017. Prior to joining the Computer Science at RPI, he was a Research Assistant Professor at the Center for Complex Network Research at Northeastern University, working with Prof. Albert-László Barabási. Dr Gao got his PhD degree in the Department of Automation at Shanghai Jiao Tong University in 2012. During his PhD studies from 2009 to 2012, he visited Prof. H. Eugene. Stanley in the Physics Department at Boston University, as well as Prof. Shlomo Havlin in the Physics Department at Bar-Ilan University in 2012. He received the NSF CAREER Award in 2021 to study the resilience of complex networks. His research focuses on using network theory, control theory, statistic physics, and operation research to understand, predict, and ultimately control complex systems' resilience and cascading failures in networks of networks. He has published over 80 papers in journals, such as *Nature, Nature Physics, Nature Ecology & Evolution, Nature Communications, Proceedings of the National Academy of Sciences, Physical Review Letters*, and more, and conferences such as AAAI, KDD, and IJCAI, with over 5000 citations on Google Scholar. Dr Gao has also been selected as the Editor board of *Scientific Reports and Physica* A, external editor of *PNAS*, distinguished referee of *EPL* and Elsevier.

Amir Bashan

Dr Amir Bashan is a principal investigator and senior-lecturer in the department of physics in Bar-Ilan university (BIU), Israel, since 2016. He completed his PhD studies in physics and network science in BIU, under the guidance of Prof. Shlomo Havlin in 2013. He then did postdoctoral research in the Channing Division of Network Medicine, Brigham and Women's Hospital and Harvard Medical School, Boston, USA, in the group of Prof. Yang-Yu Liu. Dr Bashan focuses on utilizing mathematical modeling and network theory and developing new computational methods to analyze heterogeneous high-throughput biological data, aiming to uncover general underlying principles that govern the functioning of large, complex systems.

Louis Shekhtman

Dr Louis Shekhtman is an Associate Research Scientist at Northeastern University. Dr Shekhtman finished his undergraduate studies at Northwestern Univeristy majoring in Physics and Integrated Science. He completed his PhD in Physics at Bar-Ilan University in 2020 under Prof. Shlomo Havlin. His research is focused on network science, viral dynamics, statistic physics, and most recently, philanthropic networks. He has published over 30 papers in top peer-reviewed journals, including *Proceedings of the National Academy of Sciences, Science Translational Medicine, eLife, National Science Review*, and others

Shlomo Havlin

Professor Shlomo Havlin has made fundamental contributions to the physics of complex systems and statistical physics. These discoveries have impacted many other fields such as medicine, biology, geophysics, and more. He has over 60,000 citations on ISI Web of Science and over 100,000 in Google Scholar. His h-index is 111 (140) in Web of Science (Google Scholar). Havlin has been a Highly Cited Scientist in the last three years.

He is a professor in the Physics Department at Bar-Ilan University. He received his PhD in 1972 from Bar Ilan University and he has been a professor at BIU since 1984. Also, between the years of 1999–2001 he was the Dean of the Faculty of Exact Sciences and from 1996–1999 he was the President of the Israel Physical Society.

Havlin won the Israel prize in Physics (2018), Order of the Star of Italy, President of Italy (2017), the Rothschild Prize for Physical and Chemical Sciences, Israel (2014), the Lilienfeld Prize for 'a most outstanding contribution to physics', APS, USA (2010), the Humboldt Senior Award, Germany (2006), the Distinguished Scientist Award, Chinese Academy of Sciences (2017), the Weizmann Prize for Exact Sciences, Israel (2009), the Nicholson Medal, American Physical Society, USA (2006) and many others.

His main research interests are in the field of statistical physics and complex networks, with a recent focus on interdependent networks, cascading failures, networks of networks and their implications to real-world problems. The real-world systems he studied include physiology, climate, infrastructures, finance, traffic, earthquakes and others.

IOP Publishing

Introduction to Networks of Networks

Jianxi Gao, Amir Bashan, Louis Shekhtman and Shlomo Havlin

Chapter 1

Basic concepts of single networks

1.1 Introduction

Networks, sets of nodes connected by links, can describe diverse systems, such as the Internet, the brain and our social interactions [1–35]. The Internet is a network where the nodes represent routers and the links are the cables between them. In the brain, nodes and links represent neurons and the synapses connecting them. In a social network, people are represented by nodes and the relationships between them are represented by links. The original mathematical model for networks, called random graph theory, was developed and systematically studied in the 1960s by the mathematicians Erdős and Rényi [36, 37]. It is worth noting though that several basic ideas of graph theory were actually discussed even earlier, in particular, by Rapoport [38]. However, only after the systematic analytical studies of Erdős and Rényi (ER) did random graph theory begin to receive much attention. The ER network model is based on the assumption that each pair of nodes has an equal probability to be connected with a link, leading to a Poissonian distribution in the number of links per node (degree) [36–39]. In parallel, other network topologies have been studied. Solid state physicists usually considered and studied lattice networks [40, 41], where each node has exactly the same number of links and the networks are embedded in d-dimensional Euclidean space. In addition, tree-like (non-embedded) structures, usually referred to as Cayley trees [41, 42], have also been studied to model physical systems, e.g., branched polymers. ER networks essentially equated complexity with randomness and have occupied the scientific literature since their introduction.

While graph theory is a well-established tool in mathematics and computer science, it is a poor descriptor of many modern real-world networks. Indeed, two seminal papers, one in *Nature* in 1998 by Watts and Strogatz [3] on small-world networks and the other in *Science* in 1999 by Barabasi and Albert [1] on scale-free networks, triggered the emergence of a new science—network science, which studies the properties of complex networks. These pioneering observations indicated that many real networks do not follow the ER model but rather that other fundamental organizing principles underlie many real systems.

doi:10.1088/978-0-7503-1046-8ch1

The science of complex networks grew in the beginning of the 21st century into an exciting and active area in many scientific disciplines. The new interdisciplinary field of network science [1–35] has received much attention and experienced many achievements, spanning from a better understanding of structural network properties, dynamic behaviors, and the interplay between structure and function. These achievements have been enabled by the fact that large-scale (big) data regarding social [57–65], economic [25, 61, 66–68], technological [66, 69–75], and biological [10, 11, 76–79] systems has been gathered, modeled and analyzed by applying network science tools. These modelling efforts have led to achievements in understanding the spread of epidemics [43–45], improving transportation systems [29, 46–49], improving system robustness [32], identifying organizing laws of social interactions such as friendships [50, 51] or scientific collaborations [52, 53], understanding climate phenomena such as El Niño [54–56] and determining the relationship between function and structure in physiological systems [30]. This was made possible by the information and communication revolution brought about by the rapid increase in computing power. The investigation and growing understanding of this extraordinary amount of data and the development of new models which are more closely related to real-world phenomena will hopefully enable us to make, among other advances, the infrastructures that we all use every day more efficient and robust [80]. Due to the numerous models developed, this chapter is unable to cover every aspect of networks. Rather it aims to briefly introduce the key features of networks and provide references for readers to delve deeper into areas they might be interested in.

1.2 Degree distribution—how networks are structured?

1.2.1 Types of networks

Complex networks appear in almost every aspect of science, nature and technology. While networks, in general, have diverse topologies, four common and basic model topologies frequently considered as model examples for the theoretical analysis are: lattices, random regular networks, random networks, and scale-free networks.

Lattice networks are spatially embedded graphs where each node has the same number of neighbors, i.e., each node has the same degree and the links are between nearest neighbors in space, as shown in figure 1.1(a). Note that in contrast to other

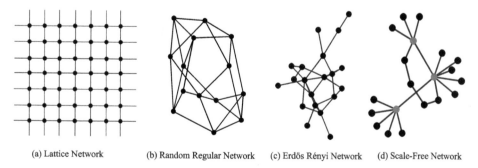

(a) Lattice Network   (b) Random Regular Network   (c) Erdős Rényi Network   (d) Scale-Free Network

Figure 1.1. Illustration of four typical network topologies: (a) lattice network, (b) random regular network, (c) Erdős Rényi network, and (d) scale-free network. In (d), the red nodes are the hubs (high degree nodes).

types of networks discussed here, the lattice network has spatial constraints since it is embedded in real space with short range links between neighboring nodes in Euclidean space. Random regular (RR) networks, demonstrated in figure 1.1(b), are random graphs where each node has the same degree.

As mentioned earlier, ER networks, also known as random graphs, were introduced and systematically analyzed by Erdős and Rényi [36, 37, 39]. The canonical ER model assumes that the network is constructed by connecting any pair of nodes chosen randomly with the same probability r. An example is shown in figure 1.1(c). The degree distribution of ER networks is Poisson.

The term 'scale-free network' (SF) was coined by Barabasi and Albert in 1999. They (and later others) discovered that many real networks often follow an approximate power-law form in their degree distribution, as demonstrated in figure 1.1(d). Some real-world networks, which can be approximated as SF networks, include the Internet [4], the WWW [5], social networks representing personal relationships between individuals [57–65], transportation networks such as airline flights [81], networks in biology [10, 11, 76, 77, 82], networks of protein–protein interactions [12], gene regulation [83], and biochemical pathways [84], and networks in physics, such as polymer networks or the potential energy landscape network [85].

1.2.2 Degree and degree distributions

The degree, k, of a node in a network is the number of neighbours or links it has to other nodes. In the small network shown in figure 1.2, there are six nodes connected to node i in the center, so $k_i = 6$.

The degree distribution is the probability distribution of the individual nodes' degrees in the whole network. It is common in analyzing networks to plot the degree distribution, or the fraction of nodes with a given degree k. In a random network, we assume that all N nodes in the network are randomly assigned a degree k from a given probability distribution $P(k)$ [86]. Figure 1.3 illustrates that regular and random regular networks have a degree distribution represented by a delta function,

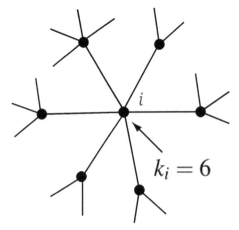

Figure 1.2. Demonstration of node degree.

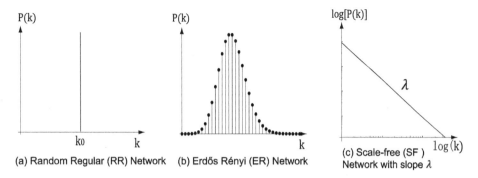

Figure 1.3. Degree distribution characteristics of different networks. (a) Random regular (RR) network, (b) Erdős Rényi (ER) network, and (c) scale-free (SF) network with slope λ.

δ_{k,k_0}, where all nodes have the same degree, k_0. ER networks follow a Poissonian degree distribution, and scale-free networks follow a power-law degree distribution.

The mathematical description of the degree distributions of these three types of networks is as follows.

The degree distribution of random regular networks (figure 1.3(a)) is

$$P(k) = \delta(k - k_0) = \begin{cases} 1 & \text{if} \quad k = k_0 \\ 0 & \text{else} \end{cases} \tag{1.1}$$

The degree distribution of ER networks (figure 1.3(b)) is

$$P(k) = \binom{N-1}{k} r^k (1 - r)^{N-1-k}, \tag{1.2}$$

and when the number of nodes, $N \to \infty$ it is Poissonian,

$$P(k) = \frac{c^k e^{-c}}{k!}, \tag{1.3}$$

where $c = \bar{k}$ is the average degree.

The degree distribution of SF networks (figure 1.3(c)) scales as a power law

$$P(k) \sim k^{-\lambda}. \tag{1.4}$$

The scale-free degree distribution, equation (1.4), may be defined between $k = m$ the minimal value of k to $k = M$, the maximal value of k, allowing for a full description.

The graphical representations of the above distributions (1.1)–(1.4) are shown in figure 1.3.

1.2.3 Generating functions

We next introduce the method of generating functions which is very useful for calculating global network properties. The generating function of the degree distribution is given by

$$G(z) = \sum_{k=0}^{\infty} P(k)z^k, \tag{1.5}$$

where z is an arbitrary complex variable. The average degree of the network $\bar{k}$ can be written as

$$\bar{k} \equiv \sum kP(k) = G'(1). \tag{1.6}$$

In the limit of an infinitely large network, $N \to \infty$, the random connection process of nodes in the network can be modeled as a branching process, in which an outgoing link from any node has a probability $kP(k)/\bar{k}$ of being connected to a node with degree k, which in turn has $k - 1$ outgoing links. The generating function of this branching process is defined as [87–90],

$$H(z) \equiv \frac{\sum_{k=0}^{\infty} P(k)kz^{k-1}}{\bar{k}} = \frac{G'(z)}{G'(1)}. \tag{1.7}$$

The generating functions of the three types of networks discussed above (figure 1.1(b)–(d)) are as follows. The generating functions of RR networks are

$$G(z) = z^k \tag{1.8}$$

and

$$H(z) = z^{k-1}. \tag{1.9}$$

The generating functions of ER networks are

$$G(z) = \exp[\bar{k}(z - 1)] \tag{1.10}$$

and

$$H(z) = \exp[\bar{k}(z - 1)]. \tag{1.11}$$

The generating functions for SF networks when the continuous power-law is discretized are [91]

$$G(z) = \frac{\sum_{m}^{M}\left[(k + 1)^{1-\lambda} - k^{1-\lambda}\right]z^k}{(M + 1)^{1-\lambda} - m^{1-\lambda}} \tag{1.12}$$

and

$$H(z) = \frac{\sum_{m}^{M}k\left[(k + 1)^{1-\lambda} - k^{1-\lambda}\right]z^{k-1}}{[(M + 1)^{1-\lambda} - m^{1-\lambda}]\bar{k}}. \tag{1.13}$$

Table 1.1. Degree distribution and generating functions of three different network topologies. N is the number of nodes in the network. For SF networks, $m \leqslant k \leqslant M$, and m, M are the minimum and maximum degrees, respectively. For random SF networks $M \ll N^{1/2}$ without considering multi-links and self-links [92].

	Regular network	ER network	SF network
$P(k)$	$P(k) = 1$	$P(k) = \binom{N-1}{k} r^k (1 - r)^{N-1-k}$	$P(k) \sim k^{-\lambda}$
$G(x)$	x^k	$\exp[\bar{k}(x - 1)]$	$\dfrac{\sum_m^M [(k+1)^{1-\lambda} - k^{1-\lambda}]x^k}{(M+1)^{1-\lambda} - m^{1-\lambda}}$
$H(x)$	$(x)^{k-1}$	$\exp[\bar{k}(x - 1)]$	$\dfrac{\sum_m^M k[(k+1)^{1-\lambda} - k^{1-\lambda}]x^{k-1}}{[(M+1)^{1-\lambda} - m^{1-\lambda}]<k>}$

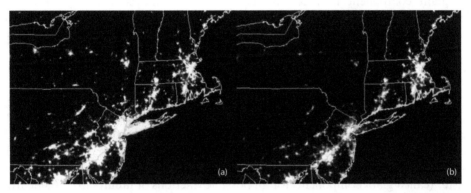

Figure 1.4. A satellite map of the US Northeastern blackout in 2003: (a) before the blackout and (b) after the blackout. The satellite map represents a real image of the US on August 14, 2003, the night of a major blackout that left an estimated 45 million people in eight U.S. states and another 10 million people in Ontario without power. Image courtesy of NOAA.

In the subsequent chapters, we will return to these results and use them to determine the stability and other properties of various networks (table 1.1).

1.3 Percolation transition—how a network collapses?

Robustness is an especially important property when it comes to infrastructures, and it is thus important that we understand and quantify their robustness in the presence of node and link failures. Empirical observations show that failures can occur in most infrastructure networks, such as those that occurred in the 2003 blackout in America, shown in figure 1.4. To determine how network structure and function can affect such failures, researchers have borrowed ideas from areas of statistical physics, such as percolation theory, phase transitions, fractals and scaling analysis.

Percolation theory from statistical physics focuses on the connectivity patterns of networks, specifically clusters of nodes that can all be reached from one another. Most interest has focused on the relative size of the largest cluster, i.e., the fraction of nodes in the largest (giant) component, P_∞, which serves as a measure of the functionality of the network. For example, it can represent how many power stations are connected to the grid, how many locations are reachable via flights, and how many routers are connected to the internet. Robustness of a network can be quantified by how resilient the size of the giant component is after a fraction of nodes fail.

As the fraction of failed nodes increases, the size of the giant component decreases. For some critical value of failed nodes, the giant component vanishes and no large sets of connected nodes remain in the network. This is referred to as the critical threshold [6, 9, 19]. As shown in figure 1.5, when we remove nodes in the network, it leads to a decrease of average degree and consequently the fraction of nodes in the giant component drops as well. When $\bar{k} \leq 1 \equiv \bar{k}_{min}$ the network is at or below its critical point. Below this point, the giant component collapses and does not scale with the network size but rather $P_\infty = 0$ for an infinite system. Since the size of the giant component is a continuous function of the connectivity, it can be determined that the system undergoes a second-order phase transition. An analogous description of this process can arise by randomly removing a fraction of $1 - p$ nodes in the network. As for the case of decreasing $\bar{k}$, there exists a critical p, $p_c = 1/k$, and when $p < p_c$ there is no giant component, i.e., $P_\infty = 0$. See sections 1.3.2 and 1.3.3 for details on the analytic results.

The robustness of a network is usually characterized by the value of the critical threshold fraction of failures leading to the collapse of the network which is the percolation threshold and can be analyzed using percolation theory [9, 19, 41, 93]. Smaller values of the critical threshold imply greater system robustness. The robustness is also characterized by the integrated size of the largest connected cluster (called giant component) for all possible fractions of failures [32]. Aside from failures of nodes, percolation was also proven useful for addressing other scenarios, such as epidemic spreading [43], efficient attacks, localized attacks, or immunization strategies [7, 8, 16, 94–97], obtaining optimal paths [98] as well as for designing robust networks [32].

1.3.1 Failure and attack

Network disintegration can occur in different ways ranging from random failures to targeted attacks, each of which can affect failures of links or nodes. Figures 1.6(a) and (c) show the original network, and figures 1.6(b) and (d) demonstrate the remaining topologies of the network after node failures and link failures, respectively. It is worth mentioning also that attacks on nodes and links can be regarded as immunization or quarantine strategies in the case of epidemics [19, 95]. In this book, we will mainly focus on node failures, however, results for link failures or combined failures are typically very similar.

Node failures mean that some nodes lose their functionality or are removed from the network, leading the original network to have disjoint components, see figure 1.6. Usually we assume that only nodes in the giant component can function, and thus all nodes that become disconnected from the giant component are regarded as failed nodes.

As discussed above, usually there are two types of node failures in a network: (i) random failures such as when some power stations of the power grid experience

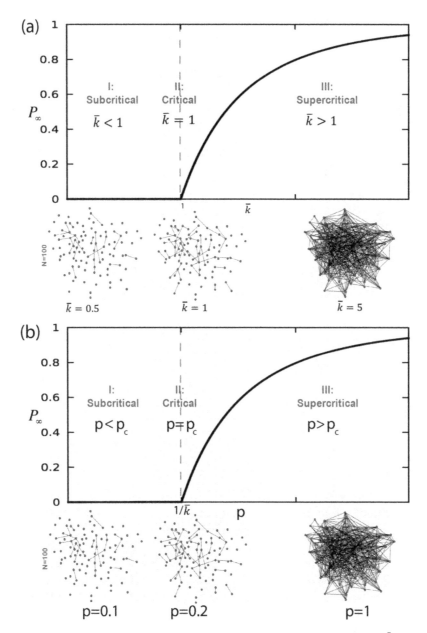

Figure 1.5. Robustness of a single ER network. (a) For an ER network with average degree $\bar{k} = 5$, there is a giant connected component. As $\bar{k}$ is decreased the giant component decreases continuously until $\bar{k}$ reaches 1, which is the critical point for ER networks. When $\bar{k} < 1$, the giant component becomes a zero fraction of the original network and disappears. (b) Similar to (a), for an ER network with average degree $\bar{k} = 5$, when $p = 1$ there is a giant connected component in the network. When we remove more than a fraction of $1 - 1/\bar{k}$ nodes, there is no longer a giant component in the network.

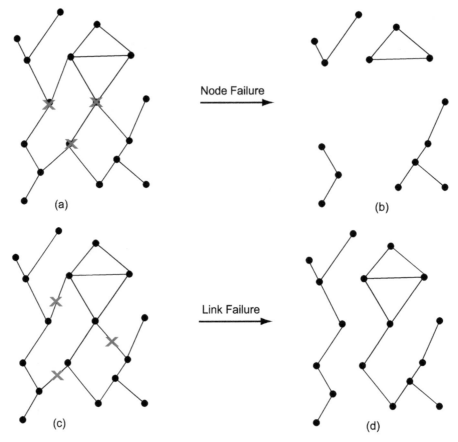

Figure 1.6. Node failures and link failures (or immunization) in a network may lead to the breaking of the network into smaller components (or herd immunization). Note that when nodes fail, their links also fail.

random technical failures (preventing them from providing electricity) and (ii) targeted attack on central nodes such as high degree nodes, e.g. central websites in the Internet being hacked. Recently, a new type of failures called 'localized attacks' was introduced in [96, 99, 100], see figure 1.7. In real-world scenarios, initial failures are in many cases due to targeted attack rather than random failures. Results on scale-free networks show that the robustness of a network is greatly reduced in cases of an attack on high degree nodes [5, 7, 8, 16, 101], localized attack [96, 99] or attacks on high betweenness nodes [84].

1.3.2 Calculating the size of the giant component

When nodes in a network are removed randomly or through targeting, the network will eventually become fragmented into many disjoint connected clusters, called components, see figure 1.6. In the initial state, figure 1.6(a), there can also be only a single component where the network is well connected or in the trivial case where each node is connected to all other nodes (complete graph). At the other extreme, if the

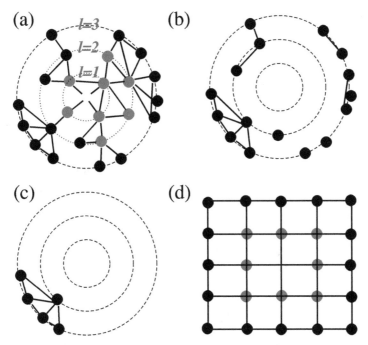

Figure 1.7. Schematic illustration of the localized attack process. (a) A fraction $1 - p$ of the nodes are chosen to be removed, starting from the root node, its nearest neighbors, next nearest neighbors, and so on (yellow represents the root node and red the other removed). (b) After removing the chosen nodes and their links, an attacked 'hole' centered around the root node is formed. (c) Only nodes in the giant component (largest cluster) remain functioning and are left in the network. (d) Localized attack on a regular lattice (here, square lattice). For a regular lattice with $N \rightarrow \infty$, one needs to attack all nodes in order for the network to collapse, i.e., $p_c \rightarrow 0$. Note, however, that if one removes a line or column of nodes the network breaks apart so for that particular type of localized attack, $p_c = 1$. Reproduced from [96], copyright 2015 The Authors. Published by IOP Publishing Ltd on behalf of the Institute of Physics and Deutsche Physikalische Gesellschaft.

network is composed of N isolated nodes, then the network has N components. In network theory, the giant component is the connected component that contains the largest number of nodes and whose size is a finite fraction of the original network of size N. We denote the fraction of nodes in the giant component of the network as P_∞. For example, the giant component in figure 1.6(b) is $P_\infty = 5/17$ and in figure 1.6(d) it is $P_\infty = 10/17$. Usually we will assume that only nodes belonging to the giant component are functional. This is since functionality often requires that every node can communicate with all other nodes such as in a communication network.

To calculate the size of the giant component, we will continue our analysis using generating functions. Let f be the probability that a randomly selected link does not lead to the giant component. If a link leads to a node with $k - 1$ outgoing links this probability is f^{k-1}. Thus, $H(f)$ in equation (1.7) also has the meaning that a randomly selected link does not lead to the giant component and hence f satisfies the recursive relation equation $f = H(z)$. The probability that a node with degree k does not belong to the giant component is f^k and hence the probability that a randomly selected node belongs to the giant component is $g = 1 - G(f)$. Once a fraction $1 - p$ of nodes is randomly removed from a random network, the generating function remains the same, but with a new argument $z = 1 + fp - p$. Accordingly, the probability that a randomly chosen node belongs to the giant component is given by [87–90, 102, 103],

$$P_\infty = pg = p(1 - G(z)) \tag{1.14}$$

and

$$f = H(z). \tag{1.15}$$

For a lattice network, where spatial embedding also plays an important role in the robustness, there is no analytical solution, but one can obtain the size of the giant component through numerical simulations. According to equations (1.1), (1.14) and (1.15) the giant component of RR networks is

$$P_\infty = p\left\{1 - \left[1 - p + p\left(1 - \frac{P_\infty}{p}\right)^{(k-1)/k}\right]^k\right\}, \tag{1.16}$$

and the giant component of ER networks is

$$P_\infty = p[1 - \exp(-\bar{k}P_\infty)]. \tag{1.17}$$

The giant component of SF networks is [6]

$$P_\infty = p\left[1 - \sum_{k=0}^{\infty} P(k)u^k\right], \tag{1.18}$$

where $u = H_1(1)$ is the smallest positive root of

$$u = 1 - p + \frac{p}{\langle k \rangle} \sum_{k=0}^{\infty} kP(k)u^{k-1}. \tag{1.19}$$

An illustrative figure of the giant components as a function of the fraction of non-removed nodes p for these four types of networks is shown in figure 1.8.

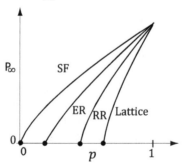

Figure 1.8. Demonstration of the giant components and the critical thresholds for random failures of four different types of networks with the same average degree. The black dots are the critical thresholds for the four networks. Note that networks with lower p_c are more robust. The lattice, due to spatial constraints, is more vulnerable compared to all other examples shown with the same average degree.

1.3.3 Calculating the critical threshold

In a random network, the removal of a small fraction of $1 - p$ randomly chosen nodes leads to a small amount of damage to the giant component P_∞ (see figure 1.5(b)). As p further decreases, there exists a critical threshold p_c, where the giant component reaches 0. For $p < p_c$, there is no giant component, while for $p > p_c$, the giant component emerges, see figure 1.8.

We now obtain p_c analytically by analyzing equation (1.15). According to equation (1.15) and $z = 1 + fp - p$, by eliminating f we obtain a recursive equation with only z,

$$\frac{1}{p} = \frac{1 - H(z)}{1 - z}. \tag{1.20}$$

We know that the system undergoes a second-order phase transition meaning that when $p = p_c$, $P_\infty = 0 = 1 - G(z)$. Using the definition of $G(z)$ in equation (1.5), we see that when $G(z) = 1$ then $z = 1$. When $z \to 1$ and $H(1) = 1$, the rhs of equation (1.20) becomes $H'(1)$, yielding

$$p_c = 1/H'(1). \tag{1.21}$$

Using equations (1.7) and (1.21), we obtain [6]

$$H'(1) = 1/(\kappa - 1), \tag{1.22}$$

where $\kappa = \langle k^2 \rangle / \bar{k}$. Thus, we obtain the critical thresholds for the three types of networks as follows.

For RR networks, $\kappa = k$, and the critical threshold is

$$p_c = \frac{1}{k - 1}. \tag{1.23}$$

For ER networks, $\kappa = \bar{k} + 1$ and the critical threshold is

$$p_c = 1/\bar{k}. \tag{1.24}$$

For SF networks when $\lambda \in (2, 3]$, $\kappa \to \infty$, and the critical threshold is $p_c = 0$. For $\lambda > 3$, κ is a finite value, and p_c is given by $p_c = 1 - (((\lambda - 2)/(\lambda - 3))m - 1)^{-1}$, where m is the minimum degree of the network [6].

1.4 Further network properties

The general framework described above has focused on the basic connectivity patterns of the network, most importantly the degrees of the nodes. However, there are several more advanced network properties that we will also consider in this book, as they too also often affect the properties of networks and networks of networks. We describe these here in brief.

The first property incorporates the fact that in many networks there are correlations between the degrees of two connected nodes. For example, in some networks it might be more likely for higher degree nodes to connect to one another more than to lower degree nodes. This is referred to as *degree–degree correlations* or *assortativity* [104, 105]. A second property, relates to the tendency of nodes to form triangles. In this sense, if a node is connected to two other nodes, there is often an increased likelihood for those two nodes to be connected to one another. For example, two friends of mine have a high likelihood to also be friends with one another. This property is called *clustering* and is especially common in social networks, though it is also present in many other networks [106]. Another property directly related to the connectivity of individual nodes is the existence of a so-called 'core' of nodes of high connectivity that are highly connected to one another. Such cores are typically found using the 'k-core' or 'k-shell' algorithm [107, 108], which works as follows. For some given value of k all nodes with degree lower than k are removed. In the reduced network the degree of each node is again calculated and once again, all nodes with fewer than k connections to other nodes in the reduced network are removed. This process starts from $k = 1$ and is repeated iteratively until all remaining nodes have at least k connections to other remaining nodes.

A network property that occurs at a slightly higher level is the existence of *communities* or groups of nodes that are tightly connected to one another, but with many fewer connections to nodes in other communities [50, 109–114]. Most of the studies in this direction have focused on identifying and grouping nodes into communities. In contrast, our main question here will focus on how community structure affects the properties of networks of networks, and in particular their robustness.

Another aspect, that will be considered in some sections of the book is the existence of *weights* on the links [115, 116]. For example, in the context of a transportation network, the weight could be the speed or the number of cars passing through a given road segment in some period of time. In many networks, the weights are highly important as they can be used to identify locations of holdups or other issues in the network that should be improved.

Finally, we mention a few properties related to paths on the network. In this sense, we are typically most interested in the *shortest path* between two given nodes. If the network is weighted, the shortest path can also incorporate any information related to the weights in which case it is regarded as an optimal path. The shortest or optimal paths are important because they inform us how information is most likely to travel and in the context of many networks such as electricity, transportation and other infrastructures, they can be used to predict traffic. Another measure, which is derived from the shortest paths is the *betweenness* which measures what fraction of shortest paths between all pairs of nodes pass through a given node or edge [117, 118]. The betweenness is often used to quantify the 'load' on a given node or edge and can be used to assess whether the node might be 'overworked' or 'overloaded' with traffic or flow [119, 120].

1.5 Spatial networks

A final property that has key effects on networks of networks is the fact that many networks are embedded in space [27]. Spatial networks are unique since the nodes each have spatial locations and links typically connect nearby nodes, which has important effects on the overall network structure and function. For example, in such networks the mean distance between nodes will often scale as $N^{1/d}$ where N is the number of nodes and d is the dimension. This is in contrast to the small-world nature of random networks where the mean distance scales logarithmically with N [3]. The simplest spatial networks are lattices that have been studied extensively in the physics literature. As such, the generating functions approach used above for random networks does not apply to spatial networks since the links between nodes are highly non-random, and instead constrained by space.

One recent model of spatial networks is referred to as the ζ-model and was proposed in Danziger *et al* [121, 122]. In this model, the lattice sites are regarded as network nodes, thereby also implying the distance from any given node to another node. Then links are randomly added between nodes of a given distance l apart. In order to control for spatial effects, the values of l are chosen from an exponential distribution such that

$$P(l) \sim e^{-l/\zeta}, \tag{1.25}$$

where ζ will control the typical length of a link. This model allows for simple control of the average degree in the network—as one can simply randomly sample larger distances of links to add—and also provides an easily tuneable parameter to control the spatial effects. Indeed if ζ approaches to the maximum distance between nodes (the size of the embedding space—lattice size), then the connections become roughly random and results for random networks are valid. Using this model, it was shown that spatial networks tend to have a larger value of p_c as ζ decreases, thus being more vulnerable, than does a random network with equivalent average degree [121]. This is due to the lack of long-range links in spatial networks, which enhance the connectivity between distance regions in a random network and increase the robustness.

A further aspect of spatial features could model a system of multiple cities with many nodes well connected within a city (leading to short distances or times to get from one place to another within a city) and then having a few long-range links to other neighboring cities. This is essentially a spatial network of communities where the communities are random networks. Such a model was considered in [123] where communities were created with pairs linked randomly within each community and then with links between communities being only between nearest neighbors (see figure 1.9). This model was shown to undergo two distinct transitions as the number of failures increases. In the first stage, the communities (or cities) become separated and then at the second stage, at a second lower p_c, the individual communities break down.

Furthermore, when dealing with spatial networks, there are also different types of failure scenarios that are worth considering, such as localized failures [99] where all the nodes in a given region fail together. Due to the crucial impact of spatial features in networks of networks, we dedicate chapter 5 to their analysis and provide details on localized attacks there.

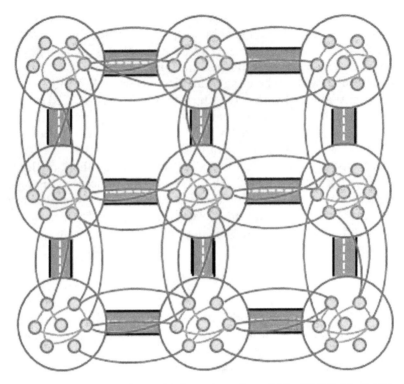

Figure 1.9. Spatial modular networks model. Reproduced from [123], CC BY 4.0. Published by IOP Publishing Ltd on behalf of the Institute of Physics and Deutsche Physikalische Gesellschaft.

References

[1] Barabási A and Albert R 1999 Emergence of scaling in random networks *Science* **286** 509–12

[2] Watts D J 2002 A simple model of global cascades on random networks *Proc. Natl. Acad. Sci. USA* **99** 5766

[3] Watts D J and Strogatz S H 1998 Collective dynamics of 'small-world' networks *Nature* **393** 440–2

[4] Faloutsos M, Faloutsos P and Faloutsos C 1999 On power-law relationships of the internet topology *ACM SIGCOMM Comput. Commun. Rev.* **29** 251–62

[5] Albert R, Jeong H and Barabási A 2000 Error and attack tolerance of complex networks *Nature* **406** 378–82

[6] Cohen R, Erez K, Ben-Avraham D and Havlin S 2000 Resilience of the internet to random breakdown *Phys. Rev. Lett.* **85** 4626–8

[7] Callaway D S, Newman M E J, Strogatz S H and Watts D J 2000 Network robustness and fragility: percolation on random graphs *Phys. Rev. Lett.* **85** 5468

[8] Cohen R, Erez K, Ben-Avraham D and Havlin S 2001 Breakdown of the internet under intentional attack *Phys. Rev. Lett.* **86** 3682–5

[9] Newman M E J 2010 *Networks: An Introduction* (Oxford: Oxford University Press)

[10] Dorogovtsev S N and Mendes J FF 2003 *Evolution of Networks: From Biological Nets to the Internet and WWW (Physics)* (New York: Oxford University Press)

[11] Milo R, Shen-Orr S, Itzkovitz S, Kashtan N, Chklovskii D and Aron U 2002 Network motifs: simple building blocks of complex networks *Science* **298** 824–7

[12] Albert R and Barabási A-L 2002 Statistical mechanics of complex networks *Rev. Mod. Phys.* **74** 47–97

[13] Newman M E J 2003 The structure and function of complex networks *SIAM Rev.* **45** 167–256

[14] Barrat A, Barthelemy M, Pastor-Satorras R and Vespignani A 2004 The architecture of complex weighted networks *Proc. Natl. Acad. Sci.* **101** 3747–52

[15] Newman M E J and Girvan M 2004 Finding and evaluating community structure in networks *Phys. Rev.* E **69** 026113

[16] Gallos L K, Cohen R, Argyrakis P, Bunde A and Havlin S 2005 Stability and topology of scale-free networks under attack and defense strategies *Phys. Rev. Lett.* **94** 188701

[17] Song C, Havlin S and Makse H A 2005 Self-similarity of complex networks *Nature* **433** 392–5

[18] Boccaletti S, Latora V, Moreno Y, Chavez M and Hwang D-U 2006 Complex networks: structure and dynamics *Phys. Rep.* **424** 175–308

[19] Cohen R and Havlin S 2010 *Complex Networks: Structure, Robustness and Function* (Cambridge: Cambridge University Press)

[20] Newman M, Barabási A-L and Watts D J 2006 *The structure and dynamics of networks* (Princeton, NJ: Princeton University Press)

[21] Satorras A and Vespignani R P 2004 *Evolution and Structure of the Internet: A Statistical Physics Approach* (Cambridge: Cambridge University Press)

[22] Caldarelli A and Vespignani G 2007 *Large Scale Structure and Dynamics of Complex Webs* (New York: World Scientific)

[23] Barrat A, Barthelemy M and Vespignani A 2008 *Dynamical Processes on Complex Networks* vol 1 (Cambridge: Cambridge University Press)

[24] West B J and Grigolini P 2011 *Complex Webs: Anticipating the Improbable* (Cambridge: Cambridge University Press)

[25] Bonanno G, Caldarelli G, Lillo F and Mantegna R N 2003 Topology of correlation-based minimal spanning trees in real and model markets *Phys. Rev.* E **68** 046130

[26] Daqing L, Kosmidis K, Bunde A and Havlin S 2011 Dimension of spatially embedded networks *Nat. Phys.* **7** 481–4

[27] Barthélemy M 2011 Spatial networks *Phys. Rep.* **499** 1–101

[28] Strogatz S H 2001 Exploring complex networks *Nature* **410** 268–76

[29] Li G, Reis S D S, Moreira A A, Havlin S, Stanley H E and Andrade J S Jr+ 2010 Towards design principles for optimal transport networks *Phys. Rev. Lett.* **104** 018701

[30] Bashan A, Bartsch R P, Kantelhardt J W, Havlin S and Ivanov P Ch 2012 Network physiology reveals relations between network topology and physiological function *Nat. Commun.* **3** 702

[31] Kitsak M, Gallos L K, Havlin S, Liljeros F, Muchnik L, Stanley H E and Makse H A 2010 Identification of influential spreaders in complex networks *Nat. Phys.* **6** 888–93

[32] Schneider C M, Moreira A A, Andrade J S, Havlin S and Herrmann H J 2011 Mitigation of malicious attacks on networks *Proc. Natl. Acad. Sci.* **108** 3838–41

[33] Li D, Leyva I, Almendral J A, Sendina-Nadal I, Buldú J M, Havlin S and Boccaletti S 2008 Synchronization interfaces and overlapping communities in complex networks *Phys. Rev. Lett.* **101** 168701

[34] Caldarelli G 2007 *Scale-free Networks: Complex Webs in Nature and Technology* (Oxford: Oxford University Press)

[35] Majdandzic A, Podobnik B, Buldyrev S V, Kenett D Y, Havlin S and Stanley H E 2014 Spontaneous recovery in dynamical networks *Nat. Phys.* **10** 34–8

[36] Rényi P and A Erdős 1959 On random graphs. 1 *Publ. Math.* **6** 290–7

[37] Erdős A and Rényi P 1960 On the evolution of random graphs *Inst. Hung. Acad. Sci.* **5** 17–61

[38] Rapoport A 1957 Contribution to the theory of random and biased nets *Bull. Math. Biophys.* **19** 257–77

[39] Bollobás B 1985 *Random Graphs* (London: Academic)

[40] Birkhoff G 1967 *Lattice theory* vol 25 (AMS Bookstore)

[41] Bunde A and Havlin S 1991 *Fractals and Disordered Systems* (New York: Springer)

[42] Flory P J 1953 *Principles of Polymer Chemistry* (Ithaca, NY: Cornell University Press)

[43] Pastor-Satorras A and Vespignani R 2001 Epidemic spreading in scale-free network *Phys. Rev. Lett.* **86** 3200

[44] Balcan D, Colizza V, Gonçalves B, Hu H, Ramasco J J and Vespignani A 2009 Multiscale mobility networks and the large scale spreading of infectious diseases *Proc. Natl. Acad. Sci.* **106** 21484

[45] Kiss I Z, Miller J C and Simon P L *et al* 2017 *Mathematics of Epidemics on Networks* 598 (Cham: Springer)

[46] Li D, Fu B, Wang Y, Lu G, Berezin Y, Stanley E H and Havlin S 2015 Percolation transition in dynamical traffic network with evolving critical bottlenecks *Proc. Natl. Acad. Sci.* **112** 669–72

[47] Zeng G, Li D, Guo S, Gao L, Gao Z, Stanley H E and Havlin S 28, 2019 Switch between critical percolation modes in city traffic dynamics *Proc. Natl. Acad. Sci.* **116** 23

[48] Zhang J, Zhao Y, Tian B, Peng L, Zhang H T, Wang B H and Zhou T 2009 Accelerating consensus of self-driven swarm via adaptive speed *Phys. A: Stat. Mech. Appl.* **388** 1237–42

[49] Serok N, Levy O, Havlin S and Blumenfeld-Lieberthal E 2019 Unveiling the inter-relations between the urban streets network and its dynamic traffic flows: planning implication *Environ. Plan. B: Urban Anal. City Sci.* **46** 1362–76

[50] Palla G, Derényi I, Farkas I and Vicsek T 2005 Uncovering the overlapping community structure of complex networks in nature and society *Nature* **435** 814–8

[51] Kossinets D and Watts G 2006 Empirical analysis of an evolving social network *Science* **311** 88

[52] Newman M E J 2001 The structure of scientific collaboration networks *Proc. Natl. Acad. Sci.* **98** 404

[53] Girvan M and Newman M E J 2002 Community structure in social and biological networks *Proc. Natl. Acad. Sci. USA* **99** 7821

[54] Gozolchiani A, Havlin S and Yamasaki K 2011 Emergence of El Niño as an autonomous component in the climate network *Phys. Rev. Lett.* **107** 148501

[55] Ludescher J, Gozolchiani A, Bogachev M I, Bunde A, Havlin S and Schellnhuber H J 2013 Improved El Niño forecasting by cooperativity detection *Proc. Natl. Acad. Sci.* **110** 11742–5

[56] Donges J F, Zou Y, Marwan N and Kurths J 2009 Complex networks in climate dynamics *Eur. J. Spec. Topics* **174** 157–79

[57] Kleinberg J 2008 The convergence of social and technological networks *Commun. ACM* **51** 66–72

[58] Liben-Nowell D and Kleinberg J 2008 Tracing information flow on a global scale using internet chain-letter data *Proc. Natl. Acad. Sci.* **105** 4633

[59] Snijders T A B, Pattison P E, Robins G L and Handcock M S 2006 New specifications for exponential random graph models *Sociol. Methodol.* **36** 99–153

[60] Handcock M S, Raftery A E and Tantrum J M 2007 Model-based clustering for social networks *J. R. Stat. Soc. Ser. A (Stat. Soc.)* **170** 301–54

[61] Jackson M O and Rogers B W 2007 Meeting strangers and friends of friends: how random are social networks? *Am. Econ. Rev.* **97** 890–915

[62] Borgatti S P, Mehra A, Brass D J and Labianca G 2009 Network analysis in the social sciences *Science* **323** 892–5

[63] Borgatti S P 2006 Identifying sets of key players in a network *Comput. Math. Org. Theory* **12** 21–34

[64] Onnela J-P, Saramäki J, Hyvönen J, Szabó G, Lazer D, Kaski K, Kertész J and Barabási A-L 2007 Structure and tie strengths in mobile communication networks *Proc. Natl. Acad. Sci.* **104** 7332–6

[65] Faust K 2006 Comparing social networks: size, density and local structure *Metodol. Zvezki* **3** 185–216

[66] Joost R 2006 Inoperability input-output modeling of disruptions to interdependent economic systems *Syst. Eng.* **9** 20–34

[67] Jackson O 2008 *Social and Economic Networks (Economics, Physics, Sociology)* (Princeton, NJ: Princeton University Press)

[68] Kenett D Y, Raddant M, Lux T and Ben-Jacob E 2012 Evolvement of uniformity and volatility in the stressed global financial village *PloS One* **7** e31144

[69] Zimmerman R 2005 Decision-making and the vulnerability of interdependent critical infrastructure *2004 IEEE Int. Conf. Syst. Man Cyber.* **5** 4059–63

[70] Mendonça D and Wallace W A 2006 *J. Infrastruct. Syst.* **12** 260

[71] Robert B and Morabito L 2008 The operational tools for managing physical interdependencies among critical infrastructures *Int. J. Critical Infrastruct* **4** 353–67

[72] Reed D A, Kapur K C and Christie R D 2009 Methodology for assessing the resilience of networked infrastructure *IEEE Syst. J* **3** 174–80

[73] Bagheri E and Ghorbani A A 2009 Uml-ci: a reference model for profiling critical infrastructure systems *Inf. Syst. Front.* **12** 115–39

[74] Mansson D, Thottappillil R and Backstrom M 2009 Methodology for classifying facilities with respect to intentional emi *IEEE Trans. Electromagn. Compatib.* **51** 46–52

[75] Johansson J and Hassel H 2010 An approach for modelling interdependent infrastructures in the context of vulnerability analysis *Reliab. Eng. Syst. Saf.* **95** 1335–44

[76] Khanin R and Wit E 2006 How scale-free are biological networks *J. Comput. Biol.* **13** 810–8

[77] Alon U 2003 Biological networks: the tinkerer as an engineer *Science* **301** 1866–7

[78] Sendiña-Nadal I, Ofran Y, Almendral J A, Buldú J M, Leyva I, Li D, Havlin S and Boccaletti S 2011 Unveiling protein functions through the dynamics of the interaction network *PLoS One* **6** e17679

[79] Gallos L K, Makse H A and Sigman M 2012 A small world of weak ties provides optimal global integration of self-similar modules in functional brain networks *Proc. Natl. Acad. Sci.* **109** 2825–30

[80] Helbing D 2013 Globally networked risks and how to respond *Nature* **497** 51–9

[81] Colizza V, Barrat A, Barthélemy M and Vespignani A 2006 The role of the airline transportation network in the prediction and predictability of global epidemics *Proc. Natl. Acad. Sci. USA* **103** 2015–20

[82] Jeong H, Tombor B, Albert R, Oltvai Z N and Barabási A-L 2000 The large-scale organization of metabolic networks *Nature* **407** 651

[83] Teichmann S A and Madan Babu M 2004 Gene regulatory network growth by duplication *Nat. Genet.* **36** 492–6

[84] Holme P, Kim B J, Yoon C N and Han S K 2002 Attack vulnerability of complex networks *Phys. Rev. E* **65** 056109

[85] Doye J P K 2002 Network topology of a potential energy landscape: a static scale-free network *Phys. Rev. Lett.* **88** 238701

[86] Molloy M and Reed B 1998 The size of the giant component of a random graph with a given degree sequence *Combin. Probab. Comput.* **7** 295–305

[87] Newman M E J, Strogatz S H and Watts D J 2001 Random graphs with arbitrary degree distributions and their applications *Phys. Rev. E* **64** 026118

[88] Newman M E J 2002 Spread of epidemic disease on networks *Phys. Rev. E* **66** 016128

[89] Buldyrev S V, Parshani R, Paul G, Stanley H E and Havlin S 2010 Catastrophic cascade of failures in interdependent networks *Nature* **464** 1025–8

[90] Parshani R, Buldyrev S V and Havlin S 2010 Interdependent networks: reducing the coupling strength leads to a change from a first to second order percolation transition *Phys. Rev. Lett.* **105** 048701

[91] Gao J, Buldyrev S V, Havlin S and Stanley H E 2012 Robustness of a network formed by n interdependent networks with a one-to-one correspondence of dependent nodes *Phys. Rev. E* **85** 066134

[92] Boguná M, Pastor-Satorras R and Vespignani A 2004 Cut-offs and finite size effects in scale-free networks *Eur. Phys. J. B* **38** 205–9

[93] Stauffer D and Aharony A 1994 *Introduction to Percolation Theory* (Boca Raton, FL: CRC Press)

[94] Chen Y, Paul G, Havlin S, Liljeros F and Stanley H E 2008 Finding a better immunization strategy *Phys. Rev. Lett.* **101** 058701

[95] Cohen R, Havlin S and Ben-Avraham D 2003 Efficient immunization strategies for computer networks and populations *Phys. Rev. Lett.* **91** 247901

[96] Shao S, Huang X, Stanley H E and Havlin S 2015 Percolation of localized attack on complex networks *New J. Phys.* **17** 023049

[97] Liu Y, Sanhedrai H, Dong G, Shekhtman L M, Wang F, Buldyrev S V and Havlin S 2020 Efficient network immunization under limited knowledge *Natl. Sci. Rev.* **09**

[98] Braunstein L A, Buldyrev S V, Cohen R, Havlin S and Stanley H E 2003 Optimal paths in disordered complex networks *Phys. Rev. Lett.* **91** 168701

[99] Berezin Y, Bashan A, Danziger M M, Li D and Havlin S 2015 Localized attacks on spatially embedded networks with dependencies *Sci. Rep.* **5** 1–5

[100] Vaknin D, Danziger M M and Havlin S 2017 Spreading of localized attacks in spatial multiplex networks *New J. Phys.* **19** 073037

[101] Moreira A A, Andrade J S Jr, Herrmann H J and Indekeu J O 2009 How to make a fragile network robust and vice versa *Phys. Rev. Lett.* **102** 019701

[102] Shao J, Buldyrev S V, Cohen R, Kitsak M, Havlin S and Stanley H E 2008 Fractal boundaries of complex networks. EPL *Europhys. Lett.* **84** 48004

[103] Shao J, Buldyrev S V, Braunstein L A, Havlin S and Stanley H E 2009 Structure of shells in complex networks *Phys. Rev.* E **80** 036105

[104] Newman M E J 2002 Assortative mixing in networks *Phys. Rev. Lett.* **89** 208701

[105] Noldus R and Van Mieghem P 2015 Assortativity in complex networks *J. Complex Netw.* **3** 507–42

[106] Saramäki J, Kivelä M, Onnela J-P, Kaski K and Kertesz J 2007 Generalizations of the clustering coefficient to weighted complex networks *Phys. Rev.* E **75** 027105

[107] Dorogovtsev S N, Goltsev A V and Mendes J F F 2006 k-core organization of complex networks *Phys. Rev. Lett.* **96** 040601

[108] Carmi S, Havlin S, Kirkpatrick S, Shavitt Y and Shir E 2007 A model of internet topology using k-shell decomposition *Proc. Natl. Acad. Sci.* **104** 11150–4

[109] Newman M E J 2006 Modularity and community structure in networks *Proc. Natl. Acad. Sci. USA* **103** 8577–82

[110] Girvan M and Newman M E J 2002 Community structure in social and biological networks *Proc. Natl. Acad. Sci.* **99** 7821–6

[111] Fortunato S 2010 Community detection in graphs *Phys. Rep.* **486** 75–174

[112] Clauset A, Newman M E J and Moore C 2004 Finding community structure in very large networks *Phys. Rev.* E **70** 066111

[113] Shai S, Kenett D Y, Kenett Y N, Faust M, Dobson S and Havlin S 2015 Critical tipping point distinguishing two types of transitions in modular network structures *Phys. Rev.* E **92** 062805

[114] Shekhtman L M and Havlin S 2018 Percolation of hierarchical networks and networks of networks *Phys. Rev.* E **98** 052305

[115] Newman M E J 2004 Analysis of weighted networks *Phys. Rev.* E **70** 056131

[116] Barthélemy M, Barrat A, Pastor-Satorras R and Vespignani A 2005 Characterization and modeling of weighted networks *Physica* A **346** 34–43

[117] Freeman S C and Freeman L C 1979 The networkers network: a study of the impact of a new communications medium on sociometric structure *Social Science Research Reports 46* Irvine, CA: University of California

[118] Dolev S, Elovici Y and Puzis R 2010 Routing betweenness centrality *J. ACM* **25** 1–27

[119] Motter A E and Lai Y-C 2002 Cascade-based attacks on complex networks *Phys. Rev.* E **66** 065102

[120] Motter A E 2004 Cascade control and defense in complex networks *Phys. Rev. Lett.* **93** 098701

[121] Danziger M M, Shekhtman L M, Berezin Y and Havlin S 2016 The effect of spatiality on multiplex networks *Europhys. Lett.* **115** 36002

[122] Bonamassa I, Gross B, Danziger M M and Havlin S 2019 Critical stretching of mean-field regimes in spatial networks *Phys. Rev. Lett.* **123** 088301

[123] Gross B, Vaknin D, Buldyrev S V and Havlin S 2020 Two transitions in spatial modular networks *New J. Phys.* **22** 053002

IOP Publishing

Introduction to Networks of Networks

Jianxi Gao, Amir Bashan, Louis Shekhtman and Shlomo Havlin

Chapter 2

From single networks to networks of networks

In this chapter we will review the motivation and some fundamental qualitative aspects of networks of networks. In later chapters, we will get into more detailed quantitative results and mathematical frameworks.

2.1 Introduction

At 03:20 A.M. local time on 28 September 2003, the biggest blackout in Italian history took place. The blackout led to disruptions in many infrastructures such as the train system, communications, and others. In particular, the failures in the power grid led to failures in the communication systems and hindered the restoration of the power grid. This was because the controllers who normally could monitor power failures lacked communication, preventing them from understanding the optimal way to transfer electricity and carry out repairs. Given the vast impact of the blackout, engineers later took up investigating and attempting to understand the root cause of the blackout. Their assessments in 2008 pointed blame at the problem of *interdependence* between the different infrastructure systems [1]. This revealed a fundamental lacking in the understanding of complex systems, in that until then, only the robustness of isolated infrastructure systems had been studied and no systematic theoretical approach had been developed for possible interdependence between the systems. Finally, in 2010, the first theoretical framework of interdependent networks was developed [2]. There, the researchers developed a framework and studied percolation of a simplified system of two networks, each representing a different infrastructure such as the power grid and communications network, but assigned dependency relations between the two infrastructures. This work led to a recognition of the new phenomenon and features that arise when multiple networks depend on one another. In parallel, other researchers [3] built a model characterizing different interrelations between systems. Specifically, their model focused on interconnections where failures in one system may be mitigated through connections to another system.

doi:10.1088/978-0-7503-1046-8ch2 2-1

These foundational works led other researchers to realize that, in fact, *many real-world systems*, could and should be modeled as multiple networks with relationships between them. With the growing scale of big data-collection and processing, more and more systems have been recognized as so-called 'networks of networks' [4–20]. These are now also referred to as multiplex networks, multi-layer networks or multidimensional networks [21–28]. This chapter consists of two main parts: the first (section 2.2) categorizes the distinguishing features of the different models that have been developed so far and the second (section 2.3) deals with the novel phenomena that arise as a result of interdependent interactions between networks.

2.2 How networks network?

The general paradigm of network science has been to simplify a complex system down to its fundamental components of nodes and links. This simplification demonstrates how those components, together with the interactions between them, lead to understanding some key phenomena of the system. However, before 2010, this paradigm had only been developed for isolated networks, while in the real-world there exist interactions between different networks, each with their own nodes and links. For such systems of systems, some key phenomena may stem from interactions *between* the networks. Sometimes these interactions between networks are of a fundamentally different nature to those within each network, requiring us to introduce new types of links.

The progress in network science can be analogized to what happened in the early 20th century regarding the study of the thermodynamics of gases. There, the simplified model of an 'ideal gas' assumed non-interacting particles and served as a basic tool for understanding fundamental system behaviors. Only later were interactions between particles (atoms or molecules) included, leading to the discovery of novel features such as phase transitions and critical phenomena. Similarly, in network science, considering interactions between networks, which are different from those within networks, also leads to fundamentally new phenomena.

In this section we discuss the basic *structural representations* of networks of networks: what systems are represented by a network of networks? When is a single network not enough? What are the different models for networks of networks and what are the main differences between them?

2.2.1 When a single network is not enough: examples of interacting networks

Let's start with a concrete example. Consider two networks: a power grid and a communication network that are embedded in the same region, suppose the same city or country. The power grid represents the physical connections that allow the transfer of electricity between power stations, transmission points and consumers. In the communication network that controls the power grid, the computers are connected by communication lines allowing transfer of information between two connected computers and through the entire network. The connections between entities of the same network, e.g., between two power stations or between two computers, can be represented by links, which can be termed 'connectivity links'.

Nodes of these two networks (the power grid and communication network) are not typically considered 'connected'—electricity cannot be transferred through communication lines and the power lines do not transfer information. Yet, they may interact with and depend upon each other. The power stations need to be monitored and controlled by computers, while computers need electrical power from the grid. These types of interrelations between elements of two different networks, which are essential for their function, can be represented through dependency links (to be discussed in section 2.2.2) between them.

Another example of interacting networks is the urban transportation system, which includes taxicabs, buses, subways, trains, etc. Each of these modes of transport is a different network, yet in contrast to the example above of a power grid and communications network, a person can move from one network to another at designated transfer stations. In other words, all links essentially represent the same function—movement of people from one place to another, and are therefore all classified as connectivity links. Nonetheless, the scale of each mode of transport, e.g. the number of passengers, the speed of travel, the cost of travel, etc, could be very different, as is the structure of each individual network. Therefore, network scientists have often naturally chosen to model these systems as *multi-layer networks* where each layer refers to a single mode of transport.

Another system that contains multiple networks is that of online social media. A single user will often have accounts on multiple social media sites such as Facebook, Twitter, Instagram, etc. Like the previous example, each of these networks is distinct yet the same person may be behind the accounts. If the person is exposed to some information via one source, he can share that information with his friends through another source.

Lastly, in some cases a single network may be capable of encompassing all the system properties, yet due to the network structure and/or node 'metadata,' it may make sense to consider the system as separate interacting networks. For example, power grids of two different cities may both be part of a larger overall network. Nonetheless, since they are geographically separated and each city may have an independent controller, it may be preferable to consider each as a separate network with interconnections between them.

2.2.2 Zoology of network of networks

Each of the scenarios explained above requires a different model in accordance with the fundamental properties of the system. In this section, we will summarize some of the models that have been developed so far and describe the coupling between the networks for each category. Each of the models leads to unique phenomena resulting from their structure, which will be discussed in section 2.3.

Interdependent networks

The first example we discuss is *interdependent networks*. This system represents scenarios where several networks each has its own independent function, but is also reliant via dependency links on one or several other networks. For example, in infrastructure systems resources from one network are often required for the

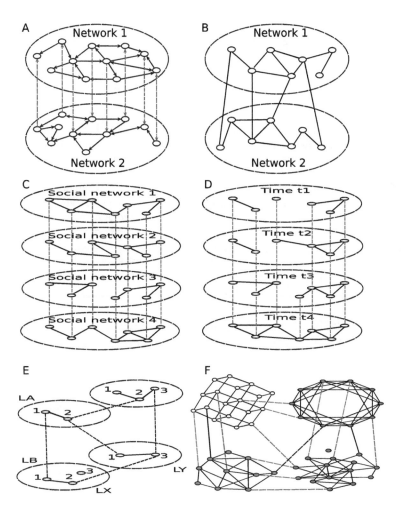

Figure 2.1. Schematic diagrams of networks of networks. (A) Interdependent networks: network 1 and network 2 are coupled by dependency links (green dashed lines). The nodes within networks are connected by connectivity links (black solid lines). The dependency links can be singly directed or bi-directed. (B) Interconnected networks: the nodes within a network and the nodes of different networks are all connected by connectivity links (black solid lines). (C) Multiplex networks: the nodes in every layer are the same, and the links of each layer represent different interacting relations. Here we illustrate, e.g., multiplex social networks: the nodes of each social network are the same actors, and different layers represent different social platforms, e.g. Facebook, Twiiter, LinkedIn etc. (D) Temporal networks: different layers of networks represent the same network system and different layers represent different times when different links may exist. The system dynamically evolves with time. The nodes connected by blue dashed lines represent a same entity at different times. (E) A network of networks combining multiple layers and interconnections between different sub-networks and layers. (F) Networks of networks with different structures, e.g. a line, a tree, a circle or other structures with or without loops. Each layer may have a different network structure, for example, lattice (nodes in light green), small-world network (nodes in blue), ER network (nodes in green) and SF network (nodes in rose red). The networks are fully or partially coupled by different interaction links: dependency links (green dashed lines), connectivity links (black solid lines), antagonistic interactions (red dashed lines), temporal relations (blue dashed lines) and other interactions or combinations of diverse interactions (black dashed lines).

Box 2.1 Dependency links:

A situation where the function of node i in one network crucially depends on the functioning of node j in another network (or even in the same network), is represented by a directed dependency link pointing from $j \rightarrow i$. This means that if j fails, then i will also fail, even if it is still connected to its own network. A special case is that of a bi-directed dependency link where i and j both depend on each other such that $i \leftrightarrow j$. If a number of nodes are all connected to each other in a single component via bi-directed dependency links they form a 'dependency group,' where the failure of a single node cripples the entire group. Trivially, the case where the dependency group spans all or a large fraction of nodes, the group is extremely unstable, but fortunately this is rare in real systems. In contrast, the case where the size of the dependency groups is restricted to 2 and a failed node leads to additional failure of only one other node is referred to as 'no feedback' [29]. As dependency links rarely form large components, they usually exist as part of a system composed of both dependency and connectivity links. The connectivity links represent the collective functioning of nodes, whereas dependency links represent a specific need for a crucial resource from particular entities.

---

functioning of nodes in other networks and vice versa (see figure 2.1). In this case, the overall system consists of distinct networks which do not provide the same resources. To model these systems, one must recognize that the type of interactions between nodes of different networks is fundamentally different from those within each network. This predicament led researchers [2] to define the concept of a *dependency link* (see Box 2.1 for details). For interdependent networks, the links within each network that enable its functioning are ordinary *connectivity* links, whereas the links between the networks are *dependency* links. Thus, in interdependent networks a node must fulfill two conditions in order to properly function: (i) be connected to its own network and (ii) that nodes in other networks on which it depends are also functional.

Interconnected networks

The case of interconnected networks refers to the case when the links between networks are of the same type as those within each network, namely both are connectivity links. This means that the same resource or information that is transferred within each network, is also transferred between the networks. Compared to each network individually, the combined network provides additional paths and enables cooperation between the individual networks. For example, power grids in two states may also have interconnections between them. Likewise, an urban transportation system within a single city can be composed of different means such as buses, trains, etc and individuals can choose a path that combines these means using transfer points (interconnections) between them.

From a structural point of view, the case of interconnected networks could be seen as similar to a single network with communities (or modular network), however, often times there are natural reasons to consider each community (or module) as a separate network. One reason could be because the links in each network have different dynamic properties. For example, trains can carry many more passengers and operate at a different frequency and time-scale compared to buses. Another scenario is where external features naturally lead to the defining of distinct networks. These could include power grids having different control systems and geographical regions.

Multiplexes
Multiplex networks refer to the case where the same nodes are connected via two or more different sets of links. Each set of links can be considered as a separate network where each node has a representation in each network. For example, the same person can have accounts and online relationships in different social media platforms, represented as nodes and links of a multiplex where each platform is a different social network and has its own links. In this case, if a person hears a rumor in one network, the person can spread the rumor in all other networks. This would represent a 'connectivity'-like relationship between the node's representations in different networks. However, sometimes there can be 'dependency'-like relationships between nodes' different representations since when a node fails in one network it may fail in all other networks [30, 31].

Multi-layer and multi-level networks
The terms multi-layer and multi-level network are general and usually refer to the case where multiple networks occupy some identical space, which can either be physical or more abstract, e.g. cyber-space. Each network is thus referred to as a single 'layer' or 'level' with the multiple networks coming together in the overall system (see, e.g. [26, 27, 32–34]). Interdependent networks where different infrastructures cover the same region would be an example of multi-layer or multi-level networks. Also, different transportation systems throughout a city can be regarded as multi-layer and multi-level networks. However, the cases of different communities in a social network or power grids in different countries with interconnections between them, would typically not fall under the category of multi-layer or multi-level networks.

2.3 Key phenomena in network of networks

Having defined various models of networks of networks, we now focus on the behaviors and phenomena that arise in them. Specifically, we are interested in differences with respect to the phenomena in single networks. Most of these key differences stem from feedback between processes taking place in the different networks. For example, in a system of two coupled networks A and B, some processes or events occurring in network A impact network B whose response propagates back to network A and so on. The nature of this feedback will be specific to the type of coupling between the networks as we will see below.

2.3.1 Cascading failures in interdependent networks

A key feature of almost any network is the robustness of the system, where on a microscopic level, a node's functionality depends on whether it is connected to the giant component. This is because isolated nodes are unable to participate in the cooperative functioning of the network. Percolation theory is a mathematical tool that allows us to calculate the probability that a node will be connected to the giant component [35, 36]. In failure scenarios, percolation theory enables us to establish a notion of robustness for an individual network, as was discussed in chapter 1.

For interdependent networks, we have a system composed of several individual networks, with dependency links (as described in Box 2.1) between them. The synergy between percolation in individual networks and coupling through dependency links, leads to *cascading failures*.

These cascading failures arise after some nodes in network A fail. This leads to structural changes in network A that cause other additional nodes to become disconnected from the giant component of network A, thus leading them to also fail. All of these failures (the initial failures and the subsequent percolation failures) lead dependent nodes in network B to also fail, see figures 2.2(a) and (b). In turn, the failures in network B will change the structure of network B and cause additional nodes in network B to become disconnected from the giant component and fail. This will then lead to further dependent nodes failing in network A and so on, see figure 2.2(c).

The domino-effect of cascading failures can either die out or accelerate. Which result occurs depends on many parameters, including the size of the initial failures,

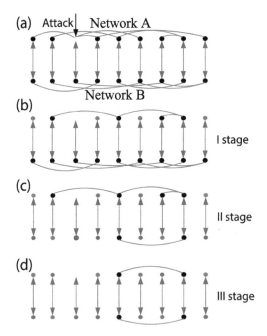

Figure 2.2. Cascading failures between two interdependent networks A and B. In (a) The black nodes represent the surviving nodes, and the yellow node represents the initially attacked node. In (b)–(d) the red nodes represent the nodes removed because they do not belong to the largest cluster and the blue nodes represent the nodes removed because they depend on failed nodes in the other network. In each stage, we first remove the nodes that do not belong to the largest cluster of the network. Next we remove the nodes that depend on the failed nodes in the other network. Notice how the failures in one network lead to dependency failures in the second network, which disconnect nodes from the giant component, leading to more failures in the first network and so on.

the structure of the individual networks, etc. If the process accelerates unabated, then the entire system will eventually collapse. In contrast, if the process dies out, the system will eventually reach a new steady state where some finite fraction of nodes are still functional, like in figure 2.2(d). The steady state consists of nodes that are both in the giant component of their respective network and have their dependent nodes also in the giant component of the other network. This set of nodes is referred to as the *mutual giant connected component*.

Percolation transition in interdependent networks. Due to the cascading failures in interdependent networks, the resulting percolation transition is strikingly different from single networks. As mentioned above, the system robustness is quantified through the size of the largest connected component under the failure of some fraction of nodes. As discussed in chapter 1, in single networks, the largest component decreases continuously with more failures, i.e., the corresponding percolation transition is continuous ('second-order'), however, in interdependent networks this transition can be abrupt, 'first-order'. This difference between continuous and abrupt transitions is fundamental for assessing the system's robustness. In a continuous transition, such as in single networks, a small number of additional failures will always result in only a small additional global failure. In contrast, cascading failures can lead to an abrupt percolation transition, so a small number of additional failures or even a single node's failure can be the difference between a highly functional and a completely failed system. In interdependent networks, even without warning, a sudden collapse of an entire interdependent system is possible.

This dramatic difference between abrupt and continuous percolation transitions directly stems from the nature of the cascading failures described above (see figure 2.3). Just above the percolation threshold the resulting cascading failures die out leaving a fraction of the system still functional, while just below the threshold the cascading failures accelerate until the system completely collapses.

Generalization of the interdependent model.
Note that the model of interdependent networks can be generalized to cases beyond ordinary percolation that have been ascribed to other network processes, e.g. k-core percolation [38, 39]. In these models, to be functional a node must both be in the k-core of its network (have k neighbors at the end of the cascade) and also have the node it depends on in the other network functional. This model led to a very rich behavior where both first-order and second-order transitions are possible depending on the exact parameter values. Moreover, it is also possible for the system to have a transition in two stages—a first-order transition followed by a continuous second-order transition [38].

Aside from k-core, other generalizations of the interdependent model include the recognition that in power grids there must be flow along the nodes otherwise they are non-functional. This led to a study of interdependent networks of random resistors [40] where if the node played no part in the electrical flow it was also considered non-functional.

Similarly, one can consider interdependence between two networks with some sort of non-linear dynamics occurring on them. In this case, the dependency links will shift the dynamic state of the nodes dragging two interdependent nodes to either being more or less closely aligned [17].

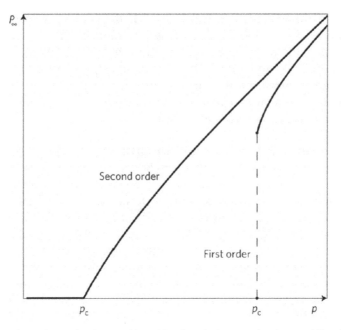

Figure 2.3. First-order and second-order transitions. Note how in the second-order transition, the change in P_∞ is continuous, whereas in the first-order transition there is an abrupt drop at p_c. Reproduced from [37], copyright 2012 with permission of Springer.

Some of these and other generalizations of the interdependent model are more deeply discussed in chapter 6.

2.3.2 Increased robustness of interconnected networks

In contrast to interdependence between networks, interconnections usually make networks *more* robust rather than less [3]. For example, if we consider two networks A and B each with some given robustness based on the structure of their links, we can then add 'interconnection' links between some nodes of the two networks. These additional links, can significantly increase the fraction of failures that are necessary for the system to collapse [3]. Essentially, this can be recognized to be a result of the fact that even if two nodes within, e.g. network A, are not connected to one another, they may both be connected to nodes that are in the same component in network B. Thus, in the system of interconnected networks, the two nodes in network A will be connected to one another through a path that goes through network B, see figure 2.4. In this manner, the interconnections increase the robustness of the two networks by forming 'new paths' through which nodes can be connected.

Furthermore, a study by Dong *et al* [42] presented a different model of interconnected networks where some number of interconnected links are distributed among a fraction of nodes that are defined in advance to be 'interconnected nodes.' This model is realistic in cases where there are some specific additional resources

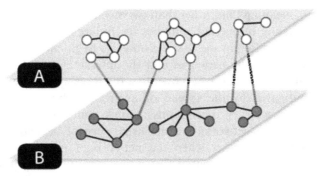

Figure 2.4. An interconnected network system with two networks: A and B. Nodes have intranetwork links within their own network, but also internetwork links connecting them to the other network. Notice how even if nodes are not connected to the giant component within their own network, they can be connected to the overall giant component via links to the other network. Reproduced with permission from [41], copyright 2012 by The American Physical Society.

required for interconnections, however, once that resource exists at a specific node, the cost of adding more links is negligible. One example of such a situation would be international flights that require an airport to have customs clearance. Similarly, intercontinental flights may involve larger planes that require longer runways. In this model, it was found that the fraction of interconnected nodes can be analogized to an 'external magnetic field' or 'percolation ghost field' from statistical physics [42–44]. Critical exponents, analogous to those from physics can then be defined and predict how the network's robustness at the critical point will scale with the fraction of interconnected nodes.

2.3.3 Dynamics on network of networks

Beyond the properties of robustness discussed in the previous two sections, several studies have incorporated *dynamics* into networks of networks [17, 40, 41, 45–49]. In this context, each node has a given dynamical state associated with it and this state changes in time based on some sort of rules (often through differential equations) taking place on the network. Typical examples include the spreading of epidemics, synchronization, transport properties, and others.

For dynamics, the nature of the links can be either connectivity links or dependency links, with both leading to different phenomena. For example, in the case of epidemics on interconnected networks, it was found that there exist three different possible states [41] where the epidemic may spread in none of the networks, some of the networks, or all of the networks, depending on the level of both interconnections and intraconnections of the network as well as the infectivity of the epidemic. For epidemics on a multiplex network see Granell *et al* [46].

For the case where the interactions between the networks are dependency links, it is first important to understand exactly how the dependency relationship is defined and how the dependency link affects the two nodes. Moreover, when discussing dynamics the possibility of *antagonistic* or *competitive* interactions was also suggested [17, 50], meaning that rather than two nodes both functioning or failing in tandem, the functioning of one node implies the failure of the other node and vice versa. This can lead to different stable states and also to global frustration depending on the specific nature of the networks and the interactions [17]. Likewise, in the context of epidemics, there can be competitive relationships where the spread of a disease is also mitigated by the spread of awareness about the disease leading individuals to take necessary precautions against contagion [46, 47]. When the interactions between the networks are the usual type of dependency links where nodes function or fail together, then the network of networks can experience explosive synchronization as the entire system can abruptly jump to the same state [17, 45]. In the next chapters, we will discuss some of these specific models and how they lead to the different resulting and rich behaviors.

References

[1] Rosato V, Issacharoff L, Tiriticco F, Meloni S, Porcellinis S and Setola R 79, 2008 Modeling interdependent infrastructures using interacting dynamical models *Int. J. Crit. Infrastruct* **4** 63

[2] Buldyrev S V, Parshani R, Paul G, Stanley H E and Havlin S 2010 Catastrophic cascade of failures in interdependent networks *Nature* **464** 1025–8

[3] Leicht E A and D'Souza R M 2009 Percolation on interacting networks arXiv:cond-mat/0907.0894

[4] Yuan X, Hu Y, Stanley H E and Havlin S 2017 Eradicating catastrophic collapse in interdependent networks via reinforced nodes *Proc. Natl. Acad. Sci.* **114** 3311–5

[5] Kenett D Y *et al* 2014 Network of interdependent networks: overview of theory and applications Networks of Networks: The Last Frontier of Complexity (Cham: Springer) 336

[6] Dong G *et al* 2013 Robustness of network of networks under targeted attack *Physical Review E 87.5* 052804

[7] Gao J *et al* 2012 Robustness of a network formed by n interdependent networks with a one-to-one correspondence of dependent nodes *Phys. Rev. E* **85** 066134

[8] Gao J, Daqing L and Shlomo H 2014 From a single network to a network of networks *Natl Sci. Rev* **1** 34–56

[9] Gao J *et al* 2013 Percolation of a general network of networks *Phys. Rev. E* **88** 062816

[10] Havlin S *et al* 2015 Percolation of interdependent network of networks *Chaos Solitons Fractals* **72** 4–19

[11] Havlin S *et al* 2014 Vulnerability of network of networks *Eur. Phys. J. Spec. Top* **223** 2087–106

[12] Liu X, Hao P and Jianxi G 2015 Vulnerability and controllability of networks of networks *Chaos Solitons Fractals* **80** 125–38

[13] Liu X, Maiorino E, Halu A, Glass K, Prasad R B, Loscalzo J, Gao J and Sharma A 2020 Robustness and lethality in multilayer biological molecular networks *Nat. Commun.* **11** 1–12

[14] Kryven I 2019 Bond percolation in coloured and multiplex networks *Nat. Commun.* **10** 1–16

[15] Reis S D S, Hu Y, Babino A, Santiago Canals Jr J S A, Sigman M and Makse H A 2014 Avoiding catastrophic failure in correlated networks of networks *Nat. Phys.* **10** 762–7

[16] Shekhtman L M, Danziger M M and Havlin S 2016 Recent advances on failure and recovery in networks of networks *Chaos, Solitons Fractals* **90** 28–36

[17] Danziger M M, Bonamassa I, Boccaletti S and Havlin S 2019 Dynamic interdependence and competition in multilayer networks *Nat. Phys.* **15** 178

[18] Smolyak A, Levy O, Shekhtman L and Havlin S 2018 Interdependent networks in economics and finance–a physics approach *Physica* A **512** 612–9

[19] Shekhtman L M, Danziger M M, Vaknin D and Havlin S 2018 Robustness of spatial networks and networks of networks *Comp. R. Phys.* **19** 233–43

[20] Klosik D F, Grimbs A, Bornholdt S and Hütt M-T 2017 The interdependent network of gene regulation and metabolism is robust where it needs to be *Nat. Commun.* **8** 1–9

[21] Aleta A and Moreno Y 2019 Multilayer networks in a nutshell *Ann. Rev. Condens. Matter Phys.* **10** 45–62

[22] Silk M J, Finn K R, Porter M A and Pinter-Wollman N 2018 Can multilayer networks advance animal behavior research? *Trends Ecol. Evol.* **33** 376–8

[23] Berlingerio M, Coscia M, Giannotti F, Monreale A and Pedreschi D 2013 Multidimensional networks: foundations of structural analysis *World Wide Web* **16** 567–93

[24] Della Rossa F, Pecora L, Blaha K, Shirin A, Klickstein I and Sorrentino F 2020 Symmetries and cluster synchronization in multilayer networks *Nat. Commun.* **11** 1–17

[25] Bianconi G 2018 *Multilayer Networks: Structure and Function* (Oxford: Oxford University Press)

[26] Kivelä M, Arenas A, Barthelemy M, Gleeson J P, Moreno Y and Porter M A 2014 Multilayer networks *J. Complex Netw.* **2** 203–71

[27] Boccaletti S, Bianconi G, Criado R, Del Genio C I, Gómez-Gardenes J, Romance M, Sendiña-Nadal I, Wang Z and Zanin M 2014 The structure and dynamics of multilayer networks *Phys. Rep.* **544** 1–122

[28] Radicchi F and Bianconi G 2017 Redundant interdependencies boost the robustness of multiplex networks *Phys. Rev.* X **7** 011013

[29] Gao J, Buldyrev S V, Havlin S and Stanley H E 2011 Robustness of a network of networks *Phys. Rev. Lett.* **107**

[30] Baxter G J, Dorogovtsev S N, Goltsev A V and Mendes J F F 2012 Avalanche collapse of interdependent networks *Phys. Rev. Lett.* **109** 248701

[31] Danziger M M, Shekhtman L M, Berezin Y and Havlin S 2016 The effect of spatiality on multiplex networks *Europhys. Lett.* **115** 36002

[32] Battiston S, Caldarelli G and Garas A 2018 *Multiplex and Multilevel Networks* (Oxford: Oxford University Press)

[33] De Domenico M, Solé-Ribalta A, Cozzo E, Kivelä M, Moreno Y, Porter M A, Gómez S and Arenas A 2013 Mathematical formulation of multilayer networks *Phys. Rev.* X **3** 041022

[34] De Domenico M, Porter M A and Arenas A 2015 Muxviz: a tool for multilayer analysis and visualization of networks *J. Complex Netw.* **3** 159–76

[35] Bunde A and Havlin S 1991 *Fractals and Disordered Systems* (New York: Springer)

[36] Stauffer D and Aharony A 1994 *Introduction to Percolation Theory* (Boca Raton, FL: CRC Press)

[37] Gao J, Buldyrev S V, Stanley H E and Havlin S 2012 Networks formed from interdependent networks *Nat. Phys.* **8** 40–8

[38] Panduranga N K, Gao J, Yuan X, Stanley H E and Havlin S 2017 Generalized model for k-core percolation and interdependent networks *Phys. Rev.* E **96** 032317

[39] Azimi-Tafreshi N, Gómez-Gardenes J and Dorogovtsev S N 2014 k-core percolation on multiplex networks *Phys. Rev.* E **90** 032816

[40] Danziger M M, Bashan A and Havlin S 2015 Interdependent resistor networks with process-based dependency *New J. Phys.* **17** 043046

[41] Dickison M, Havlin S and Stanley H E 2012 Epidemics on interconnected networks *Phys. Rev. E* **85** 066109

[42] Dong G, Fan J, Shekhtman L M, Shai S, Du R, Tian L, Chen X, Stanley H E and Havlin S 2018 Resilience of networks with community structure behaves as if under an external field *Proc. Natl. Acad. Sci.* **115** 6911–5

[43] Stanley H E 1971 *Introduction to Phase Transitions and Critical Phenomena* (New York: Oxford University Press)

[44] Reynolds P J, Stanley H E and Klein W 1977 Ghost fields, pair connectedness, and scaling: exact results in one-dimensional percolation *J. Phys. A* **10** L2

[45] Nicosia V, Skardal P S, Arenas A and Latora V 2017 Collective phenomena emerging from the interactions between dynamical processes in multiplex networks *Phys. Rev. Lett.* **118** 138302

[46] Granell C, Gómez S and Arenas A 2013 Dynamical interplay between awareness and epidemic spreading in multiplex networks *Phys. Rev. Lett.* **111** 128701

[47] Newman M E J 2005 Threshold effects for two pathogens spreading on a network *Phys. Rev. Lett.* **95** 108701

[48] Lazaridis F, Gross B, Maragakis M, Argyrakis P, Bonamassa I, Havlin S and Cohen R 2018 Spontaneous repulsion in the $A + B \to 0$ reaction on coupled networks *Phys. Rev. E* **97** 040301

[49] Duan D *et al* 2019 Universal behavior of cascading failures in interdependent networks *Proc. Natl Acad. Sci* **116** 22452–7

[50] Zhao K and Bianconi G 2013 Percolation on interacting, antagonistic networks *J. Stat. Mech. Theory Exp.* **2013** P05005

IOP Publishing

Introduction to Networks of Networks

Jianxi Gao, Amir Bashan, Louis Shekhtman and Shlomo Havlin

Chapter 3

A pair of interdependent networks

3.1 Introduction

In chapter 1, we introduced the properties of single networks which provide the basic tools to study and understand the dynamics and functioning of a pair of interacting networks. In 2010, Buldyrev et al [1] developed an analytical framework to study percolation of two interdependent networks subject to cascading failures based on a generating function formalism [3, 4]. In interdependent networks [1, 21–26], there are two different types of links: (i) *connectivity* links within each network, and (ii) *dependency* links between networks. The connectivity links connect the components within a network to perform its function and the dependency links represent the fact that a given node in one network may depend, in order to function, on a node in the other network. The case of connectivity links between the networks was studied by Leicht and D'Souza [5] and also later by Shai et al [6]. Buldyrev et al [1] found for interdependent networks a first-order, discontinuous phase transition, which is dramatically different from the second-order continuous phase transition found in isolated networks. The abrupt discontinuous transition occurs due to the cascading failures which do not appear in single isolated networks. Parshani et al [7] studied two partial interdependent networks and found that as the coupling strength (fraction of dependent nodes decreases) decreases below a critical coupling, the percolation transition becomes a continues second-order transition.

Since in real-world scenarios the initial failure of nodes may not be random but targeted, e.g., attacking the more important nodes ('hubs'), Huang et al [8] proposed a mathematical framework for understanding the robustness of interdependent networks under targeted attack, which was later extended by Dong et al [9] to targeted attack on partially interdependent networks. They [8, 9] developed a general technique that maps the targeted-attack problem in interdependent networks to the random-attack solution. Also, in real-world scenarios, each node in one of the networks may

doi:10.1088/978-0-7503-1046-8ch3

depend on several nodes in the other network, while reference [1] assumes that each node depends on a single node in the other network. Therefore, Shao *et al* [10] proposed a theoretical framework for understanding the robustness of interdependent networks with a general number of support and dependency relationships.

In many cases, high degree nodes in one network tend to depend on low degree nodes of another network which leads the coupled system to become more vulnerable. In reality, however, such as the case of interdependence between the flight network and railway network, a city with high degree in the flight network will have a high probability to have a high degree in the railway network. To better understand this phenomenon, Parshani *et al* [11] proposed an 'intersimilarity' measure between the interdependent networks. They used this measure and studied a system composed of the interdependent world-wide seaport network and the world-wide airport network, and found that as the interdependent networks become more intersimilar (e.g., high degree nodes depend on high degree and low degree on low degree) the system becomes more robust. The case in which all pairs of interdependent nodes in both networks have the same degree was solved analytically by Buldyrev *et al* [12]. The effect on percolation of coupled networks with general intersimilarity was studied analytically by Cellai *et al* [13] and Hu *et al* [14]. Hu *et al* [15] also studied a more realistic coupled network system having both dependency and connectivity links between the coupled networks, and found a mixed first-order and second-order hybrid transition. A percolation approach for a single network in the presence of dependency links has been also developed and studied [16–18]. This chapter will present some models and results on a pair of coupled networks including those related to random failures and targeted attacks, and different types of coupling relationships.

3.2 Different types of dependency between networks

In this section we will discuss how two networks can be coupled together, including an analysis of some different types of coupling and how they relate to the meaning of the interactions. Usually, when dealing with a single network with connections between the nodes, the links are *connectivity links*. In such a case, the more links there are in a network, the more robust is the network. For example, in power grid networks every link represents a wire between two buses and more links imply more possibilities for electricity to flow even if some failures occur. However, when we talk about two coupled networks, the meaning of the links between the networks may be different from the usual connectivity links. In the power grid and communication network system (that controls the power grid), the links within each network are connectivity links and the links between networks are *dependency* links. The meaning of an undirected dependency link is that when a node in one network fails (removed or attacked) the dependent node in the other network also fails. In this section we discuss the different types of coupling between the two networks and the resulting phenomena occurring in the system.

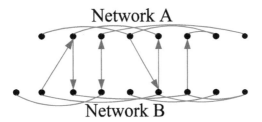

Figure 3.1. Two partially interdependent networks following a feedback condition.

3.2.1 Feedback condition

We introduce the feedback condition where the dependency links between networks are chosen randomly. The process to produce two interacting networks with a feedback condition is as follows:

(1) Generate network A with N_A nodes and network B with N_B nodes independently according to their degree distributions.

(2) In network A we randomly select $n_A = N_A q_A$ nodes, in network B we also randomly select n_A nodes, and then we randomly match them and build directed links from n_A nodes in network A and n_A nodes in network B. Thus, we obtain a fraction q_A of nodes in network A that depend on nodes in network B.

(3) Similar to (2), in network B we randomly select $n_B = N_B q_B$ nodes, in network A we also randomly select n_B nodes, and then we randomly match them and build directed links from n_B nodes in network B and n_B nodes in network A. Thus, we obtain a fraction q_B of nodes in network B that depend on nodes in network A.

As demonstrated in figure 3.1, there are $N_A = 8$ nodes in network A and there are $N_B = 9$ nodes in network B. The two networks' interactions follow a feedback condition. There is a fraction $q_A = 3/8$ of nodes in network A that depend on nodes in network B and a fraction $q_B = 4/9$ of nodes in network B that depend on nodes in network A.

3.2.2 No-feedback condition

Next we introduce the no-feedback condition in interdependent networks. In the no-feedback condition, if node a in network A depends on node b in network B, then node b in network B may either depend on node a in network A or not depend on any node in network A. The process to produce two interdependent networks with no-feedback condition:

(1) Generate network A with N_A nodes and network B with N_B nodes independently according to their degree distributions.

(2) In network A we randomly select $n_A = N_A q_A$ nodes, in network B we also randomly select n_A nodes, and then we randomly match them and create directed links from n_A nodes in network A to n_A nodes in network B. Thus, we obtain a fraction q_A of nodes in network A that depend on nodes in network B.

(3) In network B we randomly select $n_B = N_B q_B$ nodes. Now, recall that there are $n_{B,1} = n_A$ nodes in network A that already depend upon and $n_B - n_{B,1}$ nodes that are

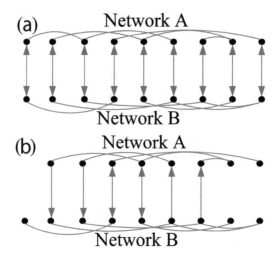

Figure 3.2. (a) Two fully interdependent networks. (b) Two partially interdependent networks with no-feedback condition.

not relied upon by any nodes in network A. For these $n_{B,1}$ nodes we change the directed links from network A to network B to bidirectional links between network A and network B. For the remaining $n_B - n_{B,1}$ nodes we randomly select $n_B - n_{B,1}$ nodes in network A (that do not already depend on a different node in network B) and randomly match them to have directed links from the nodes in network B. Note that we assume $n_B \geqslant n_A$, so that if this is not the case, the labeling of the networks A and B must be switched.

In figure 3.2(a) we show network A and network B fully interacting with the no-feedback condition where the number of nodes in each network must be the same. In figure 3.2(b), there are $N_A = 8$ nodes in network A and $N_B = 9$ nodes in network B. The two networks are interacting with a no-feedback condition. There is a fraction $q_A = 4/8$ of nodes in network A that depend on nodes in network B and a fraction $q_B = 4/9$ of nodes in network B that depend on nodes in network A.

3.2.3 Multiple support

In many cases a node in one network may interact and depend on several nodes in the other network where the interaction type is defined as requiring multiple support. In this case, the process to produce two such interdependent networks with a no-feedback condition is:

(1) Generate network A with N_A nodes and network B with N_B nodes independently according to their degree distributions.

(2) For each node i ($i = 1, \ldots, N_A$) in network A we randomly select $\tilde{k}_{A,i}$ nodes from network B and build directed links from node i pointing to them, where the $\tilde{k}_{A,i}$ are randomly chosen from a distribution $\tilde{P}_A(\tilde{k}_A)$.

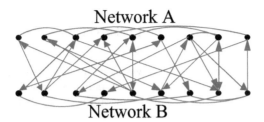

Figure 3.3. Two interdependent networks, A and B, with multiple support relationships.

(3) Similarly, for each node j ($j = 1, \ldots, N_B$) in network B we randomly select $\tilde{k}_{B,j}$ nodes from network A and build directed links from node j pointing to them, where the $\tilde{k}_{B,j}$ are randomly chosen from a distribution $\tilde{P}_B(\tilde{k}_B)$.

A demonstration of two interdependent networks with multiple support relations is shown in figure 3.3. The interacting degrees sequence of network A is {1, 1, 2, 0, 1, 1, 3, 2, 1} and the interacting degrees sequence of network B is {1, 2, 1, 0, 4, 1, 0, 1, 1}.

3.3 Random failures

An important property of networks is their stability to failures, and it is thus important that we understand and quantify their robustness in terms of node and link failures. The robustness of a single network is discussed in chapter 1. The robustness of a network is usually analyzed using percolation theory [19, 20]. In this section we will discuss how to generalize percolation theory to analyze the robustness of a pair of interdependent networks.

3.3.1 Fully interdependent networks

The most fundamental framework about two fully interdependent networks (figure 3.2(a)) was proposed in 2010 by Buldyrev *et al* [1].

Using the two fully interdependent networks from figure 3.2(a), we demonstrate the cascading failures that will happen, see figure 3.4.

Next we describe step by step how to analytically calculate the robustness of two fully interdependent networks using percolation theory.

(1) The remaining fraction of network A nodes after an initial removal of nodes is $\psi_1' \equiv p$. The initial removal of nodes will disconnect some nodes from the giant component. The remaining functional part of network A therefore contains a fraction $\psi_1 = \psi_1' g_A(\psi_1')$ of the network nodes, where $g_A(\psi_1')$ is defined in chapter 1 equations (1.14) and (1.15).

(2) Since every node from network B depends on one and only one node in network A, the number of nodes in network B that become nonfunctional is $1 - \psi_1 = 1 - \psi_1' g_A(\psi_1')$. Accordingly, the remaining fraction of network B nodes is $\phi_1' = \psi_1' g_A(\psi_1')$, and the fraction of nodes in the giant component of network B is $\phi_1 = \phi_1' g_B(\phi_1')$.

Box 3.1: The dynamic process of cascading failures of two fully interdependent networks is as follows:

(1) Build two fully interdependent networks with no-feedback conditions.

(2) Randomly remove a fraction $1 - p$ of nodes in network A, find the giant connected component of network A and remove the nodes that are not in the giant component of network A.

(3) In network B, we remove all the nodes that depend on the failed nodes in network A. Then we find the giant connected component of network B and remove the nodes not in the giant component.

(4) In network A, we remove all the nodes that depend on the failed nodes in network B. Then we find the giant connected component of network A and remove the nodes not in the giant component.

(5) Repeat (3) and (4) until there are no new nodes failure in both network A and network B.

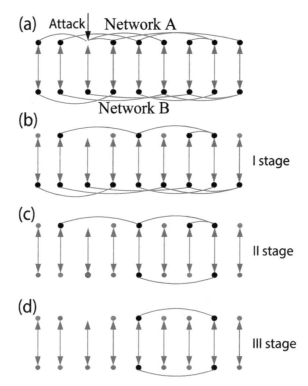

Figure 3.4. Demonstration of the dynamic process of cascading failures on two fully interdependent networks. The black nodes represent the surviving nodes, the yellow node represents the initially attacked node, the red nodes represent the nodes removed because they do not belong to the largest cluster and the blue nodes represent the nodes removed because they depend on failed nodes in the other network. In each stage, we first remove the nodes that do not belong to the largest cluster of the network. Next, we remove the nodes that depend on the failed nodes in the other network.

Following this approach we can construct the sequence, ψ_t' and ϕ_t', of the remaining fraction of nodes at each stage of the cascade of failures. The general form is given by

$$
\begin{aligned}
\psi_1' &\equiv p, \\
\phi_1' &= p g_A(\psi_1'), \\
\psi_t' &= p g_B(\phi_{t-1}'), \\
\phi_t' &= p g_A(\psi_{t-1}').
\end{aligned}
\tag{3.1}
$$

To determine the state of the system at the end of the cascade process we look at ψ_τ' and ϕ_τ' in the limit of $\tau \to \infty$. This limit must satisfy the equations $\psi_\tau' = \psi_{\tau+1}'$ and $\phi_\tau' = \phi_{\tau+1}'$ since eventually the clusters stop fragmenting and thus, the fractions of randomly removed nodes at step τ and $\tau + 1$ are equal. Denoting $\psi_\tau' = x$ and $\phi_\tau' = y$, we arrive at the stationary state to a system of two equations with two unknowns,

$$
\begin{aligned}
x &= p g_B(y), \\
y &= p g_A(x).
\end{aligned}
\tag{3.2}
$$

The giant components of networks A and B at the end of the cascade of failures are, respectively, $P_{\infty,A}$ and $P_{\infty,B}$ with the forms:

$$
\begin{aligned}
P_{\infty,A} &= \psi_\infty = x g_A(x), \\
P_{\infty,B} &= \phi_\infty = y g_B(y).
\end{aligned}
\tag{3.3}
$$

(1) Theoretical approaches for interdependent ER networks [1]. For the case of two interdependent ER networks with average degrees $\bar{k}_A$ and $\bar{k}_B$, we substitute the corresponding generating functions from equations (1.10) and (1.11). Accordingly, we obtain the generating function $g_A(x)$ and $g_B(x)$ satisfy

$$
\begin{aligned}
g_A(x) &= 1 - \exp[\bar{k}_A(f_A - 1)], \\
g_B(x) &= 1 - \exp[\bar{k}_B(f_B - 1)],
\end{aligned}
\tag{3.4}
$$

where f_A and f_B satisfy

$$
\begin{aligned}
f_A &= \exp[\bar{k}_A(f_A - 1)], \\
f_B &= \exp[\bar{k}_B(f_B - 1)],
\end{aligned}
\tag{3.5}
$$

Excluding x and y, we get a system with respect to f_A and f_B:

$$
\begin{cases}
f_A = e^{-\bar{k}_A p(f_A-1)(f_B-1)} \\
f_B = e^{-\bar{k}_B p(f_A-1)(f_B-1)}.
\end{cases}
\tag{3.6}
$$

Introducing a new variable $r = f_A^{1/\bar{k}_A} = f_B^{1/\bar{k}_B}$, we reduce the system (3.6) to a single equation

$$
r = e^{-p(r^{\bar{k}_A}-1)(r^{\bar{k}_B}-1)},
\tag{3.7}
$$

which can be solved graphically or numerically for any p. The critical case corresponds to the tangential condition

$$1 = \frac{d}{dr} e^{-p(r^{\bar{k}_A}-1)(r^{\bar{k}_B}-1)} = p[\bar{k}_A r^{\bar{k}_A} + \bar{k}_B r^{\bar{k}_B} - (\bar{k}_A + \bar{k}_B) r^{\bar{k}_A+\bar{k}_B}], \qquad (3.8)$$

from which the critical value of $r = r_c$ satisfies the transcendental equation

$$r = \exp\left[-\frac{(1 - r^{\bar{k}_A})(1 - r^{\bar{k}_B})}{\bar{k}_A r^{\bar{k}_A} + b r^{\bar{k}_B} - (\bar{k}_A + \bar{k}_B) r^{\bar{k}_A+\bar{k}_B}} \right], \qquad (3.9)$$

and the critical value of $p = p_c$ can be found from equation (3.8) to be

$$p_c = \frac{1}{\bar{k}_A r_c^{\bar{k}_A} + \bar{k}_B r_c^{\bar{k}_B} - (\bar{k}_A + \bar{k}_B) r_c^{\bar{k}_A+\bar{k}_B}}. \qquad (3.10)$$

The values of p_c and P_∞ for different $\bar{k}_A$ and $\bar{k}_B > \bar{k}_A$ are presented as function of $\bar{k}_A/\bar{k}_B$. In case $\bar{k}_A = \bar{k}_B = \bar{k}$, $f_A = f_B = f$, and f_c satisfy the equation [1],

$$f_c = \exp\left[\frac{1 - f_c}{2f_c} \right], \qquad (3.11)$$

which gives a solution $f_c = 0.284\,67$, $p_c = 2.455\,4/\bar{k}$, and the critical fraction of nodes in the mutual giant component is $P_\infty = p_c(1 - f_c)^2 = 1.256\,4/\bar{k}$. Numerical simulations of the ER networks are in excellent agreement with the theory, see below.

(2) Numerical simulations. The theory developed above can be validated by simulations [1] that generate interdependent random networks with given degree distributions. The percolation process shows an abrupt first-order phase transition, quite different from a second-order phase transition characterizing percolation of a single network, where P_∞ is a continuous function at $p = p_c$. For a finite N and p close to p_c, the giant mutually connected component exists in a particular network realization with probability $P_\infty(p, N)$. As $N \to \infty$, $P_\infty(p, N)$ converges to a Heaviside step function, $\Theta(p - p_c)$, which discontinuously changes value from zero for $p < p_c$ to one for $p > p_c$ (figure 3.5(a)). The simulation results for the value of p_c (figure 3.5(a)) agree excellently with the analytical results presented below. For two interdependent scale-free networks with power-law degree distributions, Buldyrev et al [1] show that the existence criteria for the giant component are quite different from those in a single network. For a single scale-free network with $\lambda \leqslant 3$, a giant component exists for every non-zero value of p [2]. In marked contrast, for interdependent scale-free networks, there is no giant component below the critical value $p_c \neq 0$, even for $2 < \lambda \leqslant 3$ [1]. Since low degree nodes can be easily disconnected, the advantage of a broad distribution for a single network (where $p_c = 0$) becomes a disadvantage for interdependent networks. This is since hubs in one network may depend on low degree in the other one. In figure 3.5(b) this behaviour is demonstrated by comparing simulation results for several scale-free

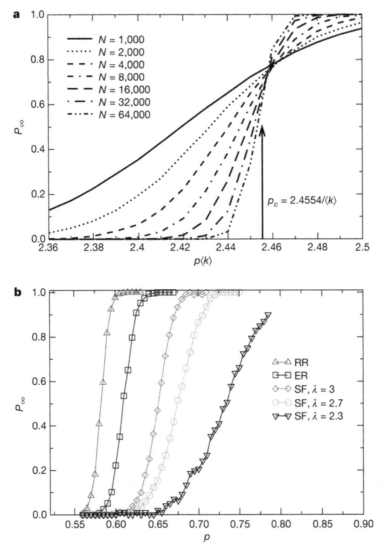

Figure 3.5. a) Numerical simulations of coupled ER networks with $\bar{k} = \bar{k}_A = \bar{k}_B$ and a finite number of nodes, N. The probability of existence of the giant mutually connected component, P_∞, is shown as function of p for different values of N. As $N \to \infty$, the curves converge to a step function. The theoretical prediction of p_c is shown by the arrow. **(b)** Simulation results for P_∞ as a function of p for coupled scale-free (SF) networks with $\lambda = 3, 2.7, 2.3$, coupled ER networks and coupled random regular (RR) networks, all with the same average degree of $\bar{k} = 4$ and $N = 50,000$. The simulation results agree very well with our analytical results. We note that the broader the distribution, the higher the value of p_c. This is in marked contrast with a single scale-free network. Reproduced from [1], copyright 2010 with permission of Springer.

networks with different λ values, an ER network and a random regular network, all with an average degree of $\bar{k} = 4$. The simulation results are in full agreement with the analytical results and show that p_c is indeed higher when the distribution becomes broader, i.e., smaller λ.

3.3.2 Partially interdependent networks

The dynamic process of two partially interdependent networks is the same as in section 3.3.1, but the two networks are partially interdependent on each other with fractions q_A and q_B of dependent nodes, respectively (see figure 3.2(b)). Next, we describe how to analyze the robustness of two partially interdependent networks by using the percolation theory step by step [7, 21, 26].

(1) The remaining fraction of network A nodes after an initial removal of nodes is $\psi_1' \equiv p$. The initial removal of nodes will disconnect some nodes from the giant component. The remaining functional part of network A therefore contains a fraction $\psi_1 = \psi_1' g_A(\psi_1')$ of the network nodes, where $g_A(\psi_1')$ is still the same as in equation (1.14).

(2) Since a fraction q_B of nodes from network B depends on nodes from network A, the number of nodes in network B that become nonfunctional is $(1 - \psi_1)q_B = q_B[1 - \psi_1' g_A(\psi_1')]$. Accordingly, the remaining fraction of network B nodes is $\phi_1' = 1 - q_B[1 - \psi_1' g_A(\psi_1')]$, and the fraction of nodes in the giant component of network B is $\phi_1 = \phi_1' g_B(\phi_1')$.

(3) Following this approach we can again construct the sequence, ψ_t' and ϕ_t', of the remaining fraction of nodes at each stage of the cascade of failures. The general form is given by

$$
\begin{aligned}
\psi_1' &\equiv p, \\
\phi_1' &= 1 - q_B[1 - pg_A(\psi_1')], \\
\psi_t' &= p[1 - q_A(1 - g_B(\phi_{t-1}'))], \\
\phi_t' &= 1 - q_B[1 - pg_A(\psi_{t-1}')].
\end{aligned}
\tag{3.12}
$$

To determine the state of the system at the end of the cascade process we look at ψ_τ' and ϕ_τ' in the limit of $\tau \to \infty$. This limit must satisfy the equations $\psi_\tau' = \psi_{\tau+1}'$ and $\phi_\tau' = \phi_{\tau+1}'$ since eventually the clusters stop fragmenting and thus the fractions of randomly removed nodes at step τ and $\tau + 1$ are equal. Denoting $\psi_\tau' = x$ and $\phi_\tau' = y$, we arrive at the stationary state to a system of two equations with two unknowns,

$$
\begin{aligned}
x &= p\{1 - q_A[1 - g_B(y)]\}, \\
y &= 1 - q_B[1 - g_A(x)p].
\end{aligned}
\tag{3.13}
$$

The giant components of networks A and B at the end of the cascade of failures are, respectively, $P_{\infty,A}$ and $P_{\infty,B}$ with the same form as equation (3.3).

(1) Analytical studies for ER networks. In the case of two ER networks, whose degrees are Poisson distributed, the problem can be solved explicitly. Suppose that the average degree of the network A is $\bar{k}_A$ and the average degree of the network B is $\bar{k}_B$. Then, $G_{A1}(\xi) = G_{A0} = \exp[\bar{k}_A(\xi - 1)]$ and $G_{B1}(\xi) = G_{B0} = \exp[\bar{k}_B(\xi - 1)]$. Accordingly, $p_B(x) = 1 - f_B$ and $p_A(x) = 1 - f_A$ and therefore system equation (3.13) becomes

$$
\begin{cases}
x = p[1 - q_A f_B] \\
y = 1 - q_B(1 - p[1 - f_A]),
\end{cases}
\tag{3.14}
$$

where f_A and f_B satisfy the transcendental equations

$$\begin{cases} f_A = \exp[\bar{k}_A x(f_A - 1)] \\ f_B = \exp[\bar{k}_B y(f_B - 1)]. \end{cases} \tag{3.15}$$

The fraction of nodes in the giant components of networks A and B, respectively, at the end of the cascade process are given by $\psi_\infty = p(1 - f_A)(1 - q_A f_B)$ and $\phi_\infty = (1 - f_B)(1 + q_B(1 - p) - p q_B f_A)$. Excluding x and y from systems (3.14) and (3.15), we obtain a system:

$$\begin{cases} f_A = e^{-\bar{k}_A p(f_A - 1)(q_A f_B - 1)} \\ f_B = e^{-\bar{k}_B(q_B(1 - p[1 - f_A]) - 1)(f_B - 1)}. \end{cases} \tag{3.16}$$

The first equation can be solved with respect to f_B and the second equation can be solved with respect to f_A

$$\begin{cases} f_B = \dfrac{1}{q_A}\left[1 - \dfrac{\log f_A}{\bar{k}_A p(f_A - 1)} \right], f_A \neq 1; \ \forall f_B, f_A = 1 \\ f_A = \dfrac{1}{q_B}\left[\dfrac{1 + q_B(p - 1)}{p} - \dfrac{\log f_B}{\bar{k}_B p(f_B - 1)} \right], f_B \neq 1; \ \forall f_A, f_B = 1. \end{cases} \tag{3.17}$$

The solutions of system (3.17) can be graphically presented on the f_A, f_B plane (figure 3.6). The solutions are presented as a crossing of either $f_B(f_A)$ or $f_A = 1$ with $f_B(f_A)$ or $f_A = 1$ and are restricted to the square $0 \leqslant f_A \leqslant 1 ; 0 \leqslant f_B \leqslant 1$. There are three different possible solutions: (i) the solution where the giant components of both networks are zero ($f_A = 1$ and $f_B = 1$); (ii) a solution for which only one of the giant components of either network A or B is zero ($f_A = 1$ and $f_B \neq 1$ or $f_A \neq 1$ and $f_B = 1$) as in figure 3.6(d) (or figure 3.6(e)); (iii) a solution for which both networks have a non-zero giant component ($f_A \neq 1$ and $f_B \neq 1$). This solution is given by the lowest intersection point of the curves. This solution may disappear in two different scenarios.

(2) Numerical simulations. Next, we show how to validate the correctness of the theory using numerical simulations, which can be achieved by removal of nodes in the partially interdependent networks system. We show an iterative process of failures for ER networks of size $N_A = N_B = 8 \times 10^5$ in figure 3.7. In figure 3.7(a), the system shows an iterative process that yields a first-order collapse for $p = 0.745\,5$, $\bar{k}_A = \bar{k}_B = 2.5$, $q_A = 0.7$ and $q_B = 0.6$. Note that p is below and very close to the critical point and q_A is large. For the same values of average degrees in both networks, when the coupling strength is $q_A = 0.2$ much smaller compared to $q_A = 0.7$ even when $q_B = 0.75$, larger than $q_B = 0.6$, we observe an iterative process of failures that leads to a continuous second-order transition. Symbols represent simulation results for different random realizations of the networks. Solid lines represent the solution of the system in equation (3.14). In figure 3.7(c), we show the fraction of nodes in network's B giant component, ϕ_∞, as a function of q_A

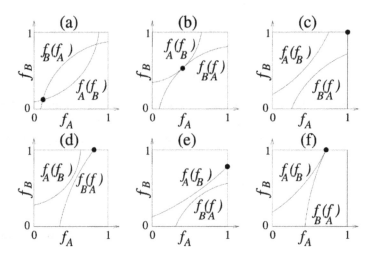

Figure 3.6. Illustrations of the different graphical solutions of the system of equations (3.17) (see text for detailed explanation of the different plots). Reproduced with permission from [7], copyright 2010 by The American Physical Society.

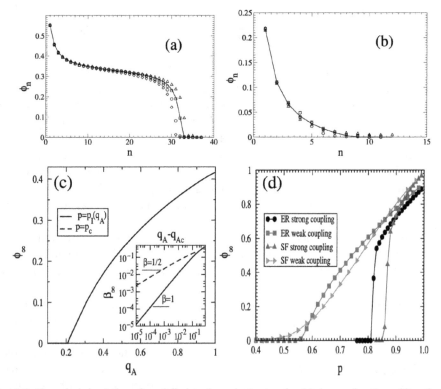

Figure 3.7. Numerical simulation of partially interdependent networks. (a) ϕ_n as a function of iterations, n, when the system exhibits a first-order phase transition. (b) ϕ_n as a function of iterations, n, when the system exhibits a second-order phase transition. (c) ϕ_∞ as a function of q_A. (d) Φ_∞ as a function of p for strong and weak interdependent ER and SF networks. Reproduced with permission from [7], copyright 2010 by The American Physical Society.

computed at $p = p_I(q_A)$, i.e., the line of the first-order phase transition. The results are obtained by solving system (3.17) with additional condition $df_A/df_B \times df_B/df_A = 1$ for $\bar{k}_A = \bar{k}_B = 3$ and $q_B = 1$. The inset in figure 3.7(c) shows the same results (solid line) as a function of $|q_A - q_{A_c}|$ yielding a straight line with slope $\phi = 1$ in a double logarithmic scale. If q_A is changed but $p = p_c$ is kept constant we obtain a straight line with slope $\phi = 0.5$ (dashed line). Figure 3.7(d) shows the simulation results for the phase transition of ϕ_∞ as a function of p for $N = 50K$. For strong coupling between the networks we observe a jump in ϕ_∞ as expected in a first-order phase transition ER (circle) and SF (triangle up). For weak coupling between the networks the change in ϕ_∞ is gradual as expected for a second- and higher order phase transitions ER (square) and SF (right rectangle).

3.3.3 Networks with multiple support

The construction of interdependent of multiple support networks is presented in section 3.2.3, see [10]. For interdependent networks with multiple support, the simplest model assumes that in order to be functional, a node in network A(B) must (i) have at least one functional support node in network B(A), and (ii) belong to the giant component of functional nodes in network A(B). According to the above assumption, the dynamic process of cascading failures is as follows.

First, we consider the cascading failure process for the two interdependent networks with multiple support links from figure 3.3. In figure 3.8 we demonstrate the series of resulting node failures after one node in the system is attacked/fails.

Next, we describe how to analyze the robustness of interdependent networks with multiple support using percolation theory [10]. The mathematical expressions for the dynamic process of cascading failures are similar to those for fully interdependent networks, but one has to use slightly different forms of generating functions,

---

Box 3.2: The dynamic process of cascading failures of two interdependent networks with multiple support is as follows:

(1) Construct an interdependent network with multiple support as in section 3.2.3.

(2) Randomly select and remove a fraction $1 - p_A$ of nodes in network A, and independently randomly select and remove a fraction $1 - p_B$ of nodes in network B. Find the giant connected component of network A and remove nodes not in the giant component.

(3) In network B, we remove the nodes that have no remaining support nodes in network A. We then find the giant connected component of network B and remove nodes that are not in the giant component.

(4) In network A, we remove the nodes that have no remaining support nodes in network B. Then we find the giant connected component of network A and remove nodes that are not in the giant component.

(5) Repeat (3) and (4) until there are no new node failures in either network A or network B.

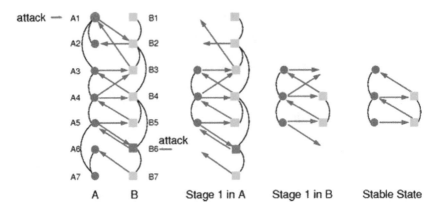

Figure 3.8. Demonstration of the dynamic process of cascading failures for two interdependent networks with multiple support links. The curved black links are connectivity links and the straight purple links are dependent links. The red nodes are initially attacked. Any nodes who have no remaining functional support nodes fail, as do nodes outside the giant component. First, we examine the nodes in network A and remove those that fail, we then move to network B and identify nodes that fail. This is done iteratively until a steady state is reached. Reproduced with permission from [10], copyright 2011 by The American Physical Society.

$$\phi_1 \equiv 1,$$
$$\psi_2' = p_A[1 - \tilde{G}_A(1 - \phi_1)],$$
$$\psi_2 = p_A g_A(\phi_2'),$$
$$\psi_t' = p_A[1 - \tilde{G}_A(1 - \phi_{t-1})], \qquad (3.18)$$
$$\psi_t = p_A g_A(\phi_t'),$$
$$\phi_t' = p_B[1 - \tilde{G}_B(1 - \psi_t)],$$
$$\phi_t = p_B g_B(\phi_t'),$$

where $\tilde{G}$ is the generating function of the support degree distribution:

$$\tilde{G}_A = \sum_{k=0}^{\infty} \tilde{P}_A(k)x^k,$$
$$\tilde{G}_B = \sum_{k=0}^{\infty} \tilde{P}_B(k)x^k. \qquad (3.19)$$

To determine the state of the system at the end of the cascade process we look at ψ_τ' and ϕ_τ' in the limit $\tau \to \infty$. This limit must satisfy the equations $\psi_\tau' = \psi_{\tau+1}'$ and $\phi_\tau' = \phi_{\tau+1}'$ since eventually the clusters stop fragmenting and thus the fractions of randomly removed nodes at step τ and $\tau + 1$ are equal. Denoting $\psi_\tau = x$ and $\phi_\tau = y$, we arrive at the stationary state for a system of two equations with two unknowns,

$$x = p_A[1 - \tilde{G}_A(1 - y)]g_A(p_A[1 - \tilde{G}_A(1 - y)]),$$
$$y = p_B[1 - \tilde{G}_B(1 - x)]g_B(p_B[1 - \tilde{G}_B(1 - x)]). \qquad (3.20)$$

The giant components of networks A and B at the end of the cascade of failures are, respectively, $P_{\infty,A} = x$ and $P_{\infty,B} = y$.

(1) The analytical solution for ER networks. In most of the cases, equation (3.20) can be solved numerically, including SF networks. However, for ER networks with average degrees $\bar{k}_A$ and $\bar{k}_B$, $G_0(x)$ and $G_1(x)$ have the same simple form. Thus, we substitute the corresponding generating function equations (1.10) and (1.11) into equation (3.20), and we can derive the percolation features for the fractions of the stable giant components of both coupled ER networks

$$\mu_\infty^A = R^A(1 - e^{-c_0^{BA}\mu_\infty^B})(1 - e^{-a\mu_\infty^A}), \tag{3.21}$$

$$\mu_\infty^B = R^B(1 - e^{-c_0^{AB}\mu_\infty^A})(1 - e^{-b\mu_\infty^B}). \tag{3.22}$$

Equations (3.21) and (3.22) are simple and can be related to the theory of random percolation of a single ER network, for which the fraction of the giant component is $\mu_\infty = R(1 - e^{-\langle k \rangle \mu_\infty})$. The coupled ER networks bring new terms $1 - e^{-c_0^{BA}\mu_\infty^B}$ and $1 - e^{-c_0^{AB}\mu_\infty^A}$. In the limit of $c_0^{AB} \to \infty$ (or $c_0^{BA} \to \infty$), the giant component of network B (or network A) does not depend on the other network and behaves similarly to the random percolation of a single network.

From equations (3.21) and (3.22), we can find μ_∞^A and μ_∞^B for a given set of parameters R^A, R^B, c_0^{BA} and c_0^{AB}. However, for some values of R^A, R^B, c_0^{BA} and c_0^{AB}, the solutions for μ_∞^A and μ_∞^B between 0 and 1 may not exist. There exist critical thresholds of R^A, R^B, c_0^{BA} and c_0^{AB} above which the two coupled ER networks have non-zero mutually connected giant components. They are represented as R_c^A, R_c^B, c_c^{BA} and c_c^{AB}. These values can be solved by finding the tangent point of the two curves (μ_∞^A is plotted as a function of μ_∞^B). The thresholds can be found from the tangential condition

$$\frac{d\mu_\infty^A}{d\mu_\infty^B}\bigg|_{equation(19)} \frac{d\mu_\infty^B}{d\mu_\infty^A}\bigg|_{equation(20)} = 1, \tag{3.23}$$

together with equations (3.21) and (3.22).

(2) Numerical simulations. Next, we compare our theoretical results obtained above to those of numerical simulations. We begin with comparing the simulations of the stages of the failure cascade in coupled ER networks with the theoretical predictions. In all simulations, we use $N^A = N^B = 10^6$. Figure 3.9 shows μ_n^A and μ_n^B as a function of n, the number of iterations, for $\bar{k}_A = \bar{k}_B = 4$, $c_0^{AB} = c_0^{BA} = 4$, $R^B = 1$ and for different values of R^A. One sees very good agreement between the theory and the simulations. Close to R_c^A, both μ_n^A and μ_n^B show large fluctuations between different realizations (shown in figures 3.9(c) and 3.9(d)). The random realizations split into two classes: one that converges to a non-zero giant component for both networks and the other that results in a complete fragmentation. The agreement

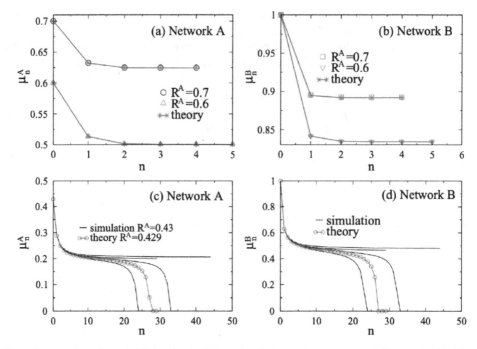

Figure 3.9. The case of coupled ER networks. Comparison between the theoretical predictions, obtained from equation (3.18), and their corresponding generating functions, and numerical simulations. (a) and (b) μ_n^A and μ_n^B at different stages n of the cascade of failures for $R^A = 0.7$ and 0.6 above $R_c^A \approx 0.43$ for both theory (lines) and simulations (symbols). One can see that both μ_n^A and μ_n^B approach stable plateau values μ_∞^A and μ_∞^B at the end of the cascade of failures. The agreement between theory and numerical simulations is very good. (c)–(d) μ_n^A and μ_n^B at different stages n of the cascade of failures for $R^A \approx R_c^A$. The bare lines represent several realizations of the simulations and the lines with symbols represent the theoretical predictions. One can see that for the early stages (small n) the agreement is good, however at large n the deviation due to random fluctuations in the actual fraction of the giant component starts to increase. The random realizations split into two classes: one that converges to a non-zero giant component for both networks and the other that results in a complete fragmentation. Reproduced with permission from [10], copyright 2011 by The American Physical Society.

between the simulations and theoretical predictions is also good for different values of R^B, a, b and c_0^{AB} and c_0^{BA}.

The fractions of the giant components of both network A (μ_∞^A) and network B (μ_∞^A) in the stable state for coupled ER networks can be found from equations (3.21) and (3.22). We solve these equations numerically for different R^A and R^B, and compare the theoretical predictions with the simulation results (figure 3.10). For simplicity, we assume $\bar{k}_A = \bar{k}_B = 4$ and that the initial fraction of nodes affected by the random attack in network A is twice as large as that in network B ($1 - R^A = 2(1 - R^B)$). We test different average degrees of inter-links for both networks $c_0^{AB} = c_0^{BA}$.

In figure 3.10, we present results for the giant components of both networks as a function of R^A and R^B. For different sets of c_0^{AB} and c_0^{BA}, we find good agreement

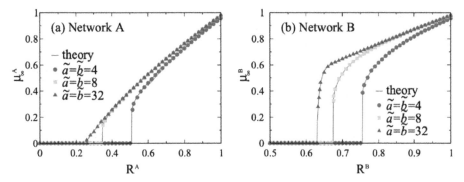

Figure 3.10. (a) The giant components, μ_∞^A and (b) μ_∞^B in the stable states as a function of R^A and R^B for coupled ER networks A and B. Several curves for $c_0^{AB} = c_0^{BA} = 4$, 8 and 32 are shown. The theory (lines) fits very well with the simulation results (symbols). One can see that for a given set of c_0^{AB} and c_0^{BA} there exist critical thresholds R_c^A and R_c^B, below which both networks will collapse and have no stable non-zero giant components. The value of R_c^A approaches the critical threshold of random percolation ($r = 1/a = 0.25$) of a single network for large values of c_0^{AB} and c_0^{BA}. The initial attack on network B is smaller than that on network A and thus $R_c^B > R_c^A$. Reproduced with permission from [10], copyright 2011 by The American Physical Society.

between the theory and simulation results. One can see the critical R_c^A and R_c^B, which are the minimum fractions of both networks needed to be kept at the beginning of the cascade of failures in order to have non-zero connected giant components for both networks at the stable state. At R_c^A and R_c^B, both μ_∞^A and μ_∞^B show an abrupt change from a finite fraction (μ_c^A and μ_c^B) to zero. As c_0^{AB} and c_0^{BA} increase, R_c^A approaches the critical threshold of random percolation of a single ER network, which is $1/a$. As expected for single networks, μ_c^A and μ_c^B approach 0 and a second-order phase transition exists for large c_0^{AB} and c_0^{BA}. However, for finite c_0^{AB} and c_0^{BA} the changes of μ_∞^A and μ_∞^B are discontinuous at R_c^A and R_c^B, indicating a first-order phase transition. This result is predicted by equations (3.21) and (3.22). We find that the theory fits well with the simulation results for the entire range of R_c^A and R_c^B for different values of c_0^{AB} and c_0^{BA}.

3.3.4 Interconnected networks

In the previous section we introduced percolation of interdependent networks where two networks are connected by dependency links. In this section we will introduce the case of interconnected networks where two networks are connected by connectivity links [5]. In this case, the links between the networks are usually beneficial for the robustness of the system. If we examine figure 3.11, we can see that considering only the links within each network would lead the giant component of each respective network to include only the nodes marked in red. However, due to the existence of the interconnection links between the networks, the small blue clusters also survive because they are directly or indirectly connected with the red

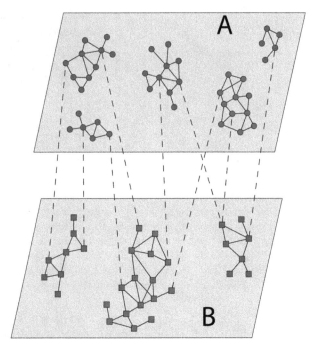

Figure 3.11. Two networks A and B are interconnected with each other. Nodes interact directly with other nodes in their immediate network, and also with nodes in the second network. Reproduced from [5] with permission of the authors.

nodes through the interconnections. Next, we follow Leicht and D'Souza [5] to study the percolation properties of such systems.

For the case of two interconnected networks, each individual network A is characterized by a multi-degree distribution, $\{P_{k_A k_B}^A\}$, where $P_{k_A k_B}^A$ is the fraction of nodes in network A that have k_A edges to nodes in network A, and k_B edges to nodes in network B. The multi-degree distribution for each network may be written in the form of a generating function:

$$G_A(x_A, x_B) = \sum_{k_A, k_B=0}^{\infty} P_{k_A k_B}^A x_A^{k_A} x_B^{k_B}. \tag{3.24}$$

Consider selecting uniformly at random an edge between a node in network B and a node in network A (i.e., a B-A edge). Let $q_{k_A k_B}^{AB}$ denote the probability of following a randomly chosen B-A edge to a node with excess B degree (which has a total B-degree of $k_B + 1$). The generating function for the distribution, $\{q_{k_A k_B}^{AB}\}$ is,

$$G_{AB}(x_A, x_B) = \sum_{k_A, k_B=0}^{\infty} q_{k_A k_B}^{AB} x_A^{k_A} x_B^{k_B} = \frac{G_A^{'B}(x_A, x_B)}{G_A^B(1, 1)}, \tag{3.25}$$

where $G_A'^B(x_A, x_B)$ denotes the first derivative of $G_A(x_A, x_B)$ with respect to x_B and and the denominator is a normalization constant so that $G_{AB}(1, 1) = 1$. Also note that $G_A'^B(1, 1)$ is the average B-degree for a node in network A.

We now consider starting from a randomly chosen A-node, rather than a random A-B edge. The generating function for the probability distribution of component sizes is,

$$H_A(x_A, x_B) = x_A G_A[H_{AA}(x_A, x_B), H_{AB}(x_A, x_B)]. \tag{3.26}$$

The preceding results regard components in the sub-critical regime where no giant connected component exists. Once a giant component emerges, the generating functions allow us to calculate properties of components *not* belonging to it. The giant component will span multiple networks and calculating its size requires accounting for the contribution from each network. Let S_A be the fraction of A-nodes belonging to the giant component. The probability that a randomly chosen A-node is *not* part of the giant component must then satisfy the following equation,

$$1 - S_A = G_A(u_{AA}, u_{AB}), \tag{3.27}$$

where u_{AB} is the probability that an A-B edge does not lead to the giant component. In addition, u_{AB} must satisfy,

$$u_{AB} = G_{AB}(u_{AA}, u_{AB}), \tag{3.28}$$

which is derived using the same self-consistency arguments that yielded equation (3.26).

All the above equations hold for a system of $l \geqslant 2$ interacting networks, and we now give a concrete example for $l = 2$ and both networks follow Poisson degree distribution with average degree k_α^α and k_β^β, respectively. Furthermore, the inter-network connectivity is described by a third Poisson degree distribution, for instance, $p_{k_\alpha k_\beta}^\alpha = [(\bar{k}_\alpha^\alpha)^{k_\alpha} e^{-\bar{k}_\alpha^\alpha}/k_\alpha!][(\bar{k}_\alpha^\beta)^{k_\beta} e^{-\bar{k}_\alpha^\beta}/k_\beta!]$. Recall that $\bar{k}_\mu^\nu$ denotes the average ν-degree for a node in network μ.

Once the giant component emerges the $u_{\nu\mu}$ which satisfy equation (3.28) are $u_{\alpha\alpha} = u_{\alpha\beta} = 1 - S_\alpha$ and $u_{\beta\beta} = u_{\beta\alpha} = 1 - S_\beta$, while S_α and S_β, respectively, the number of α-nodes and β-nodes in the giant component of the system, satisfy

$$S_\alpha = 1 - e^{-(\bar{k}_\alpha^\alpha S_\alpha + \bar{k}_\alpha^\beta S_\beta)} \tag{3.29}$$

$$S_\beta = 1 - e^{-(\bar{k}_\beta^\alpha S_\alpha + \bar{k}_\beta^\beta S_\beta)}. \tag{3.30}$$

To observe the change in connectivity of one network precipitated by an increase in connectivity of a second network attached to the first, we simulated a system of two interacting networks and fixed $\bar{k}_\alpha^\alpha, \bar{k}_\alpha^\beta$, and $\bar{k}_\beta^\alpha$ while varying $\bar{k}_\beta^\beta$ from 0 to 5 (figure 3.12). As $\bar{k}_\beta^\beta$ increases, the β-network becomes a single connected component (the traditional behavior for a single network) and $S_\beta \to 1$. However, the connectivity of α remains limited.

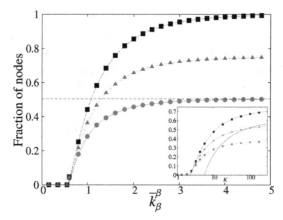

Figure 3.12. Numerical simulations and analytical results for connectivity in a system of two interacting Poisson degree distributed networks, α and β, with inter-network connectivity also Poisson distributed, as connectivity of β increases. Each network has 100,00 nodes, with $k_\alpha^\alpha = 0.4$ and $\bar{k}_\alpha^\beta = \bar{k}_\beta^\alpha = 0.5$. Shown are the fraction of α nodes, S_α (circles), β nodes, S_β (squares), and all nodes, S (triangles) in the system-wide giant component, with the dashed curves giving the analytic results, equations (3.29) and (3.29). The horizontal dashed line is the asymptotic value to which S_α approaches. (Inset) Analogous results when α has Poisson distribution with $k_\alpha^\alpha = 0.5$, inter-network edges follow a Poisson distribution with $\bar{k}_\alpha^\beta = \bar{k}_\beta^\alpha = 0.4$, but β has a power-law distribution with exponent $\lambda = 2.5$ and an exponential cutoff that we vary between $1 \leqslant \kappa \leqslant 300$. The solid curve is the result for network β when viewed in isolation. Reproduced from [5] with permission of the authors.

It can be shown that as $\bar{k}_\beta^\beta$ increases $S_\alpha \to (-1/k_\alpha^\alpha)W\left[-k_\alpha^\alpha e^{-k_\alpha^\alpha - \bar{k}_\alpha^\beta}\right] + 1$ (dashed horizontal line in figure 3.12), where W is the Lambert W function, also known as the product log.

3.3.5 Antagonistic networks

The study of interdependence between networks also led researchers to realize that there also exist other types of interactions. One example that is closely related to interdependence is *antagonistic* interactions [27]. In these interactions the fact that one node is functional requires that the antagonistic node (e.g., in another network) will not be functional. This could be the case if each of the two nodes are competing for some limited resource. This concept of antagonistic networks was later extended to competition in dynamic networks, where highly complex phenomena have been observed [28].

In the most basic model of antagonistic networks, two fully interacting networks are constructed as in figure 3.2(a) [27]. A node i belongs to the giant component of network A, if it has at least one neighbor $j \in N^A(i)$ in the giant component of network A, and has no neighbors $j \in N^B(i)$ in network B that belongs to the giant component of network B. Similarly, a node i belongs to the giant component of network B, if it has at least one neighbor $j \in N^B(i)$ in the giant component of network B, and has no neighbors $j \in N^A(i)$ in network A that belong to the giant component of network A. The percolation steady state can be found using a message passing algorithm. Each node i sends a message to each of its neighboring nodes j. A message sent from node i to node j in network A(B) is defined by $y_{i \to j}^{A(B)}$. The message $y_{i \to j}^{A(B)}$ indicates the probability that following a link (i, j) in network A(B) from j to i leads to a node i which is active in network A(B). The probability $S_i^{A(B)}$ that node i is active in network A (network B) depends on the messages $y_{k \to i}^{A(B)}$ that the neighbors k in networks A and B send to node i, i.e.,

$$
\begin{aligned}
S_i^A &= \left[1 - \prod_{k \in N_A(i)} (1 - y_{k \to i}^A) \right] \prod_{k \in N_B(i)} (1 - y_{k \to i}^B) \\
S_i^B &= \left[1 - \prod_{k \in N_B(i)} (1 - y_{k \to i}^B) \right] \prod_{k \in N_A(i)} (1 - y_{k \to i}^A).
\end{aligned}
\tag{3.31}
$$

Moreover the messages $y_{i \to j}^{A(B)}$ on a locally tree-like network are the fixed point solution $n \to \infty$ of the following iterative equations for $y_{i \to j}^{A(B),n}$,

$$
\begin{aligned}
y_{i \to j}^{A,n} &= \left[1 - \prod_{k \in N_A(i) \setminus j} (1 - y_{k \to i}^{A,n-1}) \right] \prod_{k \in N_B(i)} (1 - y_{k \to i}^{B,n-1}) \\
y_{i \to j}^{B,n} &= \left[1 - \prod_{k \in N_B(i) \setminus j} (1 - y_{k \to i}^{B,n-1}) \right] \prod_{k \in N_A(i)} (1 - y_{k \to i}^{A,n-1}).
\end{aligned}
\tag{3.32}
$$

In order to find the messages, usually the variables $y_{i \to j}^{A(B),n}$ are updated starting from given initial conditions until a fixed point of the iteration if found. At the fixed point the messages $y_{i \to j}^{A(B)} = \lim_{n \to \infty} y_{i \to j}^{A(B),n}$ satisfy the following relation:

$$
\begin{aligned}
y_{i \to j}^A &= \left[1 - \prod_{k \in N_A(i)j} (1 - y_{k \to i}^A) \right] \prod_{k \in N_B(i)} (1 - y_{k \to i}^B) \\
y_{i \to j}^B &= \left[1 - \prod_{k \in N_B(i) \setminus j} (1 - y_{k \to i}^B) \right] \prod_{k \in N_A(i)} (1 - y_{k \to i}^A).
\end{aligned}
\tag{3.33}
$$

If we average equations (3.31) and (3.33) over an ensemble of networks with degree distribution $p^A(k)$, $p^B(k)$ we get the equation for $S_{A(B)} = \langle S_i^{A(B)} \rangle$ and $S'_{A,B} = \langle y_{k \to i}^{A(B)} \rangle$, where $S_{A(B)}$ is the probability to find a node in the percolation cluster of network A (network B), and $S'_{A(B)}$ is the probability that following a link we reach a node in the percolation cluster of network A (network B). In particular, we have,

$$S_A = [1 - G_0^A(1 - S_A')]G_0^B(1 - S_B')$$
$$S_B = [1 - G_0^B(1 - S_B')]G_0^A(1 - S_A'). \tag{3.34}$$

In equation (3.34) we have used $G_0^{A(B)}(z)$ and $G_1^{A(B)}(z)$ to indicate the generating functions of network A and B defined as,

$$G_1(z) = \sum_k \frac{kp_k}{\langle k \rangle} z^{k-1}$$
$$G_0(z) = \sum_k p_k z^k, \tag{3.35}$$

where we use the degree distributions $p^A(k)$, $p^B(k)$, respectively, for network A and network B. Moreover $S_{A(B)}'$ on a locally tree-like network, satisfy the following recursive equations

$$S_A' = (1 - G_1^A(1 - S_A'))G_0^B(1 - S_B') = f_A(S_A', S_B'),$$
$$S_B' = (1 - G_1^B(1 - S_B'))G_0^A(1 - S_A') = f_B(S_A', S_B'). \tag{3.36}$$

Numerical simulations of percolation on antagonistic ER networks
In order to consider a specific example of antagonistic networks we analyse two antagonistic Poisson networks with average degree $\bar{k}_A = z_A$ and $\bar{k}_B = z_B$, respectively. In the case of a Poisson network we have $G_0(z) = G_1(z) = e^{\bar{k}(1-z)}$. Therefore we have $S_A = S_A'$ and $S_B = S_B'$. The recursive equations (3.36) become in this case,

$$S_A = (1 - e^{-z_A S_A})e^{-z_B S_B}$$
$$S_B = (1 - e^{-z_B S_B})e^{-z_A S_A}. \tag{3.37}$$

We characterize the phase diagram percolation on two antagonistic Poisson networks shown in figure 3.13. The critical lines are given by $z_A = 1$, $z_B = 1$ and by $z_B = \log z_A/(1 - 1/z_A)$ or $z_A = \log(z_B)/(1 - 1/z_B)$. In particular, we observe a first-order phase transition along the line $z_A > 1$, and $z_B = \log(z_A)/(1 - 1/z_A)$ and along the line $z_B > 1$ $z_A = \log(z_B)/(1 - 1/z_B)$ indicated as solid red lines in figure 3.13. The other lines marked as black dashed lines in figure 3.13 are critical lines of a second-order transition.

One should note that the solution $S_A' > 0$, $S_B' > 0$ in which both networks are percolating is always unstable in this case. This implies that for each realization of the percolation process, only one of the two networks is percolating. In order to demonstrate the bistability of the percolation solution in region III of the phase diagram we solved recursively equations (3.36) for $z_B = 1.5$ and variable values of z_A (see figure 3.14). We start from values of $z_A = 4$, and we solve equations (3.36) recursively. We find the solutions $S_A' = S_A'(z_A = 4) > 0$, $S_B' = S_B'(z_A = 4) = 0$. Then we lower slightly z_A and we solve again equation (3.36) recursively, starting from the initial condition $S_A'^o = S_A'(z_A = 4) + \epsilon$, $S_B'^o = S_B'(z_A = 4) + \epsilon$, and plot the result. (The small perturbation $\epsilon > 0$ is necessary in order not to end up with the trivial solution $S_A' = 0$, $S_B' = 0$.) Using this procedure we show that if we first lower the

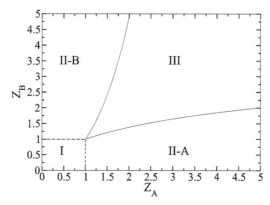

Figure 3.13. Phase diagram of the percolation process on two antagonistic Poisson networks of average degree $\bar{k}_A = z_A$ and $\bar{k}_B = z_B$, respectively. After [29], copyright 2013 IOP Publishing Ltd and SISSA Medialab srl.

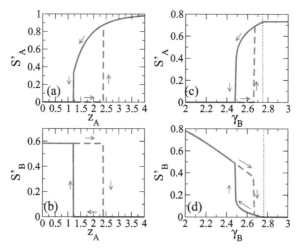

Figure 3.14. (a) and (b) The hysteresis loop for the percolation problem of two antagonistic Poisson networks with $z_B = 1.5$. (c) and (d) The hysteresis loop for the percolation problem for two antagonistic networks of different topologies: a Poisson network of average degree $z_A = 1.8$ and a scale-free networks with power-law exponent γ_B, minimal degree $m = 1$ and maximal degree $K = 100$. The hysteresis loop is performed using the method explained in the main text. The value of the parameter ϵ used in this figure is $\epsilon = 10^{-3}$. After [29], copyright 2013 IOP Publishing Ltd and SISSA Medialab srl.

value of z_A and then again we raise it, the spanning region III of the phase diagram as shown in figure 3.14(a) and (b) show a solution that displays a hysteresis loop. The hysteresis loop for the percolation problem on two antagonistic scale-free networks of different topology is shown in figure 3.14(c) and (d).

3.4 Targeted attack on partially interdependent networks

In order to study the cascading failure under targeted attack, we apply the general technique in which a targeted-attack problem can be mapped to a random-attack problem [8, 30]. A value $W_\alpha(k_i)$ is assigned to each node, which represents the probability that a node i with k_i links becomes inactive through targeted-attack. We focus on the family of functions [31]:

$$W_\alpha(k_i) = \frac{k_i^\alpha}{\sum\limits_{i=1}^{N} k_i^\alpha}, \quad -\infty < \alpha < +\infty. \tag{3.38}$$

When $\alpha > 0$, nodes with higher degree are targeted, while for $\alpha < 0$, nodes with lower degree have higher probability to fail. For $\alpha = 0$, all the nodes in the network have the same probability to fail, which is equivalent to the case of random attack.

Without loss of generality, we begin by studying the generating function and the giant component of network A after a targeted attack, which can be directly applied to network B. Next we study the generating functions of network A at each iteration.

(i) The generating function of network A is defined as

$$G_{A0}(x) = \sum_k P_A(k)x^k. \tag{3.39}$$

The generating function of the associated branching process is $G_{A1}(x) = G'_{A0}(x)/G'_{A0}(1)$ [1, 3, 7, 32]. The average degree of network A is defined as $a = \bar{k} = \sum_k P_A(k)k$.

(ii) We next remove a fraction $1 - p_1$ of nodes from network A according to equation (3.38) and remove the links of the removed nodes. Thus, we obtain that the generating function of the nodes left in network A is [4, 8, 32],

$$G_{Ab}(x) = \sum_k P_A^{p_1}(k)x^k = \frac{1}{p_1} \sum_k P_A(k)h_1^{k^\alpha} x^k, \tag{3.40}$$

where the new degree distribution of the remaining fraction p_1 of nodes $P_A^{p_1}(k) \equiv (1/p_1)P_A(k)h_1^{k^\alpha}$, where h_1 satisfies,

$$p_1 = G_\alpha(h_1) \equiv \sum_k P_A(k)h_1^{k^\alpha}, \quad h_1 \equiv G_\alpha^{-1}(p_1). \tag{3.41}$$

The average degree of the remaining nodes in network A at this stage is $\bar{k}(p_1) = \sum_k P_A^{p_1}(k)k$.

(iii) We remove the links between the failed nodes and the remaining nodes. Thus we find that the generating function of the remaining nodes is [4],

$$G_{Ac}(x) = G_{Ab}(1 - \tilde{p}_1 + \tilde{p}_1 x), \tag{3.42}$$

where $\tilde{p}_1$ is the fraction of the original links that connect to the remaining nodes, which satisfies

$$\tilde{p}_1 = \frac{p_1 N_A \bar{k}(p_1)}{N_A \bar{k}} = \frac{\sum\limits_k P_A(k)k h_1^{k^\alpha}}{\sum\limits_k P_A(k)k}. \tag{3.43}$$

Next, we can find the equivalent network A' with generating function $\tilde{G}_{A0}(x)$, such that after a fraction $1 - p_1$ of nodes are randomly removed, the new generating function of remaining nodes in A' is the same as $G_{Ac}(x)$. By solving the equation $\tilde{G}_{A0}(1 - p_1 + p_1 x) = G_{Ac}(x)$, and using equation (3.42), we obtain

$$\tilde{G}_{A0}(x) = G_{Ab}\left(1 - \frac{\tilde{p}_1}{p_1} + \frac{\tilde{p}_1}{p_1}x\right). \tag{3.44}$$

The generating function of the associated branching process is then $\tilde{G}_{A1}(x) = \tilde{G}'_{A0}(x) / \tilde{G}'_{A0}(1)$.

(iv) Thus, the targeted-attack problem on network A can be rigorously mapped to the random-attack problem on network A'. For network A, a fraction $1 - p_1$ of nodes is intentionally removed according to equation (3.38) and the fraction of nodes that belongs to the giant component is [4, 8, 33]:

$$P_A(p_1) = 1 - \tilde{G}_{A0}[1 - p_1(1 - f_A)], \tag{3.45}$$

where $f_A \equiv f_A(p_1)$ satisfies the transcendental equation,

$$f_A = \tilde{G}_{A1}[1 - p_1(1 - f_A)]. \tag{3.46}$$

For network B, a fraction $1 - p_2$ of nodes is removed according to equation (3.38) and the fraction of nodes that belongs to the giant component $p_B(p_2)$ is similar to equation (3.45), with p_1 being changed to p_2 and A being changed to B.

According to the definition of the fraction of nodes that belongs to the giant component, the dynamics of cascading failures is as follows: initially, fractions $1 - p_1$ and $1 - p_2$ of nodes are intentionally removed from network A and network B, respectively. The remaining fraction of network A nodes after an initial removal of $1 - p_1$ is $\psi'_1 = p_1$, and the remaining fraction of network B nodes after an initial removal of $1 - p_2$ is $\phi'_0 = p_2$. The remaining functional part of network A contains a fraction $\psi_1 = \psi'_1 p_A(\psi'_1)$ of network nodes. Accordingly, for the same reason, the remaining fraction of network B is $\phi'_1 = p_2[1 - q_B(1 - p_A(\psi'_1)p_1)]$, and the fraction of nodes in the giant component of network B is $\phi_1 = \phi'_1 p_B(\phi'_1)$. Then the sequence, ψ_t and ϕ_t, of the giant components, and the sequence ψ'_t and ϕ'_t, of the remaining fraction of nodes at each stage of the cascading failures, are constructed as follows:

$$\begin{aligned}
&\psi'_1 = p_A, \; \psi_1 = \psi'_1 p_A(\psi'_1), \\
&\phi'_1 = p_B, \; \phi'_1 = p_B[1 - q_B(1 - p_A(\psi'_1)p_1)], \; \phi_1 = \phi'_1 p_B(\phi'_1), \\
&\psi'_2 = p_1[1 - q_A(1 - p_B(\phi'_1)p_B)], \; \psi_2 = \psi'_2 p_A(\psi'_2), \\
&\phi'_2 = p_2[1 - q_B(1 - p_A(\psi'_2)p_A)], \; \phi_2 = \phi'_2 p_B(\phi'_2), \\
&\quad\cdots \\
&\psi'_t = p_A[1 - q_A(1 - p_B(\phi'_{t-1})p_B)], \; \psi_t = \psi'_t p_A(\psi'_t), \\
&\phi'_t = p_B[1 - q_B(1 - p_A(\psi'_t)p_A)], \; \phi_t = \phi'_t p_B(\phi'_t).
\end{aligned} \tag{3.47}$$

Next, we study the steady state of the system given by equation (3.47) after the cascading failures, which can be represented by ψ'_τ, ϕ'_τ in the limit of $\tau \to \infty$. The limit must satisfy the equations $\psi'_\tau = \psi'_{\tau+1}$, $\phi'_\tau = \phi'_{\tau+1}$ since eventually the clusters stop fragmenting and the fractions of randomly removed nodes at step n and $\tau + 1$ are equal. Denoting $\psi'_\tau = x$, $\phi'_\tau = y$, we arrive at a system of two symmetric equations:

$$x = p_A[1 - q_A(1 - p_B(y)p_B)],$$
$$y = p_B[1 - q_B(1 - p_A(x)p_A)].$$
(3.48)

And f_A, f_B can be expressed as:

$$f_A(f_B) = \frac{1}{q_B}\left[\frac{1 + q_B(p_A - 1)}{p_A} - \frac{\ln f_B}{bp_Ap_B(f_B - 1)}\right],$$
$$f_A \neq 1; \forall f_A, f_B = 1,$$
$$f_B(f_A) = \frac{1}{q_A}\left[\frac{1 + q_A(p_2 - 1)}{p_B} - \frac{\ln f_A}{ap_Ap_2(f_A - 1)}\right],$$
$$f_B \neq 1; \forall f_A, f_B = 1.$$
(3.49)

For equation (3.47), as $\alpha = 0$, figure 3.15 shows excellent agreement between computer simulations of the cascade of failures and the numerical results obtained by the analytical results of equation (3.47).

(1) The theoretical studies for $\alpha = 0$. For the special case, $\bar{k}_A = \bar{k}_B = k$, $p_A = p_B = p$, $q_A = q_B = q$, we obtain the equations:

$$f_A = f_B = f = e^{kp(f-1)[1-q+pq(1-f)]}, \quad 0 \leqslant f < 1,$$
(3.50)

and

$$\psi_\infty = \phi_\infty = p(1 - e^{-k\phi_\infty})[1 - q + pq(1 - e^{-k\phi_\infty})].$$
(3.51)

Equation (3.50) can be solved graphically as the intersection of a straight line $y = f$ and a curve $y = e^{kp(f-1)[1-q+pq(1-f)]}$. When p is small enough the curve increases very slowly and does not intersect with the straight line except at $f = 1$ which corresponds to the trivial solution. The condition for a first-order transition $(p = p^I)$ is that the derivatives of the equations of system (3.50) with respect to f are:

$$1 = f[kp^I(1 - q) + 2k(p^I)^2q(1 - f)].$$
(3.52)

And solving system (3.50) for $f \to 1$ yields the condition for the second-order transition $(p = p^{II})$:

$$kp^{II}(1 - q) = 1.$$
(3.53)

The analysis of equations (3.52) and (3.53) show that the first- and second-order transition lines coincide with each other:

$$p = p^I = p^{II} = \frac{1}{k(1 - q)}.$$
(3.54)

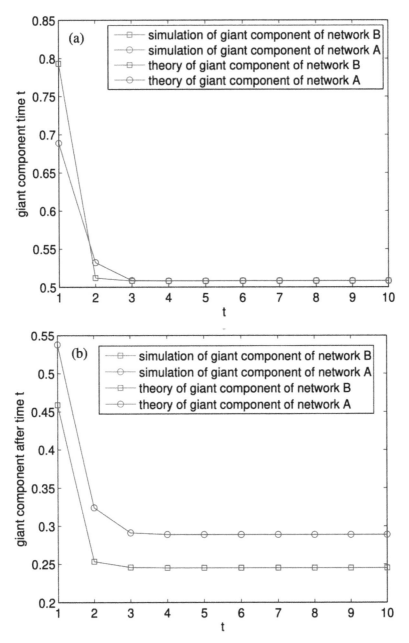

Figure 3.15. (a) Simulation and analytical results for the giant components of two fully interdependent ER networks after time t cascading failures. For each network $N = 100,000$, $\bar{k}_A = \bar{k}_B = 6$, $p_1 = 0.8$, $p_2 = 0.7$, $q_A = q_B = 1$. (b) Simulation results of the giant component of two partially interdependent ER networks after t cascading failures. For each network $N = 100,000$, $\bar{k}_A = \bar{k}_B = 6$, $q_A = 0.6$, $q_B = 0.65$, $p_1 = 0.49$, $p_2 = 0.56$. All values are the results of averaging over 10 realizations. ψ_∞ and ϕ_∞, the fraction of nodes in the giant components of networks A and B separately, after a cascade of failures. Note that the simulations results for fully and partially interdependent networks are identical to the theoretical values.

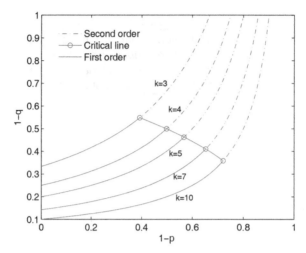

Figure 3.16. The phase transition is shown for $k = 3, 4, 5, 7$, and 10. The critical line (in red) is also graphically obtained from equation (3.55). Its tendency is to monotonically decrease with increasing average k. Reproduced with permission from [9], copyright 2010 The American Physical Society.

The critical values of p_c, q_c for which the phase transition changes from first order to second order are obtained when equations (3.50), (3.52) and (3.53) are satisfied simultaneously. Thus, we get the critical values that depend only on the average degree as,

$$
p_c = \frac{k + 1 - \sqrt{2k + 1}}{k},
$$
$$
q_c = \frac{\sqrt{2k + 1} + 1}{2k}.
$$
(3.55)

The phase transition and critical lines are graphically shown, respectively, in figure 3.16. From figure 3.16, the tendency of the critical line (in red) descends with average degree k.

(2) **The theoretical results for $\alpha \neq 0$.** When $\alpha \neq 0$, both of the two partially interdependent networks are initially attacked with probability $W_\alpha(k_i)$ (equation (3.38)). Initially, $1 - p_A$ and $1 - p_B$ fraction of nodes are targeted and removed from network A and network B, respectively. The generating functions will be defined for network A while similar equations describe network B. According to equation (3.38), $1 - p_A$ fraction of nodes are removed from network A but before the links of the remaining nodes which connect to the removed nodes are removed. The generating function of the nodes left in network A before removing the links to the removed nodes is

$$
G_{Ab}(x) = \sum_{k_1} P_{p_1}(k_1) x^{k_1} = \frac{1}{p_1} \sum_{k_1} P(k_1) h_1^{k_1^\alpha} x^{k_1},
$$
(3.56)

where the new degree distribution of the remaining fraction p_1 of nodes is $P_{p_1}(k_1) = \frac{1}{p_1} P(k_1) h_1^{k_1^\alpha}$, $G_\alpha(x) \equiv \sum_{k_1} P(k_1) x^{k_1^\alpha}$ and $h_1 \equiv G_\alpha^{-1}(p_1)$. The generating function

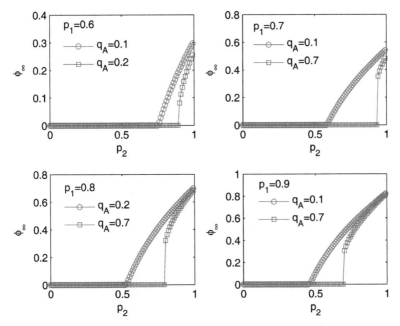

Figure 3.17. For given $p_1 = 0.6 - 0.9$, the system undergoes a first order phase transition and a second order phase transition for network B with strong and weak coupling. Reprinted with permission from [9], copyright 2010 by The American Physical Society.

of the new distribution of nodes left in network A after the links to the removed nodes are also removed is

$$G_{Ac}(x) = G_{Ab}(1 - \tilde{p}_1 + \tilde{p}_1 x), \tag{3.57}$$

where $\tilde{p}_1 = p_1 N_A \langle k_1(p_1) \rangle / N_A \langle k_1 \rangle = \sum_{k_1} P(k_1) k_1 h_1^{k_1^{\alpha}} / \Sigma_{k_1} P(k_1) k_1$ is the fraction of the original links that connect to the nodes left, $\langle k_1 \rangle$ is the average degree of the original network A, $\langle k_1(p_1) \rangle$ is the average degree of the remaining nodes before the links that are disconnected are removed (3.17). Then we can find the equivalent networks A′ and B′ with generating functions $\tilde{G}_{A0}(x)$ and $\tilde{G}_{B0}(x)$, such that after simultaneous random attack with $1 - p_1$ and $1 - p_2$ fractions of nodes, the new generating functions of nodes left in A′ and B′ are the same as $G_{Ac}(x)$ and $G_{Bc}(x)$. That is, the simultaneous targeted-attack problem on interdependent networks A and B can be solved as simultaneous random-attack problem on interdependent networks A′ and B′. By solving the equations $\tilde{G}_{A0}(1 - p_1 + p_1 x) = G_{Ac}(x)$, $\tilde{G}_{B0}(1 - p_2 + p_2 x) = G_{Bc}(x)$ and from equation (3.56), we can get

$$\tilde{G}_{A0}(x) = G_{Ab}\left(1 - \frac{\tilde{p}_1}{p_1} + \frac{\tilde{p}_1}{p_1} x\right),$$
$$\tilde{G}_{B0}(x) = G_{Bb}\left(1 - \frac{\tilde{p}_2}{p_2} + \frac{\tilde{p}_2}{p_2} x\right). \tag{3.58}$$

Simplified forms for $G_{Ab}(x)$, $G_{Ac}(x)$ and $\tilde{G}_{A0}(x)$ from equations (3.56), (3.57) and (3.58) exist for $\alpha = 1$,

$$G_{Ab}(x) = \frac{1}{p_1} \sum_{k_1} P(k_1) h_1^{k_1} x^{k_1} = \frac{1}{p_1} G_{A0}(h_1 x), \tag{3.59}$$

$$G_{Ac}(x) = \frac{1}{p_1} G_{A0}(h_1(1 - \tilde{p}_1 + \tilde{p}_1 x)), \tag{3.60}$$

$$\tilde{G}_{A0}(x) = \frac{1}{p_1} G_{A0}(h_1(1 - \frac{\tilde{p}_1}{p_1} + \frac{\tilde{p}_1}{p_1} x)), \tag{3.61}$$

where $G_{A0}(x)$ is the original generating function of network A, $h_1 = G_{A0}^{-1}(p_1)$, $\tilde{p}_1 = (G'_{A0}(h_1)/G'_{A0}(1))h_1$. For ER networks, we can also get $p_A(x) = 1 - f_A$, $p_B(y) = 1 - f_B$, where $p_A(x) = 1 - \tilde{G}_{A0}[1 - x(1 - f_A)]$, $f_A = \tilde{G}_{A1}[1 - x(1 - f_A)]$, and equations (3.59)–(3.61) become

$$\begin{aligned} x &= p_1[1 - q_A + p_2 q_A(1 - f_B)], \\ y &= p_2[1 - q_B + p_1 q_B(1 - f_A)]. \end{aligned} \tag{3.62}$$

The fraction of nodes in the giant components of networks A and B, respectively, at the end of the cascade process are then given by:

$$\begin{aligned} \psi_\infty &= p_1(1 - f_A)[1 - q_A + p_2 q_A(1 - f_B)], \\ \phi_\infty &= p_2(1 - f_B)[1 - q_B + p_1 q_B(1 - f_A)]. \end{aligned} \tag{3.63}$$

And f_A, f_B can be expressed as follows:

$$\begin{aligned} f_A(f_B) &= \frac{1}{q_B}\left[\frac{1 + q_B(p_1 - 1)}{p_1} - \frac{\ln f_B}{b p_1 p_2 h_2^2(f_B - 1)}\right], \\ & \quad f_A \neq 1; \forall f_A, f_B = 1, \\ f_B(f_A) &= \frac{1}{q_A}\left[\frac{1 + q_A(p_2 - 1)}{p_2} - \frac{\ln f_A}{a p_1 p_2 h_1^2(f_A - 1)}\right], \\ & \quad f_B \neq 1; \forall f_A, f_B = 1. \end{aligned} \tag{3.64}$$

Likewise, for targeted attack ($\alpha = 1$) on partially interdependent networks simultaneously, the phase transition changes from a first-order to a second-order percolation transition, as the coupling strength q_A is reduced. From figure 3.18, the phase transition lines are graphically presented, and the critical line (in red) descends with increasing p_A.

Both networks A and B are attacked simultaneously with probability $W_\alpha(k_i)$. When $\alpha > 0$, nodes with higher degree are more vulnerable and those nodes are intentionally attacked, when $\alpha < 0$, nodes with higher degree have lower probability to fail. Figure 3.19 shows the phase transition lines for different $\alpha > 0$ and $\alpha < 0$. The critical line (in red) is also found and it monotone increases with α.

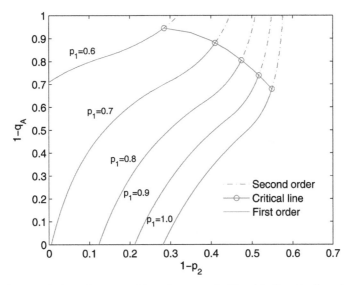

Figure 3.18. The percolation phase transition for network B with $\bar{k}_A = 3$, $\bar{k}_B = 4$, $q_B = 0.7$ and $p_A = 0.6 \sim 1.0$. The corresponding phase transition lines are shown. Also, the critical line is graphically seen (in red), and it monotonically decreases with p_A. Below the critical line, the system undergoes a first-order phase transition. As we approach the critical point, ϕ_∞ tends to 0. Above the critical line, the system undergoes a second-order transition. Reprinted with permission from [9], copyright 2010 by the American Physical Society.

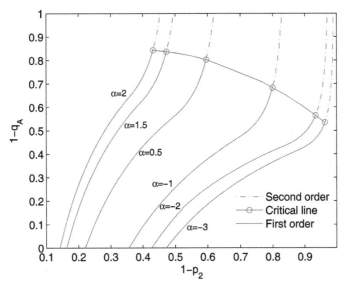

Figure 3.19. The percolation phase transition for network A with $\bar{k}_A = 3$, $\bar{k}_B = 4$, $q_B = 0.7$, $p_A = 0.8$ and $\alpha = -3, -2, -1, 0.5, 1.5, 2$. The corresponding phase transitions lines are showed. Also, the critical line is graphically seen (in red), and it monotonically increases with α. Below the critical line, the system undergoes a first order phase transition. As we approach the critical point, ψ_∞ tends to 0. Above the critical line, the system undergoes a second order transition. Reprinted with permission from [9], copyright 2010 by The American Physical Society.

References

[1] Buldyrev S V, Parshani R, Paul G, Stanley H E and Havlin S 2010 Catastrophic cascade of failures in interdependent networks *Nature* **464** 1025–8

[2] Cohen R, Erez K, Ben-Avraham D and Havlin S 2000 Resilience of the internet to random breakdown *Phys. Rev. Lett.* **85** 4626–8

[3] Newman M E J, Strogatz S H and Watts D J 2001 Random graphs with arbitrary degree distributions and their applications *Phys. Rev. E* **64** 026118

[4] Shao J, Buldyrev S V, Braunstein L A, Havlin S and Stanley H E 2009 Structure of shells in complex networks *Phys. Rev. E* **80** 036105

[5] Leicht E A and D'Souza R M 2009 Percolation on interacting networks arXiv:0907.0894v1

[6] Shai S, Kenett D Y, Kenett Y N, Faust M, Dobson S and Havlin S 2015 Critical tipping point distinguishing two types of transitions in modular network structures *Phys. Rev. E* **92** 062805

[7] Parshani R, Buldyrev S V and Havlin S 2010 Interdependent networks: reducing the coupling strength leads to a change from a first to second order percolation transition *Phys. Rev. Lett.* **105** 048701

[8] Huang X, Gao J, Buldyrev S V, Havlin S and Stanley H E 2011 Robustness of interdependent networks under targeted attack *Phys. Rev. E* **83** 065101

[9] Dong G, Gao J, Tian L, Du R and He Y 2012 Percolation of partially interdependent networks under targeted attack *Phys. Rev. E* **85** 016112

[10] Shao J, Buldyrev S V, Havlin S and Stanley H E 2011 Cascade of failures in coupled network systems with multiple support-dependence relations *Phys. Rev. E* **83** 036116

[11] Parshani R, Rozenblat C, Ietri D, Ducruet C and Havlin S 2010 Inter-similarity between coupled networks *Europhys. Lett.* **92** 68002

[12] Buldyrev S V, Shere N W and Cwilich G A 2011 Interdependent networks with identical degrees of mutually dependent nodes *Phys. Rev. E* **83** 016112

[13] Cellai D, López E, Zhou J, Gleeson J P and Bianconi G 2013 Percolation in multiplex networks with overlap *Phys. Rev. E* **88** 052811

[14] Hu Y, Zhou D, Zhang R, Han Z, Rozenblat C and Havlin S 2013 Percolation of interdependent networks with intersimilarity *Phys. Rev. E* **88** 052805

[15] Hu Y, Ksherim B, Cohen R and Havlin S 2011 Percolation in interdependent and interconnected networks: abrupt change from second to first order transition *Phys. Rev. E* **84** 066116

[16] Parshani R, Buldyrev S V and Havlin S 2011 Critical effect of dependency groups on the function of networks *Proc. Natl. Acad. Sci.* **108** 1007–10

[17] Bashan A, Parshani R and Havlin S 2011 Percolation in networks composed of connectivity and dependency links *Phys. Rev. E* **83** 051127

[18] Zhao J-H, Zhou H-J and Liu Y-Y 2013 Inducing effect on the percolation transition in complex networks *Nat. Commun.* **4** 2412

[19] Bunde A and Havlin S 1991 *Fractals and Disordered Systems* (New York: Springer)

[20] Stauffer D and Aharony A 1994 *Introduction to Percolation Theory* (Boca Raton, FL: CRC Press)

[21] Gao J, Buldyrev S V, Havlin S and Stanley H E 2011 Robustness of a network of networks *Phys. Rev. Lett.* **107** 195701

[22] Gao J, Buldyrev S V, Havlin S and Stanley H E 2012 Robustness of a network formed by n interdependent networks with a one-to-one correspondence of dependent nodes *Phys. Rev. E* **85** 066134

[23] Gao J, Li D and Havlin S 2014 From a single network to a network of networks *Natl Sci. Rev.* **1** 346–56

[24] Liu X, Stanley H E and Gao J 2016 Breakdown of interdependent directed networks *Proc. Natl Acad. Sci.* **113** 1138–43

[25] Gao J *et al* 2013 Percolation of a general network of networks 88 *Phys. Rev. E* **88** 062816

[26] Gao J, Buldyrev S V, Stanley H E and Havlin S 2012 Networks formed from interdependent networks *Nat. Phys.* **8** 40–8

[27] Zhao K and Bianconi G 2013 Percolation on interacting, antagonistic networks *J. Stat. Mech. Theory Exp.* **2013** P05005

[28] Danziger M M, Bonamassa I, Boccaletti S and Havlin S 2019 Dynamic interdependence and competition in multilayer networks *Nat. Phys.* **15** 178

[29] Zhao K and Bianconi G 2013 Percolation on interacting, antagonistic networks *J. Stat. Mech. Theory Exp.* **2013** P05005

[30] Cohen R, Erez K, Ben-Avraham D and Havlin S 2001 Breakdown of the internet under intentional attack *Phys. Rev. Lett.* **86** 3682–5

[31] Gallos L K, Cohen R, Argyrakis P, Bunde A and Havlin S 2005 Stability and topology of scale-free networks under attack and defense strategies *Phys. Rev. Lett.* **94** 188701

[32] Newman M E J 2002 Spread of epidemic disease on networks *Phys. Rev. E* **66** 016128

[33] Shao J, Buldyrev S V, Cohen R, Kitsak M, Havlin S and Stanley H E 2008 Fractal boundaries of complex networks *Europhys. Lett.* **84** 48004

Chapter 4

Robustness of networks composed of interdependent networks

4.1 Introduction

In this chapter we introduce the framework to study the robustness of a network formed by n interdependent networks. The approach to analyze this complex system and the mathematical tools are based on percolation theory and on the generating functions technique. In chapter 3 we introduced the analysis of a pair of interdependent networks, however, in many realistic examples, more than two networks depend on each other. As modern technologies enhance the dependencies between infrastructure systems, infrastructures such as water and food supply, communications, fuel, financial transactions, and power stations are becoming more and more coupled together [1–4], see figure 4.1. Thus, understanding the vulnerability due to such interdependencies is a major challenge for designing resilient infrastructures and for mitigation of cascading failures. In addition to the internal structure of each network, the interdependencies between them, i.e., the structure of the network of networks, determines the stability of the entire system. When n networks form a line or a tree-like structure through dependency links between the networks, the system becomes more vulnerable as the number of networks increases because the dependency links induce more failures in the system [5]. In the more complex case when there are loops of dependency links between the networks in the network of networks, the system becomes even more vulnerable [6]. In the following we discuss four real world examples of networks of interdependent networks.

(A) Network of interdependent infrastructure networks
Infrastructures, which affect all areas of our modern life, are usually interdependent as illustrated in figure 4.1. Examples of interdependent systems include electric power, natural gas and petroleum production and distribution, telecommunications, transportation, water supply, banking and finance systems, emergency and government services, agriculture, and other services which are critical for security and economic prosperity. Disasters ranging from hurricanes to large-scale power blackouts and

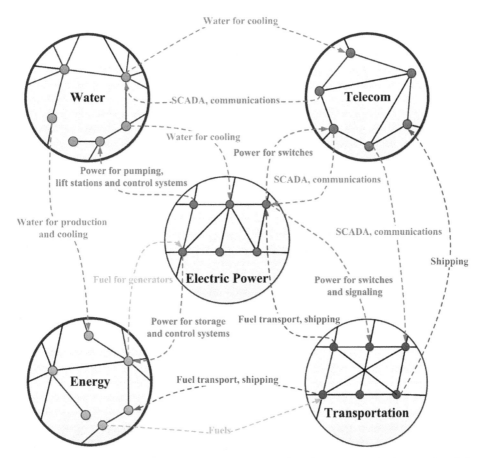

Figure 4.1. Illustration of the interdependent relationships among different infrastructures [2]. These complex relationships are characterized by multiple connections between infrastructures, feed-back and feed-forward paths, and intricate, branching topologies. The connections create an intricate web that, depending on the characteristics of its linkages, can transmit shocks throughout broad swaths of the economy and across multiple infrastructures. It is clearly incorrect to analyze or understand the behavior of a given infrastructure in isolation from the environment or other infrastructures. Rather, one must consider multiple interconnected infrastructures and their interdependencies. For example, the reliable operation of modern infrastructures depends on computerized control systems, from the SCADA system that controls electric power grids to computerized systems that manage the flow of rail cars and goods in the rail industry. In these cases, the infrastructures require information transmitted and delivered by the communication infrastructure. From [8], copyright The Author(s) 2014. Published by Oxford University Press on behalf of China Science Publishing & Media Ltd.

terrorist attacks have shown that significant catastrophic vulnerability arises from the many interdependencies across different infrastructures [2–4]. Infrastructures are frequently connected at multiple points through a wide variety of mechanisms, such that unidirectional or bidirectional dependency relationships can exist between different pairs of nodes in connected networks. For example, in California, the electric power disruptions in early 2001 affected oil and natural gas production, refinery operations, pipeline transport of gasoline and jet fuel within California and its neighboring states as well as the transportation of water from northern to central and southern regions of the state for crop irrigation. Another dramatic real-world example of a cascade of failures between infrastructures is the electrical blackout that affected all Italy on 28 September 2003: the shut-down of power stations directly led to the failure of nodes in the Supervisory Control and Data Acquisition (SCADA) communication network, which in turn caused further breakdown of power stations [3, 7], as well as breakdown of transportation systems, financial systems and health services. Identifying, understanding, and analyzing vulnerabilities due to such interdependencies are therefore urgent challenges. These challenges are greatly magnified by the breadth and complexity advances of our modern critical interdependent infrastructures [2].

(B) Network of ecological networks
Understanding the robustness of interacting networks of species in the presence of species loss is essential to shed light on the problem of species' decline and extinction. Pocock *et al* [9] studied the robustness and restoration of a network of ecological networks. They found that, overall the networks did not have strong covariance in their robustness, which suggests that ecological restoration (for example, through agri-environment schemes) benefiting one functional group will not inevitably benefit others. They also found that some individual plant species were disproportionately well linked to many other species. This type of information can be used in restoration strategies, because it identifies the plant taxa that can potentially lead to disproportionate gains in biodiversity, see figure 4.2. The application of multilayer networks to ecology continues to be developed as highlighted by Pilosof *et al* [10].

(C) Network of biological networks
Biological networks and clusters of interacting networks occur at different levels such as genes and proteins, but they may also have higher hierarchical genetic levels, for example metabolites, organelles, cells, organs, and organ systems (see figure 4.3), where each level corresponds to a network, forming a network of biological networks [11], see also [12]. Understanding the robustness of a network of biological networks may help us to avoid cascading reactions due to diseases or enable faster recovery from a disease [13, 14].

(D) Network of networks in the brain
The human brain can be viewed as a network of networks from multiple perspectives. First, the brain is known to consist of different regions or modules that are interconnected (an interconnected network view) [15–17]. In addition, the brain consists of both structural and functional layers where different nodes of the brain have different patterns of connections in each layer (a multiplex or multilayer network) [18–20]. Another example is the tangled blood distribution network which has a distinct function from the neuronal circuits of the brain, but is bidirectionally coupled to them. Understanding the different types of networks of networks in the brain could shed light on how this all-important human organ functions.

4.2 Structures of networks of networks (NON)

In this section we illustrate some models of networks of networks (NON) structures. These are networks in which each node represents a network and the links are

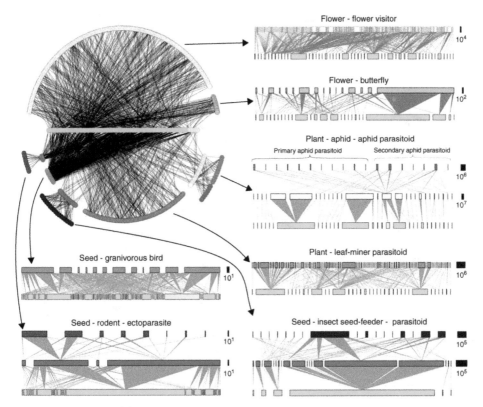

Figure 4.2. Species' interaction networks at Norwood Farm, Somerset, UK. The entire network of networks is shown at top left (in which each circle represents one species), and quantitative visualizations are shown for each of the seven quantified individual networks (in which each block is a species, and the width of blocks of each color represents relative abundance). After reference [9], reprinted with permssion from AAAS.

dependency relationships, see figure 4.4. For a network formed of fully or partially interdependent networks, the relationship between the n networks can be described by a matrix $Q = [q_{ij}]_{n \times n}$. The matrix can represent any topology including loopless NON such as chain-like and star-like NON, loop-like NON and any other complex network structure, for demonstration see figures 4.4, 4.5 and 4.6.

Loopless network of networks

We begin by studying loopless NONs including a chain-like NON, a star-like NON and general tree-like NON structures, as shown in figure 4.4(a)–(c), respectively, which represent the simplest cases of network of networks. Results on these structures will be presented in the following sections. Surprisingly, the results are the same for all of these structures and depend only on n, the number of networks in the NON.

Loop-like network of networks

We will consider here a single loop of NON, which is a basic component of many complex structures. We describe two loop-like topologies, one with unidirectional dependencies and the other having bidirectional dependencies as shown in figure 4.5.

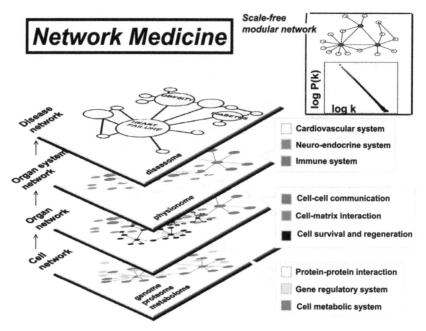

Figure 4.3. Illustration of a network of biological networks in network medicine. Networks emerge at many different levels, such as genes, transcripts, proteins, metabolites, organelles, cells, organs, and organ systems, forming a network of networks. After reference [11] with permssion from Wolters Kluwer Health Inc.

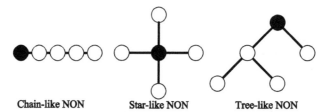

Figure 4.4. Three types of loopless NONs, each composed of five interedependent networks. Each node represents a network and the links represent the dependencies between the networks. They all have the same percolation threshold and the same giant percolation component. Reprinted with permission from [21], copyright 2011 by the American Physical Society.

Random regular network of random networks

Next we introduce a topology of a random-regular (RR) network structure which includes loops, see figure 4.6(a) and (b). In this structure each network depends on a fixed number, m, of other networks.

Replica nodes in network of networks

The differences between the dependencies assumed in tree-like and loop-like networks of networks without replica nodes are illustrated in figure 4.7(a) and (c) [5, 22]. Figure 4.7(b) shows the case of network of networks with replica nodes [23].

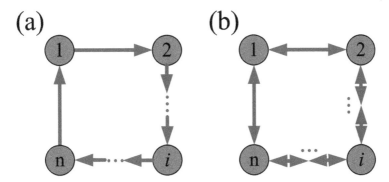

Figure 4.5. Illustration of structure of a loop-like NON. (a) Unidirectional dependencies and (b) bidirectional dependencies. Reprinted with permission from [19], copyright 2011 by the American Physical Society

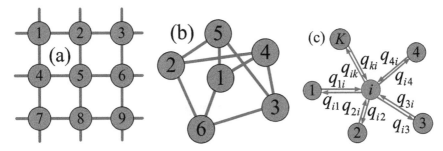

Figure 4.6. Illustration of regular and random regular (RR) NON of interdependent random networks. (a) An example of a regular network, a lattice with periodic boundary conditions composed of 9 interdependent networks represented by 9 circles. The degree of the NON is $m = 4$, i.e., each network depends on 4 networks. (b) An RR network composed of 6 interdependent networks represented by 6 circles. The degree of the NON is $m = 3$, i.e., each network depends on 3 networks. (c) Schematic representation of the dependencies of the networks. Circles represent networks in the NON, and the arrows represent the partially interdependent pairs. For example, a fraction of q_{3i} of nodes in network i depends on nodes in network 3. Pairs of networks which are not connected by dependency links do not have nodes that directly depend on each other. Reprinted with permission from [6], copyright 2013 by the American Physical Society.

In this network of networks with replica loops the dependency behavior is identical to figure 4.7(a), which is loopless, because the added dependency links are redundant and do not change the partition to sets of mutually interdependent nodes. Thus, with respect to dependency and cascading failures, figure 4.7(b) can be regarded as a tree-like network of networks figure 4.7(a).

4.3 Cascading failures in a network of networks

Consider a network formed by n interdependent networks, where each node in the NON is itself a network and each link represents a *fully* or *partially* dependent pair of networks (see figures 4.4, 4.5 and 4.6). We assume that each network i ($i = 1, 2, \ldots, n$) of the NON consists of N_i nodes which are linked through connectivity links. Two networks i and j form a partially dependent pair if a certain fraction $q_{ji} > 0$ of nodes in network i directly depend on nodes in network j, i.e.,

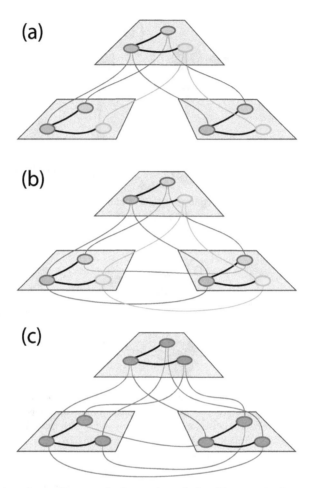

Figure 4.7. Illustration of a tree-like network of networks and a looplike network of networks. (a) In this tree-like network of networks the mutually interdependent nodes are distinguished by different colors and the tree-like topology guarantees that the size of a mutually interdependent set be exactly n (assuming $n = 3$ and full interdependency, $q = 1$, as in this example). (b) In this network of networks with loops the dependency behavior is identical to (a) because the added dependency links are redundant and do not change the partition to sets of mutually interdependent nodes. Thus, with respect to dependency and cascading failures, (b) can be regarded as a tree-like network of networks. (c) In contrast, if the loops are not closed, a situation can emerge in which all of the nodes are dependent upon one another. Reprinted with permission from [22], copyright 2014 by the American Physical Society.

nodes in network i cannot function if the corresponding nodes in network j do not function. A node in network i will not function if it is either removed or does not belong to the largest connected cluster (giant component) of network i. Dependent pairs may be connected by unidirectional dependency links pointing from network j to network i (see figure 4.6(c)). This convention indicates that nodes in network i need crucial support from specific nodes in network j,, e.g. electric power if network j is a power grid.

We assume that after an attack or failure only a fraction of nodes p_i in network i remain functional. We also assume that only nodes that belong to the giant component in network i will remain functional. When a cascade of failures occurs, nodes in network i that do not belong to the giant component of network i fail and cause nodes in other networks that depend on them to also fail. When those nodes fail, dependent nodes and isolated nodes in the other networks also fail, and the cascade can cause further failures back in network i. In order to determine the fraction of nodes $P_{\infty,i}$ in each network that remain functional (i.e., the fraction of nodes that constitute the giant component) after the cascade of failures as a function of p_i and q_{ij}, we need to analyze the dynamics of the cascading failures.

4.3.1 Dynamic process

4.3.1.1 The dynamic process of cascading failures in a loopless network of networks

In this section we introduce a specific variant [7] of the dependency among the networks participating in the NON, namely, bidirectional dependency links establishing a one-to-one correspondence between the nodes of all networks in the NON [5]. This is different from the case of network of networks with replica nodes [23] (see figure 4.7). Other variants, which include autonomous nodes [24], multiple dependency links [25], and reinforced nodes [26] have been studied along the same lines. We assume for simplicity, that the NON consists of n networks each having N nodes (figure 4.4). Each node in figure 4.4 represents a network, and each link between two networks i and j denotes the existence of one-to-one dependencies between all the nodes of the linked networks. The functioning of a node in network i depends on the functioning of one and only one node in network j ($i, j \in \{1, 2, \dots, n\}$, $i \neq j$), and vice versa (bidirectional links). If node i in network A stops functioning, the dependent node j in network B also stops functioning (and vice versa) after some time, τ_a.

(A) The effect of one-to-one correspondence

If the NON has a tree-like topology (figure 4.4), the dependency links establishing one-to-one correspondence between the pairs of directly linked networks establish a unique one-to-one correspondence between the nodes of any two networks in the NON [5]. The removal of a single node in one network thus causes the removal of the set of all n corresponding nodes each belonging to a different network. If we assume the existence of such a unique one-to-one correspondence, our approach applies not only to a tree-like NON but to a NON of any topology.

On the other hand, if in the NON, there is a mismatch in the correspondence of the nodes in the dependency links forming a loop, a failure of a single node may cause the complete collapse of all the networks forming a loop (see figure 4.7(c)). Indeed if any node A_i stops functioning then a different node A_{t_i} in the same network can stop functioning. If t_i is a transposition of the nodes $i = 1, 2, 3 \dots N$, then all the nodes forming a cycle in this transposition, which includes node i, will stop functioning. The probability for a randomly selected element to belong to a cycle of length ℓ in a random transposition of N elements follows a uniform distribution $P(\ell) = 1/N$.

As $N \to \infty$, the mathematical expectation of a fraction of elements that do not belong to the cycles to which $k = pN$ randomly selected elements belong scales as

$$\frac{1}{k+1} \sim \frac{1}{pN} \to 0. \tag{4.1}$$

Thus, the removal of an infinitesimally small fraction of nodes from a NON with a loop, will cause all the networks in the loop to collapse if no assumption on the nature of the transposition is made. Once a single network in the NON fails, all other networks in the NON will fail and hence a NON with a loop will completely disintegrate unless there is a unique one-to-one correspondence established by the dependency links among the nodes of each network, or the transposition character-izing the mismatch in the dependency links along the loop is not random. Here we restrict ourselves to the simple case of a one-to-one correspondence.

(B) Fully tree-like network of networks and multiplex networks
Multiplex networks can be produced by the following algorithm [27]: consider a multiplex network, with vertices $i = 1, 2, \ldots, N$ connected by n types of edges labeled $s = a, b, \ldots$ and the joint degree distribution is $P(q_a, q_b, \ldots)$. Viable clusters in any multiplex network may be identified by the following algorithm. (i) Choose a test vertex i at random from the network. (ii) For each type of edge s, compile a list of vertices that can be reached from i by following only edges of type s. (iii) The intersection of these n lists forms a new candidate set for the viable cluster containing i. (iv) Repeat steps (ii) and (iii) but traversing only the current candidate set. When the candidate set no longer changes, it is either a viable cluster, or contains only vertex i. (v) To find further viable clusters, remove the viable cluster of i from the network (via cutting any edges) and repeat steps (i)–(iv) on the remaining network beginning from a new test vertex. This algorithm is equivalent to finding the mutual giant component of a tree-like network of networks without considering the process of cascading failures. Furthermore, equations (1) and (2) for calculating the giant component of multiplex networks in reference [27] are the same as the steady state of tree-like network of networks derived in reference [5].

(C) The dynamic process
It is also interesting and important to analyze the dynamic process of cascading failures which can help in developing strategies to mitigate the failures by stopping the cascade at some optimal point [5, 6, 28, 29]. Note, it is also possible to study the percolation of NON by studying only the steady-state without following the dynamics of cascading [27, 30]. However, the dynamics are particularly interesting since it was previously found that the network collapse at criticality has a long plateau regime [28]. We assume that within network i, the nodes are randomly connected by connectivity links with degree distribution $P_i(k)$. We further assume that only the nodes belonging to the giant connected cluster of each network can function. Other nodes which belong to smaller clusters become non-functional within a time τ_c. For simplicity, we assume that τ_c is the same for all nodes in all networks and that $\tau_a \ll \tau_c$. However, the final state of the model does not depend on

these details, since it is completely defined by the mutually connected clusters, i.e., the clusters of the correspondent nodes in each network, which are independently connected by the connectivity links in each network of the NON.

Once a fraction $1 - p$ of nodes is removed from a single network, which we will refer to as the root network, the corresponding dependent nodes in all networks become nonfunctional within a short time interval bounded by

$$t_0 \equiv n\tau_a \ll \tau_c. \tag{4.2}$$

At time $t_1 = \tau_c + \tau_0 \approx \tau_c$, the nodes which do not belong to the giant components of the individual networks fail. Since the dependency links are random, the fraction of the corresponding nodes which simultaneously belong to the giant components in all networks is

$$\mu(t_1) = p \prod g_i(x_i(t_0)), \tag{4.3}$$

where $x_i(t_0) = p$ for every network and the functions $g_i(x_i)$ are defined by equation (1.5) in which $z = x_i$. From the point of view of each individual network this is equivalent to a random attack after which a fraction

$$x_i(t_1) = \frac{\mu(t_1)}{g_i[x_i(t_0)]}, \tag{4.4}$$

of nodes survive. This is since the fraction $\mu(t_1)$ of surviving nodes is selected from the current giant component, which currently consists of a fraction $g_i(x_i(t_0))$ of nodes. Accordingly, at time $t_2 = t_1 + \tau_c$ only the nodes of the new giant component of each network $g_i[x_i(t_1)]$ remain functional and only the set of corresponding nodes which simultaneously belong to the giant component of each network will remain functional after time τ_a. The fraction of these nodes is

$$\mu(t_2) = p \prod g_i(x_i(t_1)). \tag{4.5}$$

Thus, at each stage of the cascade, the fraction of nodes that remains functional is

$$\mu(t_{n+1}) = p \prod g_i(x_i(t_n)), \tag{4.6}$$

where $t_{n+1} = t_n + \tau_c$ and

$$x_i(t_n) = \frac{\mu(t_n)}{g_i(x_i(t_{n-1}))}. \tag{4.7}$$

At the end of the cascade, no further failures occur and $\mu_\infty = \mu(t_{n+1}) = \mu(t_n)$ is the mutual giant component of the NON. Obviously, $x_i(t_n) = x_i(t_{n+1}) \equiv x_i$, so the final state of the NON obeys $n + 1$ equations with $n + 1$ unknowns $x_1, x_2, \ldots, x_n$, and μ_∞, where

$$x_i = \mu_\infty/g_i(x_i), \tag{4.8}$$

and

$$\mu_\infty = p \prod_i^n g_i(x_i). \tag{4.9}$$

A different cascade of failures leading to the same final state emerges if $\tau_a \gg \tau_c$, where τ_a is in units of t. This cascade is easy to describe if τ_a is the same for all the nodes in all networks and if the NON has a tree-like topology in which the shortest path distance D_{ij} between any two networks of the NON can be uniquely defined. We initialize $x_i(t) = 1$ for $t \leqslant 0$. The root of the NON is the network $i = 1$ from which a fraction $1 - p$ of nodes is removed due to random failures. Accordingly, we set $x_1(0) = p$. Computing the subsequent failures at times 0, τ_a, $2\tau_a$, … starting from the root, it can be seen that the number of nodes that remain functional in each network at time $t > 0$ is

$$\mu_i(t) = x_i(t)g_i[x_i(t)], \tag{4.10}$$

where

$$x_i(t) = \min\left(p \prod_{j=1, j\neq i}^{n} g_j[x_j(t - D_{ij}\tau_a)], x_i(t - \tau_a)\right). \tag{4.11}$$

In this cascade, the state of each network changes at every second stage of the cascade. For example, the state of the root ($i = 1$) changes at times

$$t = 0, 2\tau_a, 4\tau_a… \tag{4.12}$$

while the state of the networks in the k-th shell of the root with $D_{j1} = k$, changes at times

$$t = k\tau_a, (k + 2)\tau_a, (k + 4)\tau_a… \tag{4.13}$$

For $t \rightarrow \infty$, equations (4.10) and (4.11) become equivalent to equations (4.9) and (4.8). Figure 4.8 shows the dynamics of the cascading failures at different time stages, and figure 4.9 shows how the damage spreads in the NON.

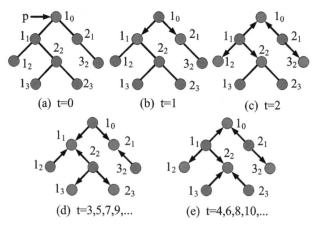

Figure 4.8. The dynamics of cascading failures at different time steps. In this figure, each node represents a network. The arrows (on the links) illustrate the direction of damage spreading from the root network to the whole NON, step by step. Reprinted with permission from [5], copyright 2012 by the American Physical Society.

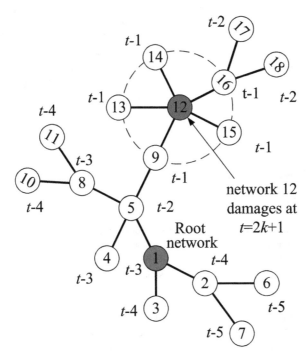

Figure 4.9. How does the damage spread in an NON system? In this figure, each node represents a network, and the connections between two networks are via fully interdependent links. The root network is network 1 (red) which is the only network in which initially a fraction $1 - p$ of nodes are removed. When examining network 12 (blue) for example, it becomes damaged at $t = 2k + 1$ ($k = 1, 2, 3, \ldots$). It receives the damage from network 8 at $t = 2k + 3$, because network 8 gets damage at $t = 2$ for the first time and its damage spreads to network 12 for the first time at $t = 5$. This agrees with equation (4.10) where network i receives damage from network j if and only if $t - D_{ij} \geq D_{1j}$. Reprinted with permission from [5], copyright 2012 by the American Physical Society.

Simulations of the cascading failures in the tree-like NON of different topologies shown in figure 4.4 for the case $\tau_c \ll \tau_a$ agree well with equations (4.10) and (4.11). Indeed figures 4.10 and 4.11 compare our theoretical results, equations (4.10) and (4.11), with simulation results for three different types of NON: ER networks, RR networks and SF networks. We find that while the dynamics are different for the three topologies shown in figure 4.4, the final P_∞ is the same as predicted from the theoretical results in equations (4.8) and (4.9).

4.3.1.2 Dynamic processes of cascading failures in a network of networks
We assume that all N_i nodes in network i are randomly assigned a degree k from a probability distribution $P_i(k)$ and the nodes are then randomly connected within each network [31].

Next, (i) each node a in network i depends with a probability q_{ji} on only one node b in network j, and (ii) if node a in network i depends on node b in network j and node b in network j depends on node c in network i, then node a coincides with node

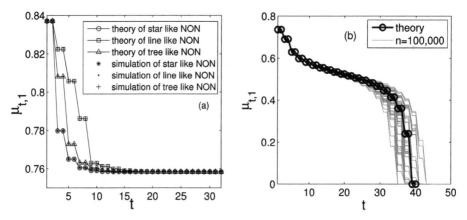

Figure 4.10. (a) Simulation results of the giant component of the root network $\mu_{t,1}$ after t cascading failures for three types of NON composed of five ER networks shown in figure 4.4. For each network in the NON, $N = 100,000$ and $\bar{k} = 5$. The chosen value of p is $p = 0.85$, and the predicted threshold is $p_c = 0.76449$ (from equations (4.43) and (4.46)). All points are the results of averaging over 40 simulated realizations. Note that the dynamics are different for the three topologies, yet the final $P_\infty \equiv \mu_{\infty,1}$ is the same, i.e., the final P_∞ does not depend on the topology of the NON (as long as it is a tree like structure). (b) Simulations of the giant component, $\mu_{t,1}$, for the tree-like NON (figure 4.4) with the same parameters as in (a) but for $p = 0.755 < p_c = 0.76449$. The figure shows 50 simulated realizations of the giant component left after t stages of the cascading failures compared with the theoretical prediction of equations (4.16) and (4.10) and (4.11). Also, note the long plateau in the size of the giant component during the cascading failures. Reprinted with permission from [5], copyright 2012 by the American Physical Society.

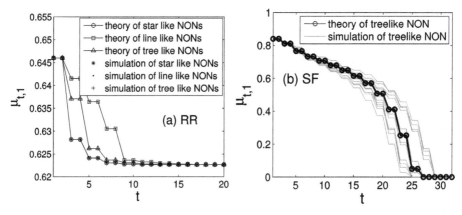

Figure 4.11. (a) Simulation results for the giant component of the root network $\mu_{t,1}$ after t cascading failures for three types of NON composed of 5 RR networks. The structures of the NON are as shown in Fig. 4.4. For each network in the NON, $N = 100,000$ and $k = 5$. The chosen value of p is $p = 0.65$, and the predicted threshold is $p_c = 0.6047$ [from Eqs. (4.55) and (4.59)]. The symbols are the results of averaging over 40 realizations. It is seen that while the dynamics is different for the three topologies, the final $P_\infty \equiv \mu_{\infty,1}$ is the same, i.e., the final P_∞ does not depend on the topology of the NON as long as it is a tree-like structure.. (b) Simulation results of the giant component of the root network $\mu_{t,1}$ after t cascading failures for a treelike NON composed of 5 SF networks shown in Fig. 4.4. For each network in the NON, N = 100, 000, $\lambda = 2.3$ and $m = 2$. The chosen value of p is $p = 0.875$ (bellow p_c). The figure shows 50 simulated realizations of the giant component left after t stages of the cascading failures compared with the theoretical prediction of Eqs. (4.62) and (4.10)-(4.11). After [5].

c, i.e., we have a no-feedback situation [5]. In section 3.2.1 we study the case of feedback, i.e., node a can be different from c in network i. The no-feedback condition prevents configurations from collapsing when all networks are still internally connected [25]. Next, we develop the dynamic process of cascading failures step by step.

At $t = 1$, in network i of the NON we randomly remove a fraction $1 - p_i$ of nodes. After the initial removal of nodes, the remaining fraction of nodes in network i, is $\psi'_{i,1} \equiv p_i$. The remaining functional part of network i therefore consists of a fraction $\psi_{i,1} = \psi'_{i,1} g_A(\psi'_{i,1})$ of the network, where $g_i(\psi'_{i,1})$ is defined by equations (1.14) and (1.15). Furthermore, we denote by $y_{ji,1}$ the fraction of nodes in network i that survive after the damage from all the networks connected to network i except network j is taken into account, so if $q_{ij} \neq 0$, $y_{ji,1} = p_j$.

At $t \geqslant 2$, all the networks receive the damage from their interdependent networks one by one. Without loss of generality, we assume that network 1 is the first, network 2 second,..., and network n is last. In figure 4.6(a), for example, since a fraction q_{21}, q_{31}, q_{41} and q_{71} of nodes of network 1 depends on nodes from network 2, 3, 4 and 7, respectively, the remaining fraction of nodes in network 1 is

$$\psi'_{1,t} = \prod_{j=2,3,4,7} [q_{j1} y_{j1,t-1} g_j(\psi'_{j,t-1}) - q_{j1} + 1], \tag{4.14}$$

and $y_{1j,t}$ $(j = 2, 3, 4, 7)$ satisfies

$$y_{1j,t} = \frac{\psi'_{1,t}}{q_{j1} y_{j1,t-1} g_j(\psi'_{j,t-1}) - q_{j1} + 1}. \tag{4.15}$$

The remaining functional part of network 1 therefore contains a fraction $\psi_{1,t} = \psi'_{1,t} g_1(\psi'_{1,t})$ of the network nodes.

Similarly, we obtain the remaining fraction of network i nodes,

$$\psi'_{i,t} = \prod_{j<i} [q_{ji} y_{ji,t-1} g_j(\psi'_{j,t}) - q_{ji} + 1] \prod_{s>i} [q_{si} y_{si,t-1} g_s(\psi'_{s,t-1}) - q_{si} + 1], \tag{4.16}$$

where $y_{ij,t}$ is

$$y_{ij,t} = \frac{\psi'_{i,t}}{q_{ji} y_{ji,t-1} g_j(\psi'_{j,t}) - q_{ji} + 1}, \tag{4.17}$$

and $y_{is,t}$ is

$$y_{is,t} = \frac{\psi'_{i,t}}{q_{si} y_{si,t-1} g_s(\psi'_{s,t-1}) - q_{si} + 1}. \tag{4.18}$$

Following this approach we can construct the sequence, $\psi'_{i,t}$ of the remaining fraction of nodes at each stage of the cascade of failures. The general form is given by

$$\psi'_{i,1} \equiv p_i,$$

$$y_{ij,1} \equiv p_i, \ q_{ij} \neq 0$$

$$\psi'_{i,t} = p_i \prod_{j<i} [q_{ji}y_{ji,t-1}g_j(\psi'_{j,t}) - q_{ji} + 1]$$

$$\prod_{s>i} [q_{si}y_{si,t-1}g_s(\psi'_{s,t-1}) - q_{si} + 1], \tag{4.19}$$

$$y_{ij,t} = \frac{\psi'_{i,t}}{q_{ji}y_{ji,t-1}g_j(\psi'_{j,t}) - q_{js} + 1},$$

$$y_{is,t} = \frac{\psi'_{i,t}}{q_{si}y_{si,t-1}g_s(\psi'_{s,t-1}) - q_{si} + 1}.$$

In figure 4.12, we compare the theoretical formulas for the dynamics, equation (4.19), and the simulation results. As seen, the theory of the dynamics (4.19) agrees well with simulations.

4.3.2 Identical steady state results for all tree-like structures

Next we study the final steady state of the NON. Equations (4.8) and (4.9) can be simplified if we introduce a new variable [32]:

$$z_i = f_i x_i + 1 - x_i. \tag{4.20}$$

Using equations (4.14) and (4.15) we obtain

$$f_i = H_i(z_i), \tag{4.21}$$

$$x_i = (1 - z_i)[1 - H(z_i)] \tag{4.22}$$

and

$$1 - z_i = p[1 - H_i(z_i)] \prod_{j=1, j\neq i}^{n} (1 - G_j(z_j)), \tag{4.23}$$

$$P_\infty \equiv \mu_\infty = p \prod_{i=1}^{n} (1 - G_i(z_i)) = \frac{[1 - G_i(z_i)](1 - z_i)}{1 - H_i(z_i)} \equiv F_i(z_i). \tag{4.24}$$

One can show that if $\bar{k}_i$, the average degree of network i, exists, then the functions $F_i(z_i)$ are analytical functions for $|z_i| < 1$ and are monotonically decreasing from $\bar{k}_i[1 - P_i(0)]/[\bar{k}_i - P_i(1)]$ at $z_i = 0$ to zero at $z_i = 1$. Selecting i such that $F_i(0)$ has the smallest value, we can solve the equations

$$F_j(z_j) = F_i(z_i), \tag{4.25}$$

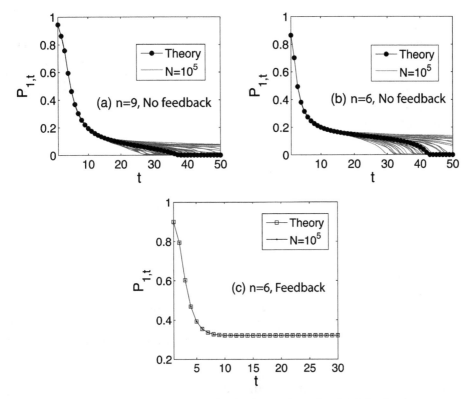

Figure 4.12. (a) Simulation results compared with the theory of equation (4.19) for the giant component of network 1, $P_{1,t}$, after t cascading failures for the lattice-like NON composed of 9 ER networks shown in figure 4.6(a). For each network in the NON, $N = 10^5$, $m = 4$ and $\bar{k} = 8$, and $q = 0.4 > q_c \doteq 0.382$ (predicted by equation (4.78)). The chosen value of p is $p = 0.945$, and the predicted threshold is $p_c^I = 0.952$ (from equation (4.75)). (b) Simulations compared with theory for the giant component, $P_{1,t}$, for the random regular NON composed of six ER networks shown in figure 4.6(b) with the no-feedback condition. For each network in the NON, $N = 10^5$, $m = 3$, $\bar{k} = 8$, $q = 0.49 > q_c \doteq 0.431\,3$ (predicted by equation (4.78)), and for $p = 0.866 < p_c^I \doteq 0.869\,6$ (from equation (4.75)). For each network in the NON, $N = 10^5$, $m = 3$ $\bar{k} = 8$, $q = 0.4 < q_{max} = 0.5$ (predicted by equation (4.97)), and for $p = 0.9 > p_c \doteq 0.578\,7$ (from equation (4.95))). The results are averaged over 20 simulated realizations of the giant component after t stages of the cascading failures which is compared with the theoretical prediction of equation (4.19). (c) Simulations compared to theory of the giant component, $P_{1,t}$, for the random regular NON composed of six ER networks shown in figure 4.6(b) with the feedback condition. For each network in the NON, $N = 10^5$, $m = 3$, $\bar{k} = 8$, $q = 0.4 < q_{max} = 0.5$ (predicted by equation (4.97)), and $p = 0.9 > p_c \doteq 0.578\,7$ (from equation (4.95)). The results are averaged over 20 simulated realizations of the giant component after t stages of the cascading failures and are compared with the theoretical prediction of equation (4.19). Reprinted with permission from [6], copyright 2013 by the American Physical Society.

with respect to z_j, and $z_j(z_i)$ can be substituted in equation (4.23) as

$$\frac{1}{p} = \frac{\displaystyle\prod_{j=1}^{n} (1 - G_j[z_j(z_i)])}{F(z_i)} \equiv R_i(z_i).$$

(4.26)

The right hand side of equation (4.26), which is $R_i(z_i)$, is an analytical function of $z_i \in [0, 1]$, such that $R_i(0) \leqslant 1$ and $R_p(z_i) \to 0$ for $z_i \to 1$. If its maximal value, R_c in this interval is greater than unity, equation (4.26) has roots in the range $z \in [0, 1)$ for $1/R_c \leqslant p \leqslant 1$. The smallest of these roots gives the physically meaningful solution from which the mutual giant component $0 < P_\infty < 1$ can be found using equation (4.24). The minimal $p = p_c = 1/R_c$, below which, the solutions cease to exist corresponds to the maximum of $R_i(z_i)$. The point z_i^c at which this maximum is achieved satisfies the equation

$$\frac{dR_i(z_i^c)}{dz_i^c} = 0. \tag{4.27}$$

It can be shown that if at least for one network in the NON, $P_i(0) + P_i(1) > 0$ (condition I), and if there exist two constants $M > 0$ and $\eta > 0$ such that for each network $\sum_{k<M} P_i(k) > \eta$ (condition II), then for sufficiently large n, $R_i(z_i)$ is less than unity for any $z \in [0, 1]$ and hence a physically meaningful solution of equation (4.26) does not exist [5]. In other words, if at least for one network there exist isolated or singly connected nodes, the NON completely disintegrates even for fully intact ($p = 1$) networks for sufficiently large n. This happens because a network which has a finite fraction of isolated and singly connected nodes it necessarily has a finite fraction of nodes which do not belong to its giant component for $p = 1$ either because these nodes do not have links at all, or because they form pairs of singly connected nodes linked to each other. These nodes will become non-functional at the first stage of the cascade and will cause the failure of a finite fraction of nodes in each network due to the one-to-one correspondence of the interdependent nodes in all networks. Because we assume that the networks are randomly connected, these failed nodes will cause the disconnection of a finite fraction of nodes in all the networks. Due to the one-to-one correspondence of interdependent nodes, the failure of these disconnected nodes will cause the failure of a union of n finite sets of dependent nodes in all the networks. Since from the point of view of each network, these n sets are randomly selected, for large enough n, the fraction of nodes that do not belong to this union will become less than the percolation threshold for a certain network. Hence, this network will entirely collapse and necessarily will cause the collapse of the entire NON.

In contrast, it can be shown that if for all networks $P_i(0) + P_i(1) = 0$, then for any n, there exists $p(n) < 1$ such that for $1 \geqslant p > p(n)$ the mutual giant component of the NON exists [5]. In other words, if there are no singly connected or isolated nodes in the entire NON, the mutual giant component will survive for sufficiently large p for any n. A simple physical reason for this is that in the absence of isolated and singly connected nodes, small isolated clusters must contain finite loops, the chances of which in a randomly connected network are infinitesimally small for $N \to \infty$. Therefore, for $p = 1$, the giant component of each network coincides with the entire network, and hence the cascade that destroys the NON can start only for $p < 1$. It can be also proven that under condition II, $p(n) \to 1$ for $n \to \infty$.

4.3.3 General stationary state

To determine the state of the system at the end of the cascade process (steady state) we look at $\psi'_{i,\tau}$ in the limit of $\tau \to \infty$. This limit must satisfy the equations $\psi'_{i,\tau} = \psi'_{i,\tau+1}$ since eventually the clusters stop fragmenting and the fractions of randomly removed nodes at steps τ and $\tau + 1$ are equal. Denoting $\psi'_{i,\tau} = x_i$, we obtain for the stationary state, a system of n equations with n unknowns

$$x_i = p_i \prod_{j=1}^{K} (q_{ji} y_{ji} g_j(x_j) - q_{ji} + 1), \qquad (4.28)$$

where the product is taken over K networks interlinked with network i by partial (or fully) dependency links (see figure 4.6(c)), and

$$y_{ij} = \frac{x_i}{q_{ji} y_{ji} g_j(x_j) - q_{ji} + 1}, \qquad (4.29)$$

is the fraction of nodes in network i that survive after the damage from all the networks interdependent with network j except network i itself are taken into account. The damage from network i itself is excluded due to the no-feedback condition. Equation (4.28) is valid for any type of interdependent NON, while equation (4.29) represents the no-feedback condition. Note that for two interdependent networks, equations (4.28) and (4.29) are equivalent to equation (13) of reference [23] for the specific case of single dependency links.

Our general framework for percolation of interdependent network of networks, equations (4.28) and (4.29), can be generalized in two ways: (i) coupling with feedback condition (ii) coupling with multiple-support.

(i) In the existence of feedback, $y_{i,j}$ is simply x_i and equations (4.28) and (4.29) become a single equation,

$$x_i = p_i \prod_{j=1}^{K} (q_{ji} x_j g_j(x_j) - q_{ji} + 1). \qquad (4.30)$$

The feedback condition leads to the extreme vulnerability of the network of interdependent networks. As we know for two fully interdependent networks with the no-feedback condition [7] if the average degree is large enough, both networks exist. However, for two fully interdependent networks with a feedback condition, no matter how large the average degree is, both networks collapse even after a single node is removed.

(ii) For the case of multiple dependency links, equation (4.28) was generalized for a pair of coupled networks by Shao *et al* [25] to be,

$$x_i = p_i \prod_{j=1}^{K} \left(1 - q_{ji} G^{ji}[1 - x_j g_j(x_j)]\right), \qquad (4.31)$$

where G^{ji} represents the generating function of the degree distribution of multiple support links through which network i depends on network j.

The term g_i reflects the topology of network i, which can be an ER network, a RR network, a scale free (SF) network, or any other network. Further, $Q = [q_{ij}]_{n \times n}$ (n is the number of networks) reflects the interactions between the networks, i.e., the topology of the NON, which can also be any type of network. Our theoretical results equations (4.28) and (4.29) are therefore general for any type of network of networks. By solving equations (4.28) and (4.29), or equation (4.30), or equation (4.31), we obtain x_i for each network in the coupled networks with the no feedback condition, the feedback condition and the multiple-support condition, respectively. Thus, we find the giant component in each network i to be

$$P_{\infty,i} \equiv x_i g_i(x_i). \tag{4.32}$$

4.4 Percolation of network of networks

4.4.1 Percolation of tree-like network of networks

For the case of a tree-like structure of n coupled networks where all the networks have the same degree distribution, all $G_i(z_i) = G_0(z_0)$ and $H_i(z_i) = H_0(z_0)$, equations (4.23)–(4.27) can be simplified to [5],

$$\frac{1}{p} = \frac{(1 - G_0(z_0))^{n-1}(1 - H_0(z_0))}{1 - z}, \tag{4.33}$$

which can be reduced to equation (1.20) for a single network if we let $z_0 = z$ and $n = 1$. We can also obtain the mutual giant component of a tree-like network of networks as

$$P_{\infty} = p(1 - G_0(z_0))^n = \frac{(1 - G_0(z_0))(1 - z_0)}{1 - H_0(z_0)}, \tag{4.34}$$

which can be reduced to equation (1.14) for a single network if we let $z_0 = z$ and $n = 1$. The critical point $z_0 = z_0^c$ satisfies

$$1 = \frac{(1 - z_0^c)H_0'(z_0^c)}{1 - H_0(z_0^c)} + (1 - z_0^c)\frac{(n-1)kH_0(z_0^c)}{1 - G_0(z_0^c)}. \tag{4.35}$$

From equation (4.33), we can rewrite the critical threshold p_c as

$$p_c = \frac{1 - z_0^c}{(1 - G_0(z_0^c))^{n-1}(1 - H_0(z_0^c))}, \tag{4.36}$$

by using z_0^c instead of z_0. When solving equation (4.35), we can obtain z_0^c, and substitute it into equation (4.36), which gives the critical threshold p_c. Next we will apply this general result for different types of specific networks.

4.4.1.1 The case of a tree-like network formed of n ER networks
(A) The general case

The case of a tree-like NON composed of n Erdős-Rényi (ER) [33–35] networks with average degrees $\bar{k}_1, \bar{k}_2, \ldots \bar{k}_i, \ldots, \bar{k}_n$ can be solved explicitly [21]. In this case, the generating functions of the n networks are defined by equation (4.16), $H_i(z_i) = G_i(z_i)$. Using equation (4.24) we obtain $F_i(z_i) = 1 - z_i$ and hence $z_i = z_j \equiv z$.

Using equations (4.24), (4.26) and (4.16) we get

$$P_\infty = 1 - z. \tag{4.37}$$

and

$$\frac{1}{p} = \frac{\displaystyle\prod_{i=1}^{n} [1 - e^{\bar{k}_i(z-1)}]}{1 - z}. \tag{4.38}$$

Hence, the mutual giant component satisfies the self-consistent equation,

$$P_\infty = p \prod_{i=1}^{n} [1 - e^{-\bar{k}_i P_\infty}]. \tag{4.39}$$

The value of mutual giant component at criticality, P_∞^c, satisfies (see equations (4.24)–(4.27))

$$\sum_{i=1}^{n} \frac{\bar{k}_i e^{-\bar{k}_i P_\infty^c}}{1 - e^{-\bar{k}_i P_\infty^c}} = \frac{1}{P_\infty^c}, \tag{4.40}$$

and hence

$$p_c = \frac{P_\infty^c}{\displaystyle\prod_{i=1}^{n} (1 - e^{-\bar{k}_i P_\infty^c})}. \tag{4.41}$$

(B) The case of NON where all networks are with the same average degree
When the n networks have the same average degree $\bar{k}$, $\bar{k}_i = \bar{k}$ ($i = 1, 2, \ldots, n$), equation (4.39) yields for the order parameter P_∞ as function of $\bar{k}$, p, and n [21]:

$$P_\infty = p[1 - \exp(-\bar{k}P_\infty)]^n. \tag{4.42}$$

The solutions of equation (4.42) for several n-values are shown in figure 4.13(a) and for several $\bar{k}$-values are shown in figure 4.13(b). As can be seen, the analytical results are in very good agreement with simulations. To determine p_c in simulations we measure the number of cascading failures (iterations) until the system reaches a steady state (see figure 4.14). As found in reference [36], when approaching criticality, the number of iterations in the cascading failures diverges. Thus the value of p where the peak occurs can be used as a good estimate for p_c. This is analogous to the case of the second-order phase transition of regular percolation, where the size of the second largest cluster diverges at p_c [37, 38]. Note that for equation (4.42) the special case $n = 1$ is the known ER second-order percolation law for a single network [33–35]. The giant component at criticality simplifies equation (4.40) to

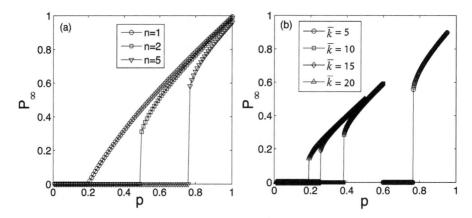

Figure 4.13. Percolation of a tree-like network of ER networks. (a) The mutual giant component P_∞ as a function of p for different values of number of networks for $\bar{k} = 5$. (b) The mutual giant component P_∞ as a function of p for different values of $\bar{k}$ for $n = 5$. The analytical results obtained using equation (4.42) agree well with simulations. Reprinted with permission from [5], copyright 2012 by the American Physical Society.

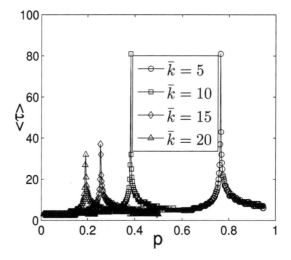

Figure 4.14. For a star-like network of 5 interdependent ER networks, the average number of iterations for reaching the convergence stage $\langle \tau \rangle$ is plotted as a function of p for different $\bar{k}$. In the simulations $N = 10^6$, and averages are obtained from 30 realizations. This feature allows us to find an accurate estimate for p_c in simulations. Reproduced from [36], copyright 2011 The Authors. Published by the National Academy of Sciences.

$$e^{-\bar{k}P_\infty^c} = [\bar{k}nP_\infty^c + 1]^{-1}. \tag{4.43}$$

If we introduce a new parameter $w = -\bar{k}P_\infty^c - 1/n$, the solution of equation (4.43) can be expressed in terms of the Lambert function $W(w)$,

$$w = W_-(-1/n \exp(-1/n)), \tag{4.44}$$

where $W_-(x)$, is the smallest of the two real roots of the Lambert equation

$$\exp(W_-)W_- = x. \tag{4.45}$$

(The largest root in this case is the trivial solution $W_+ = -1/n$.) Thus, we obtain p_c and P_∞^c by substituting $\bar{k}_i = \bar{k}$ into equations (4.40) and (4.37), with the results

$$p_c = -\frac{w}{\bar{k}[1 + 1/(nw)]^{n-1}}, \tag{4.46}$$

and

$$P_\infty^c = -(w + 1/n)/\bar{k}. \tag{4.47}$$

For $n = 1$ we obtain the known ER results $p_c = 1/\bar{k}$, and $P_\infty = 0$ at p_c (representing a second-order phase transition) [33–35]. Substituting $n = 2$ in equations (4.46) and (4.47) we obtain the exact results derived by Buldyrev *et al* [7].

Since for ER networks $P(0) + P(1) > 0$, i.e. there exist isolated and/or single connected nodes for any $\bar{k}$, the NON consisting of n ER networks for sufficiently large n must completely disintegrate even for $p = 1$ (see figure 4.15(a)). For a network composed of n ER networks where each network has average degree $\bar{k}_i$, there exist $e^{-\bar{k}_i}$ fraction of isolated nodes, as the number of networks increases the number of such isolated nodes increases, which may bring about enough damage to destroy the whole system (see also section 4.6). This occurs as the right hand side of equation (4.46) becomes greater than unity. Conversely, for each n there exists $\bar{k}_{\min}(n)$, such that for $\bar{k} < \bar{k}_{\min}(n)$ the network of n ER networks completely disintegrates even for $p = 1$. Substituting $p_c = 1$ into equation (4.46) we obtain $\bar{k}_{\min}(n)$ as a function of n,

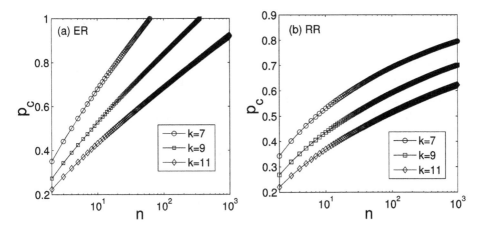

Figure 4.15. The critical threshold p_c for different $\bar{k}$ and n values for (a) a tree-like network of ER networks and (b) a tree-like network of RR networks. The analytical results for the tree-like network of ER networks are obtained from equations (4.43) and (4.46), while the results of the tree-like network of RR networks are obtained from the solution of equations (4.58) and (4.58). The results are in good agreement with simulations. In the simulations p_c was calculated from obtaining the value of p for which the number of iterations of cascading failures diverges. Reproduced from [36], copyright 2011 The Authors. Published by the National Academy of Sciences.

$$\bar{k}_{min}(n) = -\frac{w}{[1 + 1/(nw)]^{n-1}}. \tag{4.48}$$

Since for $n \to \infty$,

$$W_{-}\left[\frac{-1}{n}\exp\left(\frac{-1}{n}\right)\right] = -\ln n + o(\ln n), \tag{4.49}$$

we have

$$\bar{k}_{min}(n) = \ln n + o(\ln n). \tag{4.50}$$

Note that equation (4.48) together with equation (4.43) yields the value of $\bar{k}_{min}(1) = 1$ for $n = 1$, reproducing the known ER result that $\langle k \rangle = 1$ is the minimum average degree needed to have a giant component. For $n = 2$, equation (4.48) yields the result obtained in [7], i.e.,

$$\bar{k}_{min} = 2.455\,4. \tag{4.51}$$

In contrast, for a NON of n RR networks with $k \geqslant 2$, $P(0) + P(1) = 0$, and hence p_c approaches 1 only when $n \to \infty$ (see figure 4.15(b)), thus $k_{min}(n) = 2$ for any n (for details see section 4.4.1.2).

(C) The case of NONs with two different average degrees
We next study the case where the average degree of all n networks is not the same. Without loss of generality we assume that s networks have the same average degree $\bar{k}_2$, while the other $n - s$ networks each have average degree $\bar{k}_1$. We define $\alpha \equiv \bar{k}_1/\bar{k}_2$ where $0 < \alpha \leqslant 1$. Using equation (4.38) we can show that $f_c \equiv e^{\bar{k}_1(z_c-1)}$ satisfies

$$f_c = \exp\left[\frac{(f_c - 1)(1 - f_c^{1/\alpha})}{(n - s)f_c(1 - f_c^{1/\alpha}) + sf_c^{1/\alpha}(1 - f_c)/\alpha}\right]. \tag{4.52}$$

Results for p_c and the mutual giant component for different values of s and α are shown in figure 4.16. The case of $\bar{k}_1 \ll \bar{k}_2$ is interesting. In this limit, the s networks with large $\bar{k}_2$, due to their high connectivity, cannot cause further damage to the $n - s$ networks with $\bar{k}_1$. Thus the NON can be regarded, with respect to percolation, as a NON of only $n - s$ networks. Indeed, for $\alpha \to 0$, P_∞ as a function of p, s, n and $\bar{k}_1$ is described by equation (4.42), where n and $\bar{k}$ are replaced by $n - s$ and $\bar{k}_1$, respectively, as seen also in figure 4.16.

4.4.1.2 Analytical results for the case of tree-like network of networks composed of n RR networks
Next, we study the case of a tree-like NON composed of n random regular (RR) networks. The degree of network i is k_i. Substituting the generating function of RR networks, equations (1.8) and (1.9), into equations (4.24) and (4.26) we obtain,

$$P_\infty = p\prod_{j=1}^{n}(1 - z_j^{k_j}) \tag{4.53}$$

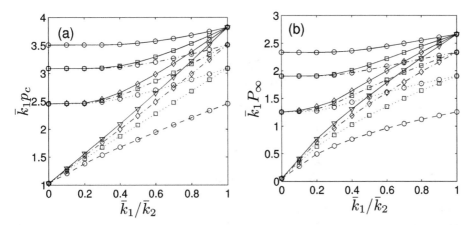

Figure 4.16. For a loopless network of n ER networks, (a) $\bar{k}_1 p_c$ and (b) $\bar{k}_1 P_\infty$ as function of the ratio $\bar{k}_1/\bar{k}_2$ for $n = 2$ (dashed), $n = 3$ (dotted), $n = 4$ (dashed dotted) and $n = 5$ (solid) and for $s = 1$ (○), $s = 2$ (□), $s = 3$ (◇) and $s = 4$ (▷), where s denotes the number of individual networks whose average degree are the same $\bar{k}_2$ while the average degree of each of the other $n - s$ networks is $\bar{k}_1$. The results are obtained using equations (4.37), (4.46), (4.47), and (4.52). Reprinted with permission from [5], copyright 2012 by the American Physical Society.

and

$$\frac{1}{p} = \frac{(1 - z_i^{k_i - 1}) \prod_{j=1, j \neq i}^{n} [1 - z_j^{k_j}]}{1 - z_i} \tag{4.54}$$

respectively. By solving equation (4.54), we obtain z_i for each network, and then we substitute z_i into equation (4.53) to obtain the mutual giant component of the tree-like NON of n RR networks.

When all n networks have the same degree k, i.e., $k_i = k$ ($i = 1, 2, \ldots, n$), $z_i = z$, the n equations, equations (4.53) and (4.54) reduce to a single equation,

$$\frac{1}{p} = \frac{(1 - z^{k-1})(1 - z^k)^{n-1}}{1 - z} \equiv R(z), \tag{4.55}$$

and the fraction of nodes in the mutual giant component is

$$P_\infty = p(1 - z^k)^n, \tag{4.56}$$

where z is the solution of equation (4.55).

For any given n and k we can plot R as a function of z. For example, for $n = 1$ and $k = 5$, R is a monotonous increasing function of z as shown in the solid line in figure 4.17. Thus, for a given p we can obtain $z = R^{-1}(1/p)$ from this solid line and then substitute z into equation (4.56) in order to obtain the mutual giant component P_∞. Furthermore, the maximum of $R = 4$ at $z = 1$, which indicates that $p_c = 1/4$ yields a second-order phase transition, because $P_\infty^c = 0$. Another example is shown for $n = 2$ and $k = 5$, for which R as a function of z shows a peak at the ○ symbol,

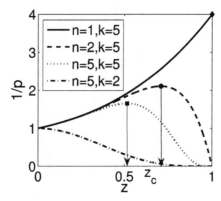

Figure 4.17. For a tree-like network composed of RR networks, we plot $1/p = R$ as a function of z for different values of k and n. All the lines are produced using equation (4.54). The filled symbols ◆, ● and ■ show the critical solutions $1/p_c$ for $k = 5$ with $n = 1$, $n = 2$ and $n = 5$, respectively. These critical thresholds coincide with the results in figure 4.18(a). The dashed dotted line shows that when $k = 2$ and $n = 5$, equation (4.54) has only a trivial solution $z = 0$ for $p = 1$. Reprinted with permission from [5], copyright 2012 by the American Physical Society.

where $R_{max} = 2.1$ and $z_c = 0.7$ yielding $p_c = 1/2.1$. Moreover, the case of $p > p_c$, gives that $R = 1/p$ has two solutions and the smaller root z has a physical meaning. We then substitute the solution into equation (4.56) and obtain the mutual giant component P_∞. In general, we can obtain P_∞ as a function of p by substituting z from equation (4.55) into equation (4.53),

$$P_\infty = p\left\{1 - \left\{p^{(1/n)} P_\infty^{(n-1)/n}\left[\left(1 - \left(\frac{P_\infty}{p}\right)^{1/n}\right)^{(k-1)/k} - 1\right] + 1\right\}^k\right\}^n.$$ (4.57)

When $k = 2$, equation (4.55) has only a trivial solution $z = 0$ for any n. When $k > 2$ and $n = 1$, $R(z)$ is an increasing function of z, so the critical threshold p_c can be obtained by substituting $z \to 1$ into equation (4.55) i.e., $p_c = 1/(k - 1)$ and $P_\infty^c = 0$ as in equation (1.16) for the second-order percolation phase transition n of a single random regular network. For $k > 2$ and $n \geqslant 2$, the critical case corresponds to the maximal $R(z)$, as shown in figure 4.17. Thus, we obtain that the value of z_c satisfies

$$1 = (1 - z_c)z_c^{k-2}\left[\frac{(n - 1)kz_c}{1 - z_c^k} + \frac{k - 1}{1 - z_c^{k-1}}\right].$$ (4.58)

Solving z_c from equation (4.58), we obtain the critical value of p_c:

$$p_c = \frac{z_c - 1}{(z_c^{k-1} - 1)(1 - z_c^k)^{n-1}}.$$ (4.59)

The numerical solutions of equation (4.57) are shown in figure 4.18. Here again, like in the ER case, for $n = 1$ we obtain the known continuous second-order percolation transition, while for $n > 1$ we obtain discontinuous, first-order transitions.

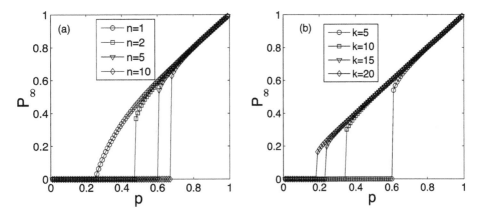

Figure 4.18. Percolation of a tree-like network of interdependent RR networks. (a) The mutual giant component P_∞ as a function of p for different values of number of networks when $k = 5$. (b) The mutual giant component P_∞ as a function of p for different values of k when $n = 5$. The analytical results obtained using equation (4.57) agree well with simulations. Reprinted with permission from [5], copyright 2012 by the American Physical Society.

Numerical solutions of p_c as a function of n are shown in figure 4.15(b). In contrast to the ER case, for RR NONs, $p_c < 1$ for any n, because for a RR network $P(0) + P(1) = 0$ (see discussion after equation (4.27) and reference [5]). Accordingly, an ER NON is significantly more vulnerable compared to an RR NON, due to the critical role played in the ER NON by singly connected nodes. Since $\lim_{n\to\infty} p_c = 1$, even RR NONs with large k become extremely vulnerable as $n \to \infty$. Indeed solving equations (4.58) and (4.59) in the limit $n \to \infty$ we obtain [39],

$$p_c = 1 - \left(1 + \frac{1}{k}\right)(kn)^{-\frac{1}{(k-1)}} + o(n^{-\frac{1}{(k-1)}}). \tag{4.60}$$

4.4.1.3 Analytical results for a network of network composed of n scale-free networks

Next we study the case of a tree-like NON composed of n scale-free (SF) networks. SF networks are characterized by a power law degree distribution, $P(k) \sim k^{-\lambda}$ with $m \leqslant k \leqslant M$, where m is the minimal degree and M is the maximal degree of a node. Reference [40] shows that it is possible to construct an uncorrelated SF network without multiple and looped links only if $M \ll \sqrt{N}$, a natural structural cutoff. However, in random SF networks, without an imposed cutoff, an expected natural cutoff for M scales as $N^{1/(\lambda-1)} \geqslant \sqrt{N}$ for $\lambda \leqslant 3$ [41]. Thus, the generating function method produces correct results in the thermodynamic limit only if M increases with the network size slower than $\sqrt{N}$. However, for interdependent SF networks with $\lambda > 2$, the general formalism of equations (4.24), (4.26), and (4.27) remains unchanged. This is true because the only singularity that can affect the behavior of these equations is the factor

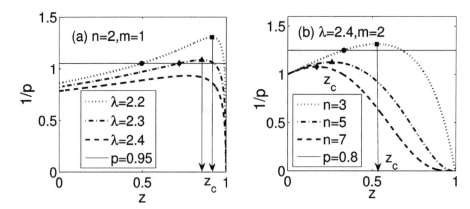

Figure 4.19. For a network composed of SF networks, we show $1/p$ as a function of z (a) for different values of λ when $n = 2$ and $m = 1$, (b) for different values of n when $\lambda = 2.4$ and $m = 2$. All lines are produced from the $R_{i,i,n}(z)$ function, equation (4.101). (a) The symbols $\bullet$ and $\blacklozenge$ show the physical solutions for $\lambda = 2.2$ and $\lambda = 2.3$ respectively when $p = 0.95$. The symbols $\bullet$ and $\blacklozenge$ show the critical solutions (z_c, p_c) for $\lambda = 2.2$ and $\lambda = 2.3$ respectively for $p = p_c$. (b) The symbol $\bullet$ shows the physical solution for $n = 3$, $p = 0.8$. The critical solutions (z_c, p_c) are shown as black symbols: $n = 7$, ($\blacklozenge$), $n = 5$ ($\blacktriangleright$) and $n = 3$ ($\blacksquare$). Reprinted with permission from [5], copyright 2012 by the American Physical Society.

$$1 - H(z) \sim (1 - z)^{\lambda - 2}. \tag{4.61}$$

Hence, $\lim_{z_i \to 1} F_i(z_i) = 0$ and $\lim_{z_i \to 1} R_i(z_i) = 0$ as for any other NON with a finite second moment of the degree distribution (figure 4.19). The critical threshold is determined by the maximum of $R_i(z_i)$ which is achieved for $z_i < 1$, for which the tail of the degree distribution is not important for obtaining an accurate result via generating functions. Hence, we expect that the analytical results of equations (4.24), (4.26) and (4.27) are correct in the thermodynamic limit for SF networks with and without a structural cutoff. Thus, we do not expect any qualitative differences in the behavior of SF NONs compared to NONs with a finite second moment. The value of the lower cutoff m is more important than λ and M for the behavior of SF NONs for $n \to \infty$. If $m = 1$, $P_i(1) > 0$, such networks completely disintegrate for sufficiently large n even for $p = 1$ (see also section 4.6).

In order to test our analytical predictions, we analyze a NON of n SF networks with the degree distribution defined by the generating function

$$G_i(z_i) = \frac{\displaystyle\sum_{m}^{M}[(k + 1)^{1-\lambda_i} - k^{1-\lambda_i}]z_i^k}{(M + 1)^{1-\lambda_i} - m^{1-\lambda_i}} \tag{4.62}$$

with the same λ, m and M for all networks. Figures 4.20(a) and (b) show the solutions for P_∞ for several values of n and m. Note that for $n \geq 2$, p_c is finite as opposed to the case of $n = 1$ where $p_c = 0$ [41]. Also, note that when the SF are partially interdependent $p_c = 0$ even for coupled networks [42].

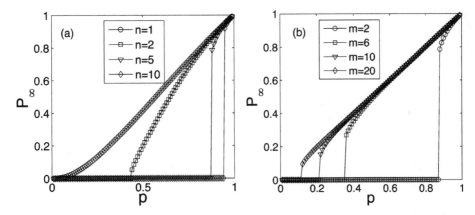

Figure 4.20. Percolation of a tree-like network composed of SF networks with exponent $\lambda = 2.3$. (a) The mutual giant component P_∞ as a function of p for different values of number of networks with $m = 2$. (b) The mutual giant component P_∞ as a function of p for different values of m when $n = 5$. The analytical results obtained using equation (4.62) agree well with simulations. Reprinted with permission from [5], copyright 2012 by the American Physical Society.

4.4.2 Percolation of an RR NON composed of random networks

4.4.2.1 The general case of an RR NON formed of random networks
In order to study the various steady-states that the system can reach after a cascade of failures, we first assume, without loss of generality, that each network depends on m other random networks, i.e., having a random regular (RR) NON formed of n random networks. We define the RR category to also include regular non-random networks in which each network has the same number of dependent networks such that the dependencies form a specific structure, e.g. a lattice of ER networks (figure 4.6(a)). We assume, for simplicity, that the initial attack on each network randomly removes a fraction $1 - p$ of the network's nodes, the partial interdependency fraction is q, and the average degree of each ER network is the same $\bar{k}$ for all networks. Because of the symmetries involved, the $nm + m$ equations in equations (4.28) and (4.29) can be reduced to two equations,

$$\begin{cases} x &= p(qyg(x) - q + 1)^m, \\ y &= p(qyg(x) - q + 1)^{m-1}. \end{cases} \tag{4.63}$$

By substituting $z = xf(x) + 1 - x$, equations (1.14), (1.15) and (4.32) into (4.63), and eliminating f, x, and y, we obtain,

$$P_\infty(z) = \frac{[1 - G(z)](1 - z)}{1 - H(z)}, \tag{4.64}$$

and

$$\left(\frac{1 - z}{1 - H(z)}\right)^{1/m}\left(\frac{1}{p}\right)^{2/m} + (q - 1)\left(\frac{1}{p}\right)^{1/m} - qP_\infty(z)\left(\frac{1 - H(z)}{1 - z}\right)^{1/m} = 0. \tag{4.65}$$

Equation (4.65) can help us to understand the percolation of a RR network formed of any interdependent random networks where all networks have the same average degree and same degree distribution.

To solve equation (4.65), we introduce an analytical function $R(z)$ for $z \in [0, 1]$ as

$$\frac{1}{p} = \frac{H(z) - 1}{z - 1}\left(\frac{1 - q + \sqrt{(1 - q)^2 + 4qP_\infty(z)}}{2}\right)^m \equiv R(z). \qquad (4.66)$$

Here, $R(z)$ as a function of z has a quite complex behaviour for various degree distributions. We present two examples to demonstrate our general results on (i) an RR network formed of interdependent ER networks and (ii) an RR network formed of interdependent SF networks.

(i) For the case of an RR network formed of ER networks we find a critical q_c such that, for $q < q_c$ the system undergoes a second-order phase transition and the critical threshold p_c depends on q and on the average degree $\bar{k}$. When $q_c < q < q_{max}$ the system experiences a first-order phase transition, and when $q > q_{max}$ there is no phase transition because the NON collapses even for a single node failure.

(ii) For the case of an RR network formed of SF networks, the phase diagram is different from the ER case, because there is no pure first-order phase transition. However, there exists an effective q_c^e, where for $q < q_c^e$, the system undergoes a second-order phase transition and the critical threshold is $p_c = 0$ when there is an infinite number of nodes in each network, i.e., the maximum degree approaches ∞. For $q_c^e < q < q_{max}$, the system experiences a hybrid transition as follows: as p decreases from 1, the giant component P_∞ as a function of p shows a sharp jump at p_{ec}^I, which is a first-order transition to a finite small value of P_∞, and then (when p further decreases) P_∞ decreases smoothly to 0. For $q > q_{max}$ there is no phase transition because all the networks in the NON collapse even for a single node failure.

4.4.2.2 RR network formed of interdependent ER networks

For ER networks [33–35], the generating function $g(x)$ satisfies [32, 43–45],

$$g(x) = 1 - \exp[\bar{k}x(f - 1)],$$
$$f = \exp[\bar{k}x(f - 1)]. \qquad (4.67)$$

Substituting equations (4.67) into equations (4.63), we get,

$$f = \exp\{\bar{k}p[qy(1 - f) - q + 1]^m(f - 1)\},$$
$$y = p[qy(1 - f) - q + 1]^{m-1}, \qquad (4.68)$$
$$P_\infty = -(\log f)/\bar{k}.$$

Eliminating y from equation (4.68), we obtain an equation for f,

$$\left[\frac{\ln f}{\bar{k}p(f - 1)}\right]^{2/m} + (q - 1)\left[\frac{\ln f}{\bar{k}p(f - 1)}\right]^{1/m} + \frac{q}{\bar{k}}\log f = 0. \qquad (4.69)$$

Considering $[\ln f / \bar{k} p (f - 1)]^{1/m}$ to be a variable, equation (4.69) becomes a quadratic equation that can be solved analytically and having only one valid solution,

$$2^m \ln f = \bar{k} p (f - 1) \left[1 - q + \sqrt{(1 - q)^2 - \frac{4q}{\bar{k}} \ln f} \right]^m. \tag{4.70}$$

From equation (4.70) and the last equation in (4.68), we determine the mutual percolation giant component for an RR network formed of ER networks,

$$P_\infty = \frac{p}{2^m} (1 - e^{-\bar{k} P_\infty}) \left[1 - q + \sqrt{(1 - q)^2 + 4q P_\infty} \right]^m. \tag{4.71}$$

Figure 4.21 shows the numerical solutions of equation (4.71) for several q and m values compared with simulations. These solutions imply that P_∞ as a function of p exhibits a second (continuous) or a first-order (abrupt) phase transition depending on the values of q and m for a given $\bar{k}$. Note, when $q = 0$ or $m = 0$, equation (4.71) is reduced to the known equation, $P_\infty = p(1 - e^{-\bar{k} P_\infty})$, for single ER networks [33–35].

From equations (4.66) and (4.71), we obtain

$$R(z) = \frac{1}{p} = \frac{(1 - e^{\bar{k}(z-1)})[1 - q + \sqrt{(1 - q)^2 + 4q(1 - z)}]^m}{2^m (1 - z)}, \tag{4.72}$$

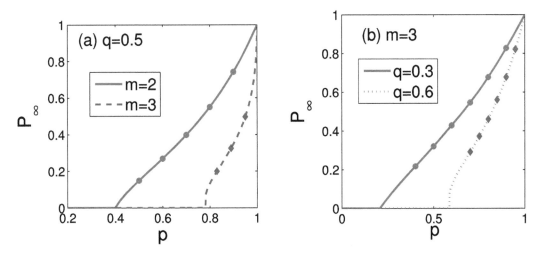

Figure 4.21. The giant component for an RR network formed of interdependent ER networks, P_∞, as a function of p, for ER networks with average degree $\bar{k} = 10$, (a) for two different values of m and $q = 0.5$, (b) for two different values of q and $m = 3$. The curves in (a) and (b) have been obtained using equation (4.71) and are in excellent agreement with simulations. The symbols are obtained from simulations by averaging over 20 realizations for $N = 2 \times 10^5$. In (a), simulation results are shown as circles ($n = 6$) for $m = 2$ and as diamonds ($n = 12$) for $m = 3$. These simulation results support our theoretical result, equation (4.71), which is interestingly independent of the number of networks n. Reprinted with permission from [6], copyright 2013 by the American Physical Society.

and

$$F(z) \equiv \frac{dR(z)}{dz} = \frac{e^{\bar{k}(1-z)} - \bar{k}(1-z)}{p(1-z)(e^{\bar{k}(1-z)} - 1)}$$
$$- \frac{2mq}{p[1 - q + \sqrt{(1-q)^2 + 4q(1-z)}]\sqrt{(1-q)^2 + 4q(1-z)}}. \tag{4.73}$$

Next we demonstrate the behaviour of equation (4.72) as shown in figure 4.22. For given $\bar{k}$ and m, when q is small, $R(z)$ is a monotonic increasing function of z, for example see the curve for $q = 0.42$. Thus, the maximum of $R(z)$ is obtained when $z \rightarrow 1$, which corresponds to a second-order phase transition threshold $p_c^{II} = 1/\max\{R(z)\} \equiv 1/R(z_c)$, where $P_\infty(p_c^{II}) = 1 - z_c = 0$. When q increases, $R(z)$ as a function of z shows a maxima at $z < 1$ and $\max\{R(z)\} > 1$, for example the case $q = 0.50$ shown in figure 4.22. Thus, the maximum of $R(z)$ is obtained when $z = z_c \in (0, 1)$ at the peak, which corresponds to a first-order phase transition threshold $p_c^{I} = 1/\max\{R(z)\} = 1/R(z_c)$, where $P_\infty(p_c^{I}) = 1 - z_c > 0$. The q value for which the first time a maxima of $R(z)$ appears at $z < 1$ is q_c i.e., the critical dependency which separates between first $(q > q_c)$ and second $(q < q_c)$-order transitions. When q further increases, $\max\{R(z)\} < 1$, which corresponds to a complete collapse of the NON. The value of q for which $\max\{R(z)\} = 1$ is q_{max}, above which the network is not stable and collapses spontaneously.

Next we analyze the different behaviors of an RR network formed of ER networks in the different regimes of q: (i) For $q < q_c$, the percolation is a continuous

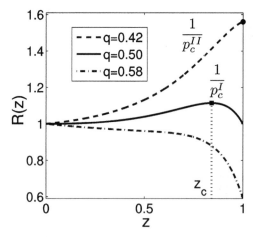

Figure 4.22. Plot of $R(z)$ as a function of z for an RR network formed of interdependent ER networks, for different values of q when $m = 3$ and $\bar{k} = 8$. All the lines are produced using equation (4.72). The symbols show the critical thresholds p_c^{II} when $q = 0.42 < q_c = 0.431\,3$ and p_c^{I} when $q = 0.5 < q_{max} = 0.546\,2$. These critical thresholds coincide with the results in figure 4.21(a). The dashed dotted line shows that when $q = 0.58 > q_{max}$ the function (4.72) has no solution for $p = 1$, which corresponds to the case of spontaneous complete collapse of the NON. Reprinted with permission from [6], copyright 2013 by the American Physical Society.

second-order transition which is characterized by a critical threshold p_c^{II}. (ii) The range of $q_c < q < q_{max}$ is characterized by an abrupt first-order phase transition with a critical threshold p_c^{I}. (iii) For $q > q_{max}$ no transition exists due to the spontaneous collapse of the system. Next, we analyze in detail the parameters characterizing the three regimes.

(i) Obtaining p_c^{II}. For a given m and $\bar{k}$, when q is sufficiently small, there exists a critical threshold p_c^{II} such that, when p increases above p_c^{II}, P_∞ continuously increases from zero to non-zero values and below p_c, $P_\infty = 0$. Here, P_∞ as a function of p exhibits a second-order phase transition. In order to evaluate p_c^{II} we analyze equation (4.73). When q is sufficiently small $dR(z)/dz > 0$, the maximum value of $R(z)$ is obtained when $z \to 1$. Thus, we obtain the critical threshold for the second-order phase transition, p_c^{II}, by substituting $z \to 1$ into equation (4.72),

$$p_c^{II} = \frac{1}{\bar{k}(1-q)^m}. \tag{4.74}$$

(ii) Obtaining p_c^{I}. According to equation (4.73), when q increases, $R(z)$ as a function z becomes not monotonous and a maxima appears, which corresponds to the condition for a first-order phase transition, i.e., when $\frac{dR(z)}{dz} = 0$. Furthermore, for a given p, the smallest of these roots gives the physically meaningful solution from which the giant component $0 < P_\infty(p_c) < 1$ can be found using equation (4.71).

By solving z_c from $F(z_c) = 0$ of equation (4.73), we obtain the critical threshold for first-order phase transition p_c^{I} as

$$p_c^{I} = \frac{2^m(1-z_c)}{(1 - e^{\bar{k}(z_c-1)})[1 - q + \sqrt{(1-q)^2 + 4q(1-z_c)}]^m}. \tag{4.75}$$

It should also be noted that other models have observed similar behaviors with multiple phase transitions such as Bianconi *et al* [46]. Next, we study the critical coupling strength q_c, i.e., the critical coupling that distinguishes between first- and second-order transitions. We find that P_∞ undergoes a second-order transition as a function of p when $q < q_c$, a first-order transition when $q_c < q < q_{max}$, and no phase transition (the system is unstable for any p) when $q > q_{max}$. By definition, when a system changes from second-order to first-order at the critical point, q, m, and $\bar{k}$ satisfy $p_c^{I} = p_c^{II}$, i.e., both conditions for the first-order and second-order phase transition should satisfy,

$$\lim_{z \to 1} \frac{dR(z)}{dz} = 0. \tag{4.76}$$

From equations (4.73) and (4.76), we obtain

$$2qm - \bar{k}(1-q)^2 = 0. \tag{4.77}$$

Solving equation (4.77), we find that the physically meaningful q_c is

$$q_c = \frac{\bar{k} + m - (m^2 + 2\bar{k}m)^{1/2}}{\bar{k}}. \tag{4.78}$$

(iii) Calculating q_{max}. Here we calculate the critical coupling q_{max}, above which ($q > q_{max}$) the system is unstable and collapses for any p. From equation (4.72), the system is unstable for any p, when $R(z) \leqslant 1$. We therefore, can obtain q_{max} by satisfying equation (4.73) and the equation $p_c^I = 1$. Thus, we obtain q_{max} as

$$q_{max} = \frac{(a^{1/m} - 1)^2}{2(1 - 2z_c - a^{1/m})}, \tag{4.79}$$

where a satisfies

$$a = \frac{1 - e^{\bar{k}(z_c-1)}}{2^m(1 - z_c)}, \tag{4.80}$$

and z_c can be solved by substituting equation (4.79) into equation (4.73) and set $p = 1$, $F(z_c) = 0$, which is one equation with only one unknown z_c.

In figure 4.23 we obtain numerical solutions of $P_\infty(p_c)$. We can see that for fixed m and $\bar{k}$, there exist two critical values of coupling strength, q_c and q_{max}. For $q < q_c$, $P_\infty(p_c) = 0$ representing a second-order phase transition, while for $q_c < q < q_{max}$, $P_\infty(p_c) > 0$ representing a first-order phase transition. When $q > q_{max}$, $P_\infty(p_c) = 0$ meaning the NON collapses and there is no phase transition ($p_c = 1$). Figure 4.24 shows the phase diagram of an RR network formed of ER networks for different values of m and $\bar{k}$. As m decreases and k increases, the region for $P_\infty > 0$ increases, showing improved robustness.

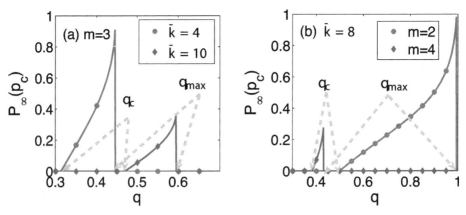

Figure 4.23. The giant component at p_c and $P_\infty(p_c)$ for an RR NON formed of ER networks, as a function of q. The curves are (a) for $m = 3$ and two different values of $\bar{k}$, and (b) for $\bar{k} = 8$ and two different values of m. The curves are obtained using equations (4.71) and (4.74) and are in excellent agreement with simulations (symbols). Panels (a) and (b) show the location of q_{max} and q_c for two values of m. Between q_c and q_{max} the transition is first order represented by $P_\infty(p_c) > 0$. For $q < q_c$ the transition is second order since $P_\infty(p_c) = 0$ and for $q > q_{max}$ the NON spontaneously collapses ($P_\infty(p_c) = 0$) and there is no phase transition ($p_c = 1$). Reprinted with permission from [6], copyright 2013 by the American Physical Society.

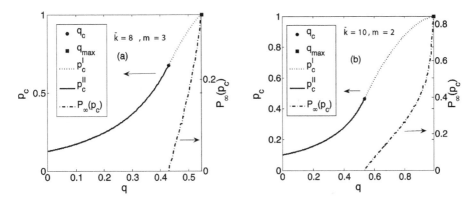

Figure 4.24. The phase diagram for a RR NON formed of ER networks, (a) for $m = 3$ and $\bar{k} = 8$, (b) for $m = 2$ and $\bar{k} = 10$. The solid curves show the second-order phase transition (predicted by equation (4.78)) and the dashed-dotted curves show the first-order phase phase transition, leading $P_\infty(p_c)$ at q_c from zero to non-zero values (on the right y-axis). As m decreases and $\bar{k}$ increases, the region for $P_\infty > 0$ increases, showing improved robustness. The circle shows the tri-critical point q_c, below which a second-order transition occurs and above which a first-order transition occurs. The square shows the critical coupling q_{max}, above which the NON spontaneously collapses even for $p = 1$. Reprinted with permission from [6], copyright 2013 by the American Physical Society.

4.4.2.3 The case of RR NON formed of interdependent scale-free (SF) networks

We analyze here NONs composed of SF networks with a power law degree distribution $P(k) \sim k^{-\lambda}$. The corresponding generating function is

$$G(z) = \frac{\sum_{s}^{M}[(k + 1)^{1-\lambda} - k^{1-\lambda}]z^k}{(M + 1)^{1-\lambda} - s^{1-\lambda}} \tag{4.81}$$

where s ($s = 2$ assumed here) is the minimal degree cutoff and M is the maximal degree cutoff.

SF networks approximate many real networks such as the internet, airline flight patterns, and patterns of scientific collaboration [47–50]. When SF networks are fully interdependent [7], $p_c > 0$, even for the case $\lambda \leqslant 3$ in contrast to a single network for which $p_c = 0$ [41]. We study percolation of a RR network formed of interdependent SF networks by substituting their degree distribution into equation (1.5) and obtaining their generating functions. We assume, for simplicity, that all the networks in the NON have the same λ, s and M, and use equation (4.65) to analyze the percolation of an RR NON formed of interdependent SF networks.

The generating function of the branching process is defined as $H(z) = G'(z)/G'(1)$. Substituting $H(z)$ and equation (4.81) into equation (4.66), we obtain the function $R(z)$ for an RR network of SF networks. As shown in figure 4.25, we find three regimes based on the coupling strength q:

(i) When q is small ($q < q_c^e$), $R(z)$ is a monotonically increasing function of z, the system shows a second-order percolation transition, and the critical threshold p_c^{II}

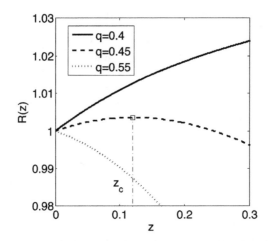

Figure 4.25. For an RR NON formed of SF networks, we show $R(z)$ as a function of z for different values of q for $m = 3$, $\lambda = 2.3$, $s = 2$ and $M = 1000$. (i) When q is small ($q = 0.4 < q_c$), $R(z)$ is a monotonically increasing function of z, and the system undergoes a second-order percolation transition. (ii) When q is larger ($q_c < q = 0.45 < q_{max}$), $R(z)$ as a function of z has a peak at z_c which corresponds to a hybrid phase transition. The square symbol represents the critical point of the sharp jump (z_c). (iii) When q is even larger ($q = 0.55 > q_{max}$), $R(z)$ decreases with z initially, and then increases with z, which corresponds to a system collapse. Reprinted with permission from [6], copyright 2013 by the American Physical Society.

is obtained when $z \to 1$ which corresponds to $R(1) = \max\{R\} = \infty = 1/p_c^{II}$, i.e., $p_c^{II} = 0$.

(ii) When q is larger and in the range $q_c^e < q < q_{max}$, $R(z)$ as a function of z shows a peak which corresponds to a sharp jump in P_∞ to a significantly lower value of P_∞ at z_c with a hybrid transition, because $\max\{R\} \neq R(z_c)$. This is different from the ER case. Furthermore, the effective critical threshold (sharp jump) is $p_{ec}^I = 1/R(z_c)$, while for p below this sharp jump the system undergoes a smooth second-order phase transition and the critical threshold is zero, similar to (i). Thus, when z is greater than some value, $R(z)$ increases with z again and reaches $\max\{R\}$ when $z \to 1$, which indicates that when p decreases to just below p_{ec}^I, P_∞ jumps in a first-order transition to a finite smaller value and then decreases smoothly to 0 as p approaches 0;

(iii) When q is above q_{max}, $R(z)$ first decreases with z, and then increases with z, which corresponds to a system collapse.

Next we analyze the three regimes more rigorously.

(i) When q is small ($q < q_c^e$), $R(z)$ is a monotonically increasing function of z, the maximum of $R(z_c)$ is obtained when $z_c \to 1$, which corresponds to $P_\infty = 0$,

$$\max\{R\} = \lim_{z\to 1} \frac{H(z) - 1}{z - 1}(1 - q)^m \doteq H'(1). \tag{4.82}$$

This is since when $M \to \infty$, $\max\{R\} \to \infty$, $p_c^{II} = 0$ when $q < q_c^e$.

(ii) As q increases ($q \geqslant q_c^e$), $R(z)$ as a function of z shows a peak corresponding to $R(z) = R(z_c)$, $dR/dz = 0$ (with the smaller root having the physical meaning), where

$R = R_c = 1/p_{ec}^I > 1$. This corresponds to the effective critical threshold where P_∞ as a function of p experiences an abrupt jump. Furthermore, we define

$$P_\infty^- = \lim_{p \to p_{ec}^I, p < p_{ec}^I} P_\infty(p), \qquad (4.83)$$

and

$$P_\infty^+ = \lim_{p \to p_{ec}^I, p > p_{ec}^I} P_\infty(p). \qquad (4.84)$$

For the case of a pure first-order phase transition there is just a sharp jump, $P_\infty^- = 0$, but for the hybrid transition in our case $P_\infty^- > 0$. After the sharp jump, P_∞ decreases smoothly to 0 as p approaches zero. For the case of two partially interdependent SF networks, see Zhou et al [42].

(iii) As q increases further ($q > q_{max}$), $dR(z)/dz$ at $z = 0$ becomes negative, thus the NON will collapse even when a single node is initially removed. So the maximum value of q is obtained as

$$\left. \frac{dR(z)}{dz} \right|_{z \to 0} = 0. \qquad (4.85)$$

Using equations (4.64), (4.66) and (4.85), we obtain

$$\frac{dR(z)}{dz} = -\frac{G'(z)R(z)}{1 - G(z)} - \frac{R(z)P_\infty'(z)}{P_\infty(z)}$$
$$+ \frac{2mR(z)}{1 - q + \sqrt{(1-q)^2 + 4qP_\infty(z)}} \frac{qP_\infty'(z)}{\sqrt{(1-q)^2 + 4qP_\infty(z)}} \qquad (4.86)$$

When $q = q_{max}$, $P_\infty(z)|_{z \to 0} = 1$ and $P_\infty'(z)|_{z \to 0} = -1$, so we get

$$q_{max} = \frac{1}{m - 1}. \qquad (4.87)$$

In figure 4.26 we show the excellent agreement between analytical and simulation results.

4.5 Comparing feedback and no-feedback conditions

The above detailed analysis considers the case of no feedback since even for two *fully* interdependent networks with a feedback condition (fb), both networks will completely collapse even if a single node fails. However, in the case of partially interdependent networks when q is sufficiently small even with feedback, removal of a single node will not destroy the NON. For the case of the feedback, equation (4.63) becomes

$$x = p(qxg(x) - q + 1)^m. \qquad (4.88)$$

Substituting $z = xf(x) + 1 - x$ and equations (1.5)–(1.7) into equation (4.88) and eliminating x, we obtain

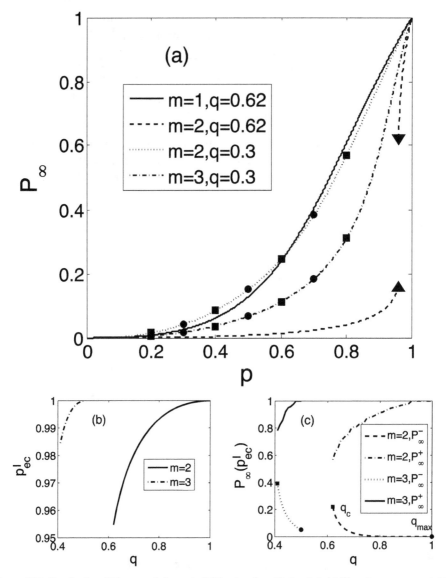

Figure 4.26. Results for a RR network formed of SF networks with $\lambda = 2.5$. (a) The giant component P_∞ as a function of p for different values of m and q. (b) The critical threshold p_{ec}^I and (c) the corresponding giant component at the threshold $P_\infty(p_{ec}^I)$ as a function of coupling strength q for $m = 2$ and $m = 3$. The symbols in (a) represent simulation results, obtained by averaging over 20 realizations of $N = 2 \times 10^5$ with the number of networks $n = 6$ (squares) and $n = 4$ (circles). The lines are the theoretical results obtained using equations (4.65) and (1.5)–(1.7). We can see in (a) that the system experiences a hybrid phase transition for $m = 2$ and $q_c^e < q = 0.62 < q_{max} = 1/(m - 1)$. When $q < q_c^e$ the system undergoes a second-order phase transition and the critical threshold is $p_c^{II} = 0$. However, in the simulations when p is small (and not zero) P_∞ is not equal to 0. This happens because $p_c^{II} = 0$ is valid only when the network size is $N = \infty$ and $M = \infty$, but in simulations we have finite systems. Furthermore, when $q_c^e < q < q_{max}$ the system shows a hybrid transition shown in (a) and (c), and when $q > q_{max}$ all the networks collapse even if one node fails. We call this a hybrid transition because $P_\infty^- > 0$, which is different from the case of ER networks with first-order phase transition where $P_\infty^- = 0$. Reprinted from [6], copyright 2013 by the American Physical Society.

$$\frac{1}{p} = \frac{1 - H(z)}{1 - z}(1 - q + qP_\infty)^m. \tag{4.89}$$

For ER networks, we obtain an equation for f,

$$\ln f = \bar{k}p\left(1 - q - q\frac{\ln f}{\bar{k}}\right)^{-m}(f - 1). \tag{4.90}$$

By substituting $P_\infty = -(\log f)/\bar{k}$, we can determine the mutual giant component for an RR network of ER networks with feedback condition via,

$$P_\infty = p(1 - e^{-\bar{k}P_\infty})(1 - q + qP_\infty)^m. \tag{4.91}$$

Figure 4.27 shows numerical solutions of equation (4.91) for several q and m values, which are in excellent agreement with simulations, presented as symbols. These solutions imply that P_∞ as a function of p exhibits only a second-order phase transition. Indeed, from equation (4.91) and substituting $P_\infty = z$ ($z \in [0, 1]$), we obtain

$$R(z) = \frac{1}{p} = \frac{(1 - e^{-\bar{k}z})}{z}(1 - q + qz)^m, \tag{4.92}$$

and

$$\frac{dR(z)}{dz} = \frac{\bar{k}z - e^{\bar{k}z} + 1}{pz(e^{\bar{k}z} - 1)} - \frac{mq}{p(1 - q + qz)}. \tag{4.93}$$

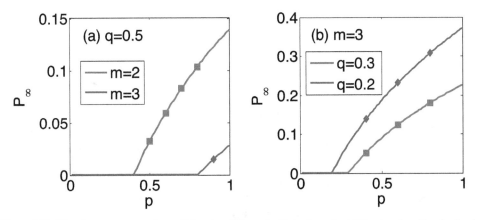

Figure 4.27. The giant component for an RR network formed of interdependent ER networks with a feedback condition. We show P_∞, as a function of p for an average degree $\bar{k} = 10$ for each of the ER networks. Plot of the analytical and simulation results for (a) two values of m for $q = 0.5$, and (b) two values of q when $m = 3$. The curves in (a) and (b) are obtained using equation (4.91) and are in excellent agreement with simulations. The symbols are obtained from simulations of the topology in figure 4.6(b) when $m = 3$ and $n = 6$ interdependent networks and for $m = 2$ (forming a circular loop) by averaging over 20 realizations for $N = 2 \times 10^5$. Reprinted with permission from [6], copyright 2013 by the American Physical Society.

Next, we prove that $R(z)$ is a decreasing function of z, i.e., $dR(z)/dz < 0$. It is easy to see that

$$\frac{d}{dz}(\bar{k}z - e^{\bar{k}z} + 1) = \bar{k} - \bar{k}e^{\bar{k}z} \leqslant 0, \tag{4.94}$$

and the equality condition is satisfied only when $z = 0$, so $\bar{k}z - e^{\bar{k}z} + 1 < 0$. Thus, we obtain that $R(z)$ is a monotonically decreasing function of z, which is very different from the no feedback case. The maximum of $R(z)$ is obtained only when $z \to 0$, which corresponds to the critical value of p_c,

$$p_c = \frac{1}{\bar{k}(1 - q)^m}, \tag{4.95}$$

which is the same as equation (4.74). Thus, the second-order threshold of no feedback p_c^{II} is the same as the p_c of the feedback case, which is also shown in figure 4.28(a). However, the feedback case is still significantly more vulnerable compared to the no-feedback case. Figures 4.28(b) and (c) show P_∞ for $p = 1$ i.e., the giant component in each network of the NON when there are no node failures, as a function of q. We can see that for the no-feedback case (figure 4.28) the system still has a very large giant component when both m and q are large, but for the feedback case, there is no giant component when both m and q are large. This happens because of the singly connected nodes and isolated nodes in each network [5] see also section 4.6.

Substituting $p_c \leqslant 1$ into equation (4.95), we obtain $\bar{k} \geqslant 1/(1 - q)^m$ or $q \leqslant 1 - (1/\bar{k})^{1/m}$, which represents the minimum $\bar{k}$ and maximum q for which a phase transition exists,

$$\bar{k}_{\min} = \frac{1}{(1 - q)^m}, \tag{4.96}$$

and

$$q_{\max} = 1 - (1/\bar{k})^{1/m}. \tag{4.97}$$

Equations (4.96) and (4.97) demonstrate that the NON collapses when q and m are fixed and $\bar{k} < \bar{k}_{\min}$. Likewise, the NON also collapses when m and $\bar{k}$ are fixed with $q > q_{\max}$, i.e., there is no phase transition in these zones as the system collapses even for $p = 1$. However, $q_{\max}$ of the feedback case is smaller than that of the no-feedback case as seen in figure 4.29(a), where the feedback case is more vulnerable than the no-feedback case. In figure 4.29(b) we show that increasing $\bar{k}$ or decreasing m will increase $q_{\max}$, i.e., increase the robustness of NON.

Next we study an RR NON formed of RR networks with degree k. We substitute the generating functions of RR networks equations (1.8) and (1.9) into equation (4.91), and obtain a recursive relation for the giant component of an RR network of RR networks

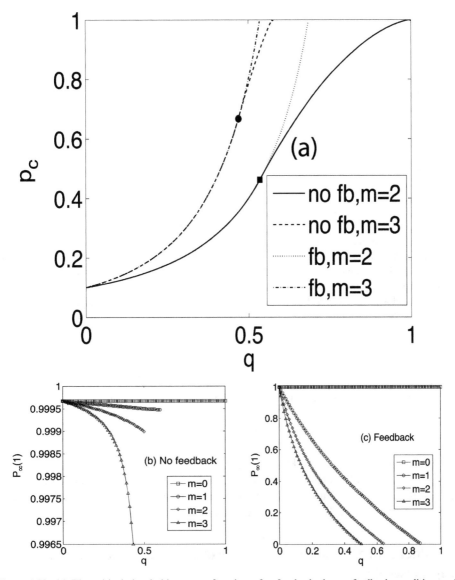

Figure 4.28. (a) The critical threshold p_c as a function of q for both the no-feedback condition and the feedback condition for $\bar{k} = 10$. For the no feedback condition, the parts of the curves bellow the symbols show p_c^{II} and above the symbols show p_c^{I}. For the feedback condition, there is only a p_c for a second-order transition, and p_c^{II} for the no feedback case is equal to p_c of the feedback case, but this does not mean that these two cases have equal vulnerability. (b) $P_\infty(1)$ as a function of q for different values of m when $\bar{k} = 8$ with the no-feedback condition. (c) $P_\infty(1)$ as a function of q for different values of m when $\bar{k} = 8$ with the feedback condition. Note that when $q = 0$, $P_\infty(1) = 1 - exp(-\bar{k})$ for all m and for both the feedback and no-feedback cases. Comparing (b) and (c), we can see that the feedback case is significantly more vulnerable than the no-feedback case, because $P_\infty(1)$ for the no-feedback case is much smaller compared to that of the feedback case. Reprinted with permission from [6], copyright 2013 by the American Physical Society.

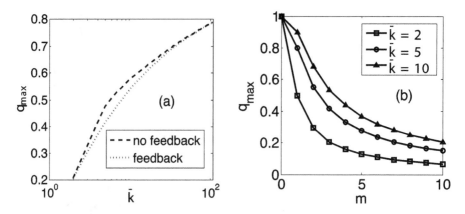

Figure 4.29. (a) The maximum value of coupling strength q_{max} as a function of $\bar{k}$ for the case of feedback condition and no-feedback condition when $m = 3$. We can see that q_{max} of the no-feedback case is larger than that of the feedback case, which indicates that the no-feedback case is more robust compared to the feedback case. (b) The maximum value of the coupling strength q_{max} as a function of m with the feedback condition for different values of $\bar{k}$, which shows that increasing $\bar{k}$ or decreasing m will increase q_{max}, i.e., increase the robustness of the NON. Reprinted with permission from [6], copyright 2013 by the American Physical Society.

$$1 - \left[1 - \frac{P_\infty}{p(1 - q - qP_\infty)}\right]^{\frac{1}{k}} = p\left\{1 - \left[1 - \frac{P_\infty}{p(1 - q - qP_\infty)}\right]^{\frac{k-1}{k}}\right\} \quad (4.98)$$

$$(1 - q + qP_\infty)^m.$$

We find that the RR networks are very different from the ER networks, and the system undergoes a first-order phase transition for large q and a secondorder phase transition for small q, as shown in figure 4.30. Furthermore, this analytical result can be reduced to the single RR network case equation (1.16) when $m = 0$.

4.6 Vulnerability of network of networks for a large number of networks

An interesting question is how vulnerable the NON becomes when the number of networks, $n \to \infty$. For sufficiently large n, will the system collapse even for $p = 1$ as was true for the tree-like network of ER networks shown in figure 4.15(a)? Or for any n, there exists $p(n) < 1$ such that, for $p(n) < p < 1$ the NON has a non-zero mutual giant component, like the tree-like network of RR networks shown in figure 4.15(b)? We will show that such a $p(n)$ exists if and only if $P_j(0) + P_j(1) = 0$ where $1 \leqslant j \leqslant n$ (condition I), provided that all the networks of the NON have a finite fraction of nodes of finite degree: namely there exist constants $\eta > 0$ and $M \geqslant 0$ such that for any j

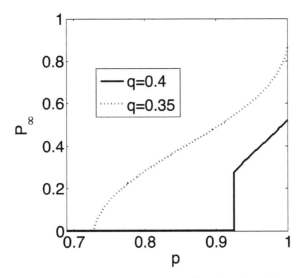

Figure 4.30. The giant component for an RR network formed of interdependent RR networks with a feedback condition. We show P_∞ as a function of p for a RR NON with $k = 6$ and $m = 3$, for different values of q. The curves are obtained using equation (4.98), showing a first-order phase transition when q is large but a second-order phase transition when q is small. Reprinted with permission from [6], copyright 2013 by the American Physical Society.

$$\sum_{k=0}^{M} P_j(k) \geqslant \eta \qquad (4.99)$$

(condition II).

In order to show this, we must first show that in equation (4.25), $F_j(z_j) = F_i(z_i)$ define a unique monotonically increasing function $z_j = F_j^{-1}(F_i(z_i))$ for $z_i \in [0, 1]$ if $F_i(0) \leqslant F_j(0)$ or for $z_i \in [z_{ij}, 1]$, where $F_i(z_{ij}) = F_j(0)$ if $F_i(0) > F_j(0)$. In order to prove this, we must show, that $F_i(z_i)$ is a monotonically decreasing function for $z_i \in [0, 1]$. This will follow from the monotonic increase of the function $(1 - H_i(z))/(1 - z)$ for $z \in [0, 1)$, because $1 - G_i(z)$ monotonically decreases. Indeed,

$$\frac{\mathrm{d}}{\mathrm{d}z} \frac{1 - H_i(z)}{1 - z} = \frac{[1 - H_i(z) - (1 - z)H_i'(z)]}{(1 - z)^2} = \frac{H_i''(z)}{2} > 0 \qquad (4.100)$$

where $0 < z < 1$, which follows from the Taylor expansion formula with a residual term. This is since $H_i''(z) > 0$ for any degree distribution except the trivial cases $P_i(m) = 0$ for $m > 1$, for which the giant component does not exist even for an isolated network. Thus, $F_i(z)$ monotonically decreases.

We next show that if $P_j(0) + P_j(1) = 0$ for all $1 \leqslant j \leqslant n$, the NON has a non-zero giant component for any n provided that $\bar{k}_j > 2$ for each network. The last condition excludes degenerate loop-like networks for which each node has a degree of 2. Among all j we can select $j = i$, such that $F_i(0) \leqslant F_j(0)$. Then, for any $z_i \in [0, 1]$ we have $1 \geqslant z_j(z_i) \geqslant 0$ and we can represent equation (4.26) as

$$R_{i,\ell,n}(z_i) = R_{i,i,n}(z_i) = \frac{\displaystyle\prod_{j=1,j\neq\ell}^{n}(1 - G_j[z_j(z_i)])(1 - H_\ell[z_\ell(z_i)])}{1 - z_\ell(z_i)} = \frac{1}{p}. \qquad (4.101)$$

If $P_j(0) + P_j(1) = 0$ for any j then $H_j(0) = G_j(0) = 1$. Hence $F_i(0) = F_j(0)$ for any i and j and we can select any i, so that $z_j(z_i)|_{z_i=0} = 0$ and $R_{i,\ell}(0) = 1$. Moreover,

$$F_i'(0) = -1 + \frac{2P_i(2)}{\bar{k}_i} < 0 \qquad (4.102)$$

and

$$\frac{dz_j}{dz_i} = \left(1 - \frac{2P_i(2)}{\bar{k}_i}\right)\Big/\left(1 - \frac{2P_j(2)}{\bar{k}_j}\right) > 1 - \frac{2P_i(2)}{\bar{k}_i} = C_1 > 0. \qquad (4.103)$$

Finally

$$\left.\frac{dR_{i,i,n}(z_i)}{dz_i}\right|_{z_i=0} = 1 - \frac{2P_i(2)}{\bar{k}_i} > 0. \qquad (4.104)$$

Hence the maximum $R_{i,\ell}(z_{i,m})$ must reach its maximum value $r = R_{i,\ell}(z_{i,m}) > 1$ at $z_i = z_{i,m}$ where $0 < z_{i,m} < 1$, for any n. Accordingly, equation (4.101) has a nontrivial solution for $1/r < p < 1$, and the NON has a nonzero mutual giant component for sufficiently large p for any n.

Next we show that if $P_j(0) + P_j(1) = 0$ for all $j = 1, 2, ...n$, then a NON has a non-zero giant component for any n for $p_c \leqslant p \leqslant 1$, and if condition II is satisfied then $p_c \to 1$ for $n \to \infty$. Suppose for $n = 2$, the maximum of $R_{i,\ell,2}(z_i)$ is r_2. Given $\delta > 0$ we will find $L > 0$ such that for $n > L$, $R_{i,\ell,n} < 1 + \delta$. Because $R_{i,\ell,2}(z_i)$ has finite derivatives, we can select $z_* < C_0\delta$ such that $R_{i,\ell,2}(z_*) < 1 + \delta$. Because $dz_j/dz_i > C_1$, and the second derivative of $z_j(z_i)$ does not exceed a constant C_2 for any j for $z \in [0, z_*]$, it is clear that $z_j(z_*) > C_1 z_* - z_*^2 C_2/2$, where C_2 is some constant. Thus, we can select $\tilde{z}_* < z_*$ such that $z_j(\tilde{z}_*) > z_* C_3$. Hence, if condition II is satisfied $1 - G_j(z_j(z_*)) < 1 - \eta(\delta C_0 C_3)^M$ and hence when $n > L = \ln[(1 + \delta)/r_2]/\ln[1 - \eta(\delta C_0 C_3)^M] + 2$, $R_{i,\ell,n}(z_i) < 1 + \delta$, for any $z_i \in [0, 1]$.

Suppose now that the function $R_{i,\ell,2}(0) < 1$ and condition II is satisfied. In this case for sufficiently large n, $R_{i,\ell,n}(z_i) < 1$ for any $z_i \in [0, 1]$. Again, let r_2 be the maximum of $R_{i,\ell,n}(z_i)$. Since $R_{i,\ell,2}(z_i)$ is an analytical function, $R_{i,\ell,2}(z_i) < 1$ for $z_i < z_*$. Making analogous considerations as before, we can see that for $n > \ln[1/r_2]/\ln[1 - \eta(z_* C_3)^M] + 2$, $R_{i,\ell,n}(z_i) < 1$ for any $z_i \in [0, 1]$.

Now we will show that if for a network r, $P_r(0) > 0$ then $R_{i,\ell,2}(0) < 1$. In order to show this we will use the identity

$$R_{i,\ell,2}(0) = [1 - H_i(0)][1 - G_\ell(z_\ell(0))]. \qquad (4.105)$$

If $F_\ell(0) = F_i(0)$, we can select $\ell = r$. If $r = \ell$ we have $1 - G_\ell(z_\ell(0)) < 0$. If $r = i$, then $F_i(0) < F_\ell(0)$. Thus $z_\ell(0) > 0$ and hence $1 - G_\ell(z_\ell(0)) < 1$.

Now we will show that if for a network $j = r$, $P_r(1) > 0$, then $R_{i,\ell,2}(0) < 1$. If $F_\ell(0) = F_i(0)$, we select $i = r$. If $r = i$ our proposition follows from equation (4.105) because $1 - H_i(0) < 1$. If $r = \ell$, it means that $F_i(0) < F_\ell(0)$. Thus $z_\ell(0) > 0$ and hence $1 - G_\ell(z_\ell(0)) < 1$.

References

[1] Peerenboom F R and Whitfield R 2001 Recovering from disruptions of interdependent critical infrastructures *CRIS/DRM/IIIT/NSF Workshop Mitigating the Vulnerability of Critical Infrastructures to Catastrophic Failures*

[2] Rinaldi S M, Peerenboom J P and Kelly T K 2001 Identifying, understanding, and analyzing critical infrastructure interdependencies *IEEE Control Syst.* **21** 11–25

[3] Rosato V, Issacharoff L, Tiriticco F, Meloni S, Porcellinis S and Setola R 2008 Modeling interdependent infrastructures using interacting dynamical models *Int. J. Crit. Infrastruct.* **4** 63–79

[4] Vespignani A 2010 The fragility of interdependency *Nature* **464** 984–5

[5] Gao J, Buldyrev S V, Havlin S and Stanley H E 2012 Robustness of a network formed by *n* interdependent networks with a one-to-one correspondence of dependent nodes *Phys. Rev. E* **85** 066134

[6] Gao J, Buldyrev S V, Stanley H E, Xu X and Havlin S 2013 Percolation of a general network of networks *Phys. Rev. E* **88** 062816

[7] Buldyrev S V, Parshani R, Paul G, Stanley H E and Havlin S 2010 Catastrophic cascade of failures in interdependent networks *Nature* **464** 1025–8

[8] Gao J, Li D and Havlin S 2014 From a single network to a network of networks *Natl. Sci. Rev.* **1** 346–56

[9] Pocock M J O, Evans D M and Memmott J 2012 The robustness and restoration of a network of ecological networks *Science* **335** 973–7

[10] Pilosof S, Porter M A, Pascual M and Kéfi S 2017 The multilayer nature of ecological networks *Nat. Ecol. Evol.* **1** 1–9

[11] De Keulenaer G W, Brutsaert D L, Borlaug B A and Redfield M M *et al* 2011 Systolic and diastolic heart failure are overlapping phenotypes within the heart failure spectrum *Circulation* **123** 1996–2005

[12] Bashan A, Bartsch R P, Kantelhardt J W, Havlin S and Ch Ivanov P 2012 Network physiology reveals relations between network topology and physiological function *Nat. Commun.* **3** 702

[13] Liu X *et al* 2020 Robustness and lethality in multilayer biological molecular networks. *Nat. Commun.* **11** 6043

[14] Liu X *et al* 2022 Network resilience *Phys. Rep.* **971** 1–108

[15] Sporns O and Betzel R F 2016 Modular brain networks *Annu. Rev. Psychol.* **67** 613–40

[16] Gallos L K, Makse H A and Sigman M 2012 A small world of weak ties provides optimal global integration of self-similar modules in functional brain networks *Proc. Natl. Acad. Sci.* **109** 2825–30

[17] Markov N T, Ercsey-Ravasz M, Van Essen D C, Knoblauch K, Toroczkai Z and Kennedy H 2013 Cortical high-density counterstream architectures *Science* **342** 1238406

[18] Van Mieghem P 2016 Interconnectivity structure of a general interdependent network *Phys. Rev. E* **93** 042305

[19] Battiston F, Nicosia V, Chavez M and Latora V 2017 Multilayer motif analysis of brain networks *Chaos* **27** 047404

[20] De Domenico M, Sasai S and Arenas A 2016 Mapping multiplex hubs in human functional brain networks *Front. Neurosci.* **10** 326

[21] Gao J, Buldyrev S V, Havlin S and Stanley H E 2011 Robustness of a network of networks *Phys. Rev. Lett.* **107** 195701

[22] Shekhtman L M, Berezin Y, Danziger M M and Havlin S 2014 Robustness of a network formed of spatially embedded networks *Phys. Rev. E* **90** 012809

[23] Bianconi G, Dorogovtsev S N and Dorogovtsev J F F 2015 Mutually connected component of networks of networks with replica nodes *Phys. Rev. E* **91** 012804

[24] Parshani R, Buldyrev S V and Havlin S 2010 Interdependent networks: reducing the coupling strength leads to a change from a first to second order percolation transition *Phys. Rev. Lett.* **105** 048701

[25] Shao J, Buldyrev S V, Havlin S and Stanley H E 2011 Cascade of failures in coupled network systems with multiple support-dependence relations *Phys. Rev. E* **83** 036116

[26] Yuan X, Hu Y, Stanley H E and Havlin S 2017 Eradicating catastrophic collapse in interdependent networks via reinforced nodes *Proc. Natl. Acad. Sci.* **114** 3311–5

[27] Baxter G J, Dorogovtsev S N, Goltsev A V and Mendes J F F 2012 Avalanche collapse of interdependent networks *Phys. Rev. Lett.* **109** 248701

[28] Zhou D, Bashan A, Cohen R, Berezin Y, Shnerb N and Havlin S 2014 Simultaneous first- and second-order percolation transitions in interdependent networks *Phys. Rev. E* **90** 012803

[29] Smolyak A, Levy O, Vodenska I, Buldyrev S and Havlin S 2020 Mitigation of cascading failures in complex networks *Sci. Rep.* **10** 1–12

[30] Son S-W, Bizhani G, Christensen C, Grassberger P and Paczuski M 2012 Percolation theory on interdependent networks based on epidemic spreading *Europhys. Lett.* **97** 16006

[31] Molloy M and Reed B 1998 The size of the giant component of a random graph with a given degree sequence *Combin. Probab. Comput.* **7** 295–305

[32] Shao J, Buldyrev S V, Braunstein L A, Havlin S and Stanley H E 2009 Structure of shells in complex networks *Phys. Rev. E* **80** 036105

[33] Rényi P and A Erdős 1959 On random graphs I. *Publ. Math.* **6** 290–7

[34] Erdős A and Rényi P 1960 On the evolution of random graphs *Inst. Hung. Acad. Sci.* **5** 17–61

[35] Bollobás B 1985 *Random Graphs* (London: Academic)

[36] Parshani R, Buldyrev S V and Havlin S 2011 Critical effect of dependency groups on the function of networks *Proc. Natl. Acad. Sci.* **108** 1007–10

[37] Bunde A and Havlin S 1991 *Fractals and Disordered Systems* (New York: Springer)

[38] Stauffer D and Aharony A 1994 *Introduction to Percolation Theory* (Boca Raton, FL: CRC Press)

[39] Bashan A, Parshani R and Havlin S 2011 Percolation in networks composed of connectivity and dependency links *Phys. Rev. E* **83** 051127

[40] Boguná M, Pastor-Satorras R and Vespignani A 2004 Cut-offs and finite size effects in scale-free networks *Eur. Phys. J. B* **38** 205–9

[41] Cohen R, Erez K, Ben-Avraham D and Havlin S 2000 Resilience of the internet to random breakdown *Phys. Rev. Lett.* **85** 4626–8

[42] Zhou D, Gao J, Stanley H E and Havlin S 2013 Percolation of partially interdependent scale-free networks *Phys. Rev. E* **87** 052812

[43] Newman M E J, Strogatz S H and Watts D J 2001 Random graphs with arbitrary degree distributions and their applications *Phys. Rev.* E **64** 026118

[44] Newman M E J 2002 Spread of epidemic disease on networks *Phys. Rev.* E **66** 016128

[45] Shao J, Buldyrev S V, Cohen R, Kitsak M, Havlin S and Stanley H E 2008 Fractal boundaries of complex networks *Europhys. Lett.* **84** 48004

[46] Bianconi G and Dorogovtsev S N 2014 Multiple percolation transitions in a configuration model of a network of networks *Phys. Rev.* E **89** 062814

[47] Barabási A-L and Albert R 1999 Emergence of scaling in random networks *Science* **286** 509–12

[48] Colizza V, Barrat A, Barthélemy M and Vespignani A 2006 The role of the airline transportation network in the prediction and predictability of global epidemics *Proc. Natl. Acad. Sci. USA* **103** 2015–20

[49] Albert R and Barabási A-L 2002 Statistical mechanics of complex networks *Rev. Mod. Phys.* **74** 47–97

[50] Daqing L, Kosmidis K, Bunde A and Havlin S 2011 Dimension of spatially embedded networks *Nat. Phys.* **7** 481–4

Chapter 5

Spatially embedded interdependent networks

5.1 Introduction

In the previous chapters we have discussed systems of interdependent networks where space restrictions have not been considered. These models represent a family of complex systems in which the spatial location of the nodes and the link length are not relevant or not even defined, such as the cases of proteins interaction networks [1, 2] and the World Wide Web [3, 4]. In contrast, as discussed in chapter 4 regarding *single networks*, the structural properties and dynamical processes in spatially embedded networks are markedly different from non-embedded networks [5]. In this chapter we show the effect of the spatial embedding on a network of networks, where some or all of the interacting networks are spatially embedded.

Most real-world infrastructure systems are embedded in a two-dimensional (2D) space. Examples include, ground transportation infrastructures such as road networks and railways [6–8], electrical power networks, gas and oil pipelines, water supply and sewage disposal, telephone land lines and exchange systems, the Internet and communication lines. Also, biological systems such as the neural network in the brain and the blood distribution network are embedded in a 3D space [9, 10].

The main feature of these spatial networks is that their links represent real physical connections, where usually a cost is associated with the length of each link. Therefore, most of the links end up being relatively short compared to the system size (figure 5.1). In general, the dimension of a network is determined by how much the links are restricted to connect only nearby nodes [5, 11]. Thus, an important consequence of the short-range nature of the links in a spatial network is that its dimension can be regarded as the dimension of the embedding space. For example, in mathematical models of spatial networks, such as regular lattices and in random geometric networks [12], the distance between two connected nodes has a given characteristic length. A realistic example is a power grid network where the links have a characteristic length following an exponential distribution [11, 13].

doi:10.1088/978-0-7503-1046-8ch5

Figure 5.1. Many infrastructures are embedded in 2D space with high degree of interdependence between their functions. Credit: timallenphoto, fuyu liu, WR7 and SGR/Shutterstock.com.

The dimension of a network is a fundamental quantity that characterizes its structure and its basic physical properties, and, in particular, its robustness, which is commonly studied using percolation theory, as discussed in chapter 4. Based on universality principles, percolation models in any 2D network with a characteristic length scale of links, belong to the same universality class [11, 14]. Thus, to obtain the main features of an arbitrary system of interdependent networks embedded in 2D space, one can model these spatially embedded networks as 2D regular lattices. In section 5.4 we discuss spatial networks with arbitrary 2D structures. Note that in many cases, real spatial networks in 2D space tend to have a lower average degree than a square lattice [5]. In section 5.7 we discuss how the results of percolation models are affected by having lower connectivity.

Spatial restrictions can also affect other key components that define the robustness of systems of interdependent networks. When the nodes of the networks are located in space, the dependencies between them will also be affected by space. Just like the connectivity links discussed above, the dependency links may also have a finite characteristic length, figure 5.1. In addition, the initial damage can be localized affecting all nodes and links within a certain area (e.g., due to a hurricane, tsunami, or an earthquake); or spread over the entire territory (e.g., an electromagnetic pulse caused by solar flares).

Accordingly, models of interdependent networks can incorporate different aspects of spatial embedding:

- **Semi-spatial model:** Both individual networks are spatially embedded, i.e. the connectivity links have a finite characteristic length, while the dependency links do not (figure 5.2(a) where the dependency links have no length limitations). Alternatively, one network is spatially embedded while the other network is not.
- **Fully spatial model:** Both networks as well as their dependencies are spatially embedded. That is, both connectivity and dependency links are short-range (e.g. figure 5.2(a) where the dependency links are also of limited length). This model naturally introduces three fundamental quantities which are unique to spatial networks:
  - the length of the connectivity links;
  - the length of the dependency links;
  - the radius of the initial damage, in the case of geographically localized attacks.

In this chapter, we address the effect of these spatial models and their fundamental quantities in regards to the robustness of a network of networks. In section 5.2 we discuss the semi-spatial model and show how the unique properties of spatial structures of connectivity links affect the robustness. In section 5.3 we discuss

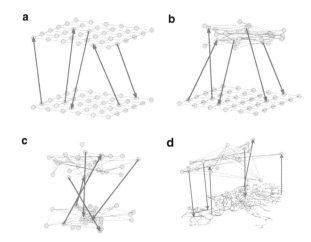

Figure 5.2. A system of interdependent networks is characterized by the structure (dimension) of the single networks as well as by the dependency coupling between the networks. In random networks with no space restrictions, such as Erdös–Rényi (ER) and random-regular (RR), the connectivity links (blue lines) do not have a defined Euclidean length. In contrast, in spatially embedded networks nodes are connected only to nodes in their geometrical neighborhood creating a 2D grid, modeled here as a square lattice. The (red) arrows represent directed dependency relations between nodes in different networks, which can be of different types: (a) coupled lattices (b) coupled lattice-random networks (c) coupled random networks (d) real-world spatial network (power grid of Europe) coupled with a random network. Models (b) and (d) belong to the same universality class. Reproduced from [15], copyright 2013 with permission of Springer.

the general semi-spatial case of a network composed of spatial networks. In section 5.4 we introduce space restriction also on the dependency links (fully-spatial model). We show that in the fully-spatial model the process of cascading failures is fundamentally different from the case of non-spatial or semi-spatial models. In particular, we discuss the effects of the two characteristics: the length of the dependency links (section 5.5) and the length of the connectivity links (section 5.6). Next, we show in section 5.7 the effect of spatial correlated attacks and compare between the effects of localized and non-localized random attacks.

5.2 The extreme vulnerability of semi-spatial interdependent networks

In this section, we study the robustness of a 'semi-spatial' system of two interdependent networks where at least one of the single networks is spatially embedded, while the dependencies between the two networks are not restricted by space, see figure 5.2(a) and (b). In chapter 3 we have shown that a basic characteristic of interdependent *random* networks is that above a critical fraction, q_c, of interdependent nodes, even a single node failure can invoke cascading failures that may abruptly fragment the system. However, below this 'critical dependency,' q_c, a failure of a fraction of nodes (infinite number of nodes when $N \to \infty$) leads only to small damage to the system. Therefore, as long as the fraction of interdependent nodes is below the critical dependency, q_c, the system is in a 'safe mode' with no risk of abrupt collapse. In this case the transition is continuous. Here we show that in semi-spatial systems, in contrast to non-embedded systems, there is no such critical dependency and any small fraction of interdependent nodes leads to an abrupt collapse. In such systems, there is no 'safe mode'.

In this section, we review analytic and numeric studies of the stability of systems composed of two interdependent spatially embedded networks using a simplified model of two interdependent lattices, where the dependency links are between random nodes in the different lattices (figure 5.2(a)). In a system of interdependent spatial and not-spatial networks the dependency links between lattice nodes and nodes of a random network are clearly not affected by space since the random network has no spatial embedding (figure 5.2(b)). In figure 5.2(b), only the connectivity links in the bottom network have spatial constraints.

5.2.1 Percolation transition in semi-spatial interdependent networks

Consider a system of two interdependent networks, $i = 1$ and $i = 2$, where a fraction $1 - p_i$ of nodes in each network is initially randomly removed (the case where only one network is initially attacked was described in section 3.3.2). We assume that only the nodes which belong to the giant component of the remaining networks constituting a fraction $P_{\infty,i}(p_i)$ of the original network remain functional. Each node that has been removed or disconnected from the giant component causing its dependent node in the other network to also fail. This leads to further disconnections in the other network and to cascading failures back and forth between the networks. The size of the networks' giant components at the end of the cascade is given by $P_{\infty,i}(x_i)$, where x_i are the solutions of the self-consistent equations [16]

$$x_1 = p_1 q_1 P_{\infty,2}(x_2) + p_1(1 - q_1) \tag{5.1}$$

$$x_2 = p_2 q_2 P_{\infty,1}(x_1) + p_2(1 - q_2), \tag{5.2}$$

where q_i is the fraction of nodes in network i that depend on nodes in the other network. Here we assume no restrictions on the selection of the directed dependency links. The results for the case of the 'no-feedback-condition', where the dependency links are bidirectional [16], are qualitatively the same [15]. The function $P_{\infty,i}(x)$ can be obtained either analytically or numerically from the percolation behavior of a *single* network.

For simplicity, we focus on a symmetric case, where both networks have the same degree distribution $P(k)$ and same topology, and where $p_1 = p_2 \equiv p$ and $q_1 = q_2 \equiv q$. Still, the results are valid for any system of interdependent spatially embedded networks (like planar graphs) which belongs to the same universality class. In particular, in order to study the role of spatial embedding, we compare the percolation transition in the case of a pair of interdependent lattices (figure 5.2(a)) to the case of a pair of interdependent RR networks (figure 5.2(c)). The RR networks have the same degree distribution, $P(k) = \delta_{k,4}$, as the lattices with the only difference being that the lattice networks are embedded in space, in contrast to the RR networks.

In the symmetric case, equations (5.1) and (5.2) can be reduced to a single equation

$$x = pqP_{\infty}(x) + p(1 - q), \tag{5.3}$$

where the size of the giant component at steady state is $P_{\infty}(x)$. For any values of p and q, the solution of equation (5.3) can be graphically presented as the intersection between the curve $y = pqP_{\infty}(x) + p(1 - q)$ and the straight line $y = x$ representing the right-hand-side and the left-hand-side of equation (5.3), respectively, as demonstrated in figure 5.3. The form of $P_{\infty}(x)$ for conventional percolation is obtained from numerical simulations of a single lattice and analytically for a single RR network [17].

5.2.2 In semi-spatial interdependent networks $q_c = 0$

From the solution of equation (5.3) we obtain $P_{\infty}(p)$ as a function of p for different values of q. This $P_{\infty}(p)$ is the new percolation behavior for a system of interdependent networks, shown in figure 5.4(a), for the case of coupled lattices and in figure 5.4(b) for the case of coupled RR networks. In the case of interdependent lattices, only for $q = 0$, i.e., no coupling between the networks (the single network limit), does the transition become continuous, while for any $q > 0$ the collapse is abrupt and takes the form of a first-order transition. In marked contrast, in the case of interdependent RR networks, for $q > q_c \cong 0.43$ the transition is abrupt, while for $q < q_c$ the transition is continuous.

The discontinuity in $P_{\infty}(p)$ is a result of a discontinuity of $x(p)$, represented graphically as the tangential touching point of the curve and the straight line (see figure 5.3(a)). At this point, $p \equiv p^\star$ is the new percolation threshold in the case of

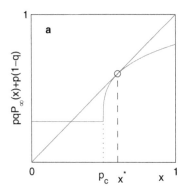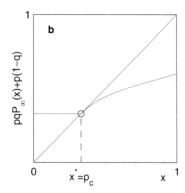

Figure 5.3. Schematic solution of the critical point of (a) coupled lattices and (b) coupled RR networks. The left-hand-side and right-hand-side of equation (5.3) are plotted as a straight (red) line and a (blue) curve, respectively. The tangential touching point, x^*, marked with a (black) circle, represents the new percolation threshold in the system of interdependent networks. In the case of coupled lattices (panel a), due to the infinite slope of the curve at p_c, x^* is always larger than p_c and, thus, there is always (for any $q > 0$) a discontinuous jump in the size of the giant component as p decreases. In contrast, in coupled random networks (panel b) the slope of the curves is finite for any value of x. Therefore, there exists $q < q_c$ for which x^* is equal to p_c, leading to a continuous transition in the size of the giant component. Reproduced from [15], copyright 2013 with permission from Springer.

interdependent networks, and $x = x^\star$ determines the size of the giant component at the transition, $P_\infty^\star \equiv P_\infty(x^\star)$, which abruptly jumps to zero as p slightly decreases. Figure 5.4(c) and (d) shows the divergence of the number of interations (NOI) at the critical threshold of the first order transition. The condition for a first-order transition $p = p^\star$, for a given q, is thus given by solving equation (5.3) together with its tangential condition,

$$1 = p^\star q P'_\infty(x^\star). \tag{5.4}$$

The size of the giant component at the transition, $P_\infty^\star$, depends on the coupling strength q such that reducing q leads to a smaller value of $x^\star$ and thus a smaller discontinuity in the size of the giant component. In general, $P_\infty(x)$ of a single network has a critical threshold at $x = p_c$ such that $P_\infty(x \leqslant p_c) = 0$ while $P_\infty(x > p_c) > 0$ with $P_\infty(x > p_c)$ monotonically increasing with x [14]. As long as $x^\star > p_c$, the size of the discontinuity is larger then zero. However, for a certain critical coupling $q \equiv q_c$, $x^\star \to p_c$ and the size of the jump becomes zero (see figure 5.3(b)). In this case the percolation transition becomes continuous.

Therefore, the critical dependency q_c below which the discontinuous transition becomes continuous, must satisfy equations (5.3) and (5.4) for $x \to p_c$ given by

$$\begin{aligned} p_c &= p^\star(1 - q_c) \\ 1 &= p^\star q_c P'_\infty(p_c). \end{aligned} \tag{5.5}$$

A dramatically different behavior between random and spatial coupled networks can be derived from equations (5.5). This difference is a consequence of the critical

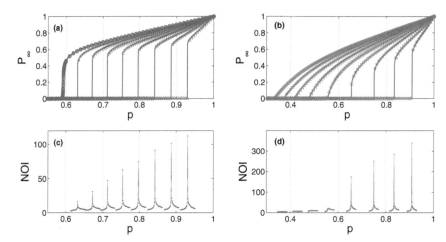

Figure 5.4. Percolation transition of interdependent lattices compared to interdependent random networks. The size of the giant component P_∞ at steady state after random failure of a fraction $1 - p$ of the nodes for (a) two interdependent lattice networks with periodic boundary conditions (PBC) and for (b) two RR networks. All networks are of size 16×10^6 nodes and the same degree distribution $P(k) = \delta_{k,4}$. The coupling between the lattices and between the RR networks changes from $q = 0$ to $q = 0.8$ with steps of 0.1 (from left to right). Note that for $q \to 1$, $p_c \to 1$ in both interdependent lattices and interdependent RR networks because the dependency links form a large cluster, leading to complete collapse of the system for any initial failure (this is different from the case of the 'no-feedback-condition' [18]). The solid lines are the solutions of equation (5.3) and the symbols represent simulation results. A characteristic behavior in a first-order percolation transition in coupled networks is the sharp divergence of the number of iterations (NOI) when p approaches $p^\star$ [19] as seen for (c) coupled lattices for any $q > 0$ and for (d) coupled RR networks for $q > q_c$. Models of coupled lattices with periodic boundary conditions (PBC) have the same behavior as models without PBC [15]. Reproduced from [15], copyright 2013 with permission from Springer.

behavior of percolation in a single network. In the case of a single random network, the derivative $P'_\infty(x)$ is finite for any value of x. This allows an exact solution of equation (5.5), yielding a finite non-zero value for q_c. In contrast, for the case of a single lattice network the derivative of $P_\infty(x)$ diverges at the critical point, $P'_\infty(p_c) = \infty$, and equation (5.5) yields $q_c = 0$. Therefore, from equation (5.5) it follows that any coupling $q > 0$ between lattices leads to an abrupt first-order transition. Figure 5.3 demonstrates how the infinite slope of the percolation curve of a single lattice leads to a discontinuous percolation transition for any $q > 0$ in coupled lattices.

The behavior of the percolation order parameter of a single network near the critical point is defined by the critical exponent β, where $P_\infty(x \to p_c^+) = A(x - p_c)^\beta$. Since for a single 2D lattice $\beta = 5/36 < 1$, it follows that $P'_\infty(x)$ diverges for $x \to p_c^+$ for all networks embedded in 2D space [14, 20–23]. In contrast, for random networks, such as ER and RR, $\beta = 1$ which yields a finite value of $P'_\infty(p_c)$ [14, 21] and therefore a finite value for q_c. Note that since $\beta < 1$ for percolation in lattices in dimensions $d < 6$, it follows that $q_c = 0$ for any $d < 6$. Only for $d > 6$, where $\beta = 1$, will q_c be finite.

We next study the effect of spatial embedding, comparing the size of the network at criticality, that is the size of the jump, in three models: (i) two non-embedded coupled RR networks ($k = 4$), (ii) two coupled lattices and (iii) a lattice coupled with

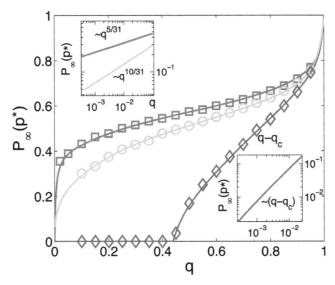

Figure 5.5. The size of the abrupt collapse in coupled interdependent lattices compared to coupled random networks. Comparison of the size of the giant component at criticality $P_\infty^\star \equiv P_\infty(p^\star)$ for two coupled lattices (squares), coupled lattice and RR networks (circles) and two coupled RR networks (diamonds) as a function of the coupling strength q. The RR networks have the same degree as the lattice, $k = 4$ for all nodes. While for random networks with $q < q_c = 0.43$ the size of the networks at criticality is zero, in coupled lattice networks the system abruptly collapses for any finite $q > 0$. Note also the significant differences in the network sizes at the transition. The coupled lattices collapse from a significantly larger giant component compared to the coupled-RR case. The solid line represents the theory for coupled interdependent lattices given by equations (5.5) and (5.5), and the symbols are from simulations. The solid line for coupled RR networks represents the theory derived in Parshani *et al* [24]. The insets show that the scaling behavior (as obtained from equations (5.7) and (5.8)) in the case of coupled lattices and coupled lattice-RR for $q \to q_c = 0$ is $P_\infty^\star \sim q^{5/31}$ and $P_\infty^\star \sim q^{10/31}$ respectively, while for coupled RR networks, $P_\infty^\star \sim (q - q_c)$. Reproduced from [15], copyright 2013 with permission of Springer.

non-embedded RR network. The last model is relevant to real-world systems in which a spatially embedded network is coupled to a non-embedded network, such as in the case of a power grid (embedded in 2D space) coupled to a communication network (non-embedded) studied in [22]. Figure 5.5 shows the size of the giant component at criticality $P_\infty^\star$ as a function of coupling strengths q for all three models, demonstrating the significantly increased vulnerability of the lattice network in the coupled system compared with the coupled random networks. For coupled lattice-lattice and coupled lattice-RR systems $P_\infty^\star > 0$ for *any* $q > 0$, while for a coupled RR–RR system $P_\infty^\star = 0$ for $q < q_c = 0.43$. Moreover, in coupled lattices even for weak coupling, the size of the discontinuity is relatively large. For example, for $q = 0.1$ the size of the network just before the collapse is about 0.42 of the original network.

5.2.3 Critical exponents of the percolation transition

Figure 5.5 suggests that when $q \to q_c^+$ there exists a scaling regime which can be evaluated as follows. We expect the scaling of the size of discontinuity near the critical coupling to behave as,

$$P_\infty^\star(q) \sim \left(q - q_c\right)^{\beta^\star} \text{as } q \to q_c^+.$$ (5.6)

The size of the giant component at the transition is $P_\infty^\star = P_\infty(x^\star)$ where $x^\star$ is the solution of equation (5.3) together with its tangential condition, equation (5.4). We solve these equations for $q = q_c + \delta$, $x^\star = p_c + \epsilon$ and $p^\star = p_c + \Delta$, where δ, ϵ, $\Delta \to 0$. Near the critical point $P_\infty(x \to p_c) = A(x - p_c)^\beta$, and thus, $P_\infty'(x \to p_c) = A\beta(x - p_c)^{\beta-1}$, where A is a constant. Equations (5.3) and (5.4) become

$$\left(p_c + \epsilon\right) = \left(p_c + \Delta\right)\left(1 - q_c - \delta\right)$$ (5.7)

$$1 = \left(p_c + \Delta\right)\left(q_c + \delta\right)P_\infty'(p_c + \epsilon) = A\beta\left(p_c + \Delta\right)\left(q_c + \delta\right)\epsilon^{\beta-1}.$$ (5.8)

In the case of coupled lattices $q_c = 0$, thus, from equation (5.7) it follows that near the critical coupling, $p^\star = p_c$. Therefore, from equation (5.8) it follows that $\epsilon \sim \delta^{1/(1-\beta)}$ and the scaling behavior of the size of the giant component at criticality for $q \to 0$ is

$$P_\infty^\star \sim q^{\beta/(1-\beta)} = q^{5/31}.$$ (5.9)

The small value of the exponent, $\beta^\star = 5/31$, demonstrates analytically the sharp increase of $P_\infty^\star$ with q, for very small q values, as seen in figure 5.5. This small value of β for a single lattice is indeed the origin of the critical role of dependencies and the extreme vulnerability of spatially embedded interdependent networks.

In the case of a square lattice coupled to a RR network with $k = 4$ with the same $q_1 = q_2 = q$, similar analytical treatment to equations (5.1) and (5.2) yields that $P_\infty^\star \sim q^{2\beta/(1-\beta)} = q^{10/31}$. This larger critical exponent expresses the fact that the singularity in the case of a lattice coupled to a random network is slightly weaker compared to the singularity of the symmetric case of coupled lattices. However, the fact that $\beta^\star < 1$ indicates that even a weak coupling between spatial networks leads to relatively large-scale collapses. For the case of coupled random networks or for lattices in $d \geqslant 6$, however, for $q \to q_c$ the discontinuity size does not have a singular point since $P_\infty^\star \sim (q - q_c)$, i.e., $\beta^\star = 1$. The above approximations are numerically validated, as shown in the insets of figure 5.5.

5.3 Semi-spatial model of network of networks

The analysis in the previous section in this chapter was restricted to a pair of interdependent spatially embedded networks. In this section we present a generalization to a network of semi-spatial networks, i.e., we have many networks, where each network is spatially embedded but the dependency links between the networks are still random. Figure 5.6 illustrates the various topologies of a system consisting of n (>2) spatially embedded networks which are interdependent.

In contrast to the case of non-embedded networks which was discussed in chapter 4, where the apparatus of *generating functions* can often be used to evaluate the size of the giant component of the individual networks at each step of the cascading failures

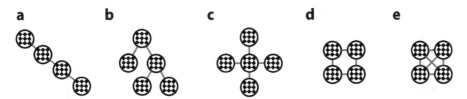

Figure 5.6. Several examples of possible structures of the network of spatially embedded networks. Red links represent dependency relations between the spatial networks. Examples include (a) a line, (b) a tree, (c) a star, (d) an RR network of networks where each network has $m = 2$ dependencies, (e) and an RR network of networks with $m = 3$. Reprinted with permission from [25], copyright 2014 by the American Physical Society.

process, in the case of spatial networks the percolation behavior of each individual network is given only as a general function, which can be evaluated numerically, as was done in the previous section. Therefore, the analytical treatment presented in chapter 4 has to be generalized.

5.3.1 Tree-like network of interdependent networks

We begin by examining results for a tree-like network of networks where the length of dependency links is unconstrained. In chapter 3 we derived P_∞ of the cascading failure of two interdependent networks as a function of iteration count. It can be shown that if a fraction $1 - p$ of nodes are removed from each network and p_i is the fraction of survived nodes, at the ith iteration $p_i = p^2 P_\infty(p_{i-1})/p_{i-1}$. For n networks in a tree-like configuration a node is in the mutual giant component if it and the $n - 1$ nodes it depends on are all in their respective networks' giant components. Thus $g(p_i) = P_\infty(p_{i-1})/p_{i-1}$, the probability for a node to be in the giant component after $1 - p_i$ fraction of nodes are removed, must be raised to the $n - 1$ power since each node has $n - 1$ dependencies. This gives

$$p_i = p^n \left(\frac{P_\infty(p_{i-1})}{p_{i-1}} \right)^{n-1}. \tag{5.10}$$

Each iteration represents reducing all networks to their giant components and removing nodes which have dependencies outside the giant component. The next iteration then removes nodes that fail due to having dependencies outside the previous giant component and again reduces each network to its giant component. The process repeats until a steady state is reached. In the limiting case of only a single network, $n = 1$, we get $p_i = p$ and there is no cascading effect. Further if $n = 2$, we obtain the previous results [22].

An alternative method of analysis involves observing how the failures propogate across the links in the network of networks (see figure 4.9) [26]. The initial attack on each network occurs at $t = 1$. A node which depends on a failed node then fails at $t = 2$ and in general for a node that failed at $t = t_n$, its dependent nodes fail at $t = t_n + 1$. Simulations of the giant component after a number of iterations and at a certain time t are shown to fit well with the theoretical equations, see figure 5.7.

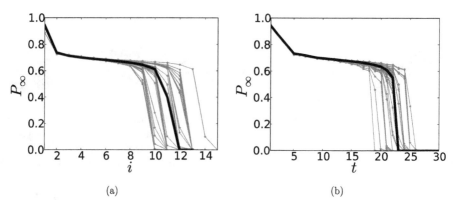

(a) (b)

Figure 5.7. Theory is shown as the thick black curve which is compared with 40 simulated realizations on lattices of size $N = 500 \times 500$, shown as lighter curves with symbols. (a) P_∞ as a function of the number of iterations is shown to fit well with the theory of equation (5.10). These results are for five networks in a line, yet for this method the shape of the tree has no effect on the number of iterations. (b) P_∞ as a function of t according to the method in Gao *et al* [26] for five networks in a line. The simulation results fit well with the theory. Reproduced with permission from [25], copyright 2014 by the American Physical Society.

We examine what happens to p_i when $i \to \infty$ and the system reaches steady state. We define $x \equiv p_\infty$ and note that as in the previous section, x represents the total fraction of non-removed nodes after the cascade considering also those removed due to interdependencies. For a given fraction of nodes, $1 - p$, removed from the network of networks, $1 - x$ is the fraction that would have to be removed from a single network to obtain an equivalent giant component. Solving for x we get

$$x = p\sqrt[n]{P_\infty(x)^{n-1}}.\tag{5.11}$$

In figure 5.8 we observe that the theory agrees with simulations for all values of p. We also see there that close to p_c, the percolation threshold, the system collapses through a long cascade in the form of a plateau [48]. The number of iterations at p_c and the value of p_c both increase as the number of networks increases.

To calculate p_c we must find where the two sides of equation (5.11) are tangent at their intersection. We take the derivatives of both sides and get

$$\frac{n}{n-1}P_\infty(x_c) = x_c P_\infty'(x_c)\tag{5.12}$$

$$p_c = \frac{x_c}{P_\infty(x_c)^{(n-1)/n}}\tag{5.13}$$

where $P_\infty'(x_c)$ is the derivative of $P_\infty(x_c)$.

If a fraction $1 - p$ of nodes is removed from only a single network, then p^n in all the above equations is replaced with p. This gives

$$x = \sqrt[n]{pP_\infty(x)^{n-1}}.\tag{5.14}$$

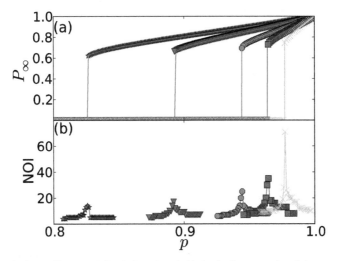

Figure 5.8. (a) Both theory (lines) and simulations (symbols) for lattice networks of size $N = 250 \times 250$ with tree-like dependencies are shown. These results are again for a network of networks in a line, yet the results are the same for other tree formations. Results are shown for $n = 2$ (stars), $n = 3$ (triangles), $n = 5$ (circles), $n = 7$ (squares), and $n = 10$ ('x's). As seen, all of the transitions are abrupt first-order transitions and the simulations fit well with the theory. Further, increasing the number of networks is seen to quickly increase p_c indicating that the system becomes more vulnerable as n increases. (b) Here we observe that the number of iterations it takes for the system to arrive at steady state diverges at p_c. The number of iterations at p_c increases both with the number of networks, n, and the size of the networks, N. Reproduced with permission from [25], copyright 2014 by the American Physical Society.

$$\frac{n}{n-1}P_\infty(x_c) = x_c P'_\infty(x_c) \tag{5.15}$$

$$p_c = \frac{x_c^{1/n}}{P_\infty(x_c)^{(n-1)/n}}. \tag{5.16}$$

Results for n networks according to equations (5.15) and (5.16) are shown in figure 5.9 as the top curve ($q = 1.0$).

5.3.2 Star-like network of interdependent networks

If we restrict the shape of the tree to be in a star formation (see figure 5.6(c)) we can also give an analytic solution for any value of the coupling q. In this case a fraction $1 - p$ of the nodes are removed only from the central network. Based on Gao *et al* [16] the equations for this system are [25],

$$x_1 = p\left(q\frac{P_{\infty_2}(x_2)}{x_2} - q + 1\right)^{n-1}$$

$$x_2 = pq\frac{P_{\infty_1}(x_1)}{x_1}\left(q\frac{P_{\infty_2}(x_2)}{x_2} - q + 1\right)^{n-2} - q + 1 \tag{5.17}$$

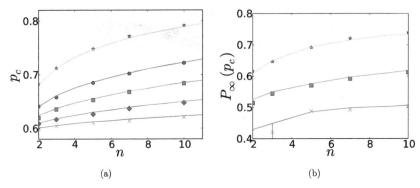

Figure 5.9. (a) The critical threshold p_c as a function of the number of networks in a star formation is plotted as a function of n, the number of networks, for $q = 0.5$ ('x's), $q = 0.6$ (diamonds), $q = 0.7$ (squares), $q = 0.8$ (circles), and $q = 1.0$ (stars). A fraction $1 - p$ of nodes are removed only from the central network. Simulations on lattices with $N = 250 \times 250$ ($n > 2$) or $N = 500 \times 500$ ($n = 2$) show excellent agreement with the theory. (b) $P_\infty(p_c)$, the size of the giant component at criticality is shown as a function of the number of networks (symbols are as before). Simulations on lattices of size $N = 500 \times 500$ fit well with the theory. Where shown, errorbars represent one standard deviation. Reproduced with permission from [25], copyright 2014 by the American Physical Society.

where subscript 1 refers to the central network and subscript 2 refers to all the other networks. Results of theory and simulations for p_c and $P_\infty(p_c)$ are in excellent agreement and can be seen in figure 5.9. Note that for $q = 1$ equation (5.17) reduces to equation (5.11).

5.3.3 Random regular network formed of interdependent spatially embedded networks

The results in chapter 4 showed that for a random-regular dependency configuration the actual number of networks, n, is irrelevant, rather the results depend only on m the number of networks each network in the RR depends on. In this case if all nodes are interdependent ($q = 1$) a failure of a single node can propagate from network to network unhindered due to the the loops and eventually lead the entire system to collapse. We therefore study the case $q < 1$ and remove a fraction $1 - p$ of the nodes from all the networks. We recall the results of equation (4.63),

$$\begin{cases} x = p(qyg(x) - q + 1)^m, \\ y = p(qyg(x) - q + 1)^{m-1} \end{cases} \tag{5.18}$$

where y represents the percolation damage from the other networks. The system in equation (5.18) can be solved by eliminating y from the second equation and obtaining a single equation for x. After substituting $g(x) = P_\infty(x)/x$ we obtain

$$P_\infty(x)p^{2/m}q = x^{2/m} + (xp)^{1/m}(q - 1) \tag{5.19}$$

which can be solved self consistently for x to obtain $P_\infty(x)$ [25]. Note that when $m = 1$ and $q = 1$, equation (5.19) reduces to the case of the pair of interdependent lattices with the 'no-feedback condition'.

From equation (5.19) we can get p_c by rearranging equation (5.19) to

$$p_c = \left[\frac{x_c^{1/m}}{2qP_\infty(x_c)} \left(q - 1 \pm \sqrt{(q - 1)^2 + 4qP_\infty(x_c)} \right) \right]^m \tag{5.20}$$

by noting that equation (5.19) is quadratic in $p^{1/m}$. To calculate x_c we take derivatives of both sides of equation (5.19) and obtain

$$mx_c q P_\infty'(x_c) p_c^{2/m} = 2x_c^{2/m} + p_c^{1/m} (q - 1) x_c^{1/m}. \tag{5.21}$$

We then substitute equation (5.20) into equation (5.21) to arrive at

$$mx_c P_\infty'(x_c) \left(q - 1 \pm \sqrt{(q - 1)^2 + 4qP_\infty(x_c)} \right)^2 =$$
$$8qP_\infty(x_c)^2 + 2(q - 1)P_\infty(x_c) \tag{5.22}$$
$$\cdot \left(q - 1 \pm \sqrt{(q - 1)^2 + 4qP_\infty(x_c)} \right).$$

which can be solved numerically for x_c.

As discussed in chapter 4, in RR networks of networks there is some maximum coupling q_{max} above which $p_c = 1$ and removing even a single node will lead the entire network to collapse. We can solve for q_{max} for the case of spatial networks by using equation (5.19) and setting $p = 1$. This gives

$$q_{max} = \frac{x_{max}^{2/m} - x_{max}^{1/m}}{P_\infty(x_{max}) - x_{max}^{1/m}}. \tag{5.23}$$

We can then solve for x_{max} using equation (5.22). Explicitly,

$$mx_{max} P_\infty'(x_{max})(x_{max}^{2/m} - x_{max}^{1/m}) =$$
$$- x_{max}^{3/m} + P_\infty(x_{max})(2x_{max}^{2/m} - x_{max}^{1/m}). \tag{5.24}$$

After we have x_{max} we substitute it into equation (5.23) and obtain q_{max}. If $m = 1$ we obtain a value of $q_{max} > 1$ which is unphysical for our system implying that for this case there is no q_{max} that will lead to a collapse.

5.4 Fully-spatial interdependent networks: propagation of cascading failures

In the previous sections, we discussed interdependence between two lattice networks yet where the dependency links are randomly assigned. However, this case neglects the fact that dependency links are also likely to have spatial restrictions. If two infrastructures are both spatially embedded and there is additional cost for longer links, then both the connectivity links and the dependency will be between nearby nodes. This case was first addressed in Li et al [27], where they restricted dependency links to some finite length. They found that for short dependency lengths, the mutual percolation transition is continuous. As the dependency length increases, the critical threshold p_c increases as well until at some critical dependency length, the transition becomes abrupt. After this point, p_c gradually decreases. This feature was explained in [27] due to the competition between the correlation length and the dependency length. The maximal p_c, maximal vulnerability, represents the case where both are the same which is a type of resonance.

Alternatively, one can consider a spatial model where one varies the length of the connectivity links as opposed to having a square lattice where connectivity links are all of length one. As discussed earlier in section 5.1, all spatial networks in the same embedding space belong to the same universality class. Nonetheless, a model with varying connectivity link lengths will better represent real-world infrastructure as opposed to the lattice model [28]. With this in mind, Danziger *et al* proposed a new model where the length of the connectivity links in each network follows an exponential distribution [29]. The dependency links are then assigned between corresponding nodes in two different networks, i.e., they have zero length, leading to a multiplex structure. This is also realistic since typically a necessary resource from another network will come from its closest source.

Surprisingly, despite the differences, qualitatively similar behaviors have been found for both models, i.e., varying the length of dependency links [27] and varying the length of connectivity links [29] (figure 5.10). The reason for this similarity stems from the fact that in both cases, the failures spread in a spatial manner. That is, the damage spread either by the dependency links (figure 5.10(a)) or connectivity links (figure 5.10(b)) with a characteristic length r or ζ, respectively. Specifically, the propagation of any local damage can directly spread only to a characteristic distance, leading to a similar spatial propagation phase diagram, figure 5.10(c).

In spatial networks, for certain parameter conditions to be detailed in subsequent subsections, cascading failures occur in a qualitatively unique manner compared to non-spatial interdependent networks. The key feature of this propagation can be illustrated by considering the microscopic cascade following the failure of an individual node. Consider what happens after the failure of node a_1 in network A. Suppose, its failure leads to other failures that cascade back to network A leading node a_2 to fail. For random networks, a_1 and a_2 will be two completely uncorrelated nodes chosen at random. However, in the case of two fully-spatial interdependent networks, the nodes a_1 and a_2 will be nearby (spatially correlated). When many nodes fail in the same spatial area of network A, the additional failures in the next cascade step will also be in the same area, and so on in further cascade steps. Thus, the damage during the cascading failures spreads locally, just like a forest fire, which is very different from the cascading processes in non-spatial networks, see figure 5.11. This growth of the damage is analogous to nucleation processes in phase transitions [30].

When researchers investigated the two fully-spatial models [27, 29] previously mentioned, they found that if there are numerous local failures in some region, a hole can form in the network. This hole then initiates a new type of cascade where at each stage of the cascade, additional failures occur primarily near the boundary of the hole. This leads the hole to grow until it consumes the entire system (see figure 5.11). The conditions leading to the initial formation of the hole can either be due to random failures or due to a geographically localized attack.

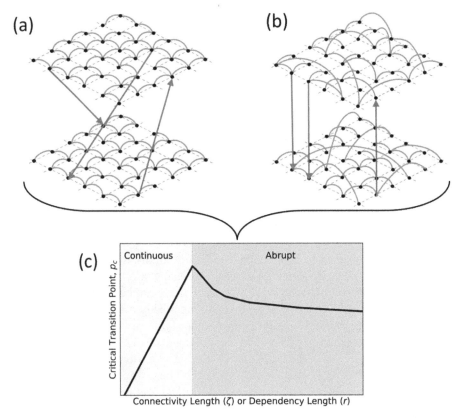

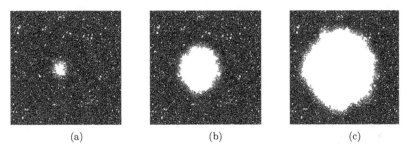

Figure 5.10. Similar effects of dependency length and connectivity length in a system of interdependent spatial networks. (a, b) Illustration of two models of fully-spatial interdependent networks. Blue links represent connectivity links within each spatially embedded network and red links represent directed inter-dependency relations between elements in the two networks. In (a) the connectivity links have the same length (ζ equals one lattice unit) and the lengths of the dependency links are taken from a distribution with finite scale (dependency length, r). In (b) the dependency relations are between elements at the same spatial location ($r = 0$) but the connectivity links have a characteristic length ζ. Finally, in (c) we show that both of these structures lead to the same phase diagram where there is a peak in the value of p_c, at which point the transition shifts from continuous (below a characteristic length at the peak of p_c) to abrupt (above this length).

Figure 5.11. Propagation of failures in fully-spatial interdependent networks. Here we show three snapshots (a), (b) and (c), of the failures in one network, which is part of a fully-spatial interdependent system. We see that a small hole of local failures propagates spatially outward in time. This leads an initially small area of failures to ultimately spread to the entire network, causing its complete collapse. Reprinted with permission from [27], copyright 2012 by the American Physical Society.

It the following subsections, we discuss in more detail the conditions where this occurs for each model.

5.5 Effect of dependency link length, the r-model

In this section we study the first example of a fully-spatial model of interdependent networks. In this model: (i) within each network nodes are connected only to the nodes in their spatial vicinity in a lattice structure, and (ii) the dependency links establishing the interdependence between the nodes in different networks are not random but have a maximal length r in each axis. A demonstration of r can be seen in figure 5.12.

This model consists of two identical square lattices A and B of linear size L and $N = L^2$ nodes with periodic boundary conditions. In each lattice, node A_i located at (x_i, y_i) in lattice A is connected to node B_j located at (x_j, y_j) in lattice B via a dependency link, under the constraint $|x_i - x_j| \leqslant r$ and $|y_i - y_j| \leqslant r$ (figure 5.12). The parameter r can be understood to represent the maximum distance that a resource from one network can travel to support a node in the other network. Note that the discussion in section 5.2 represents the limit of $r \to \infty$ (or $r = L$). It can be easily understood that the limiting case of $r = 0$ represents a system of two perfectly overlapping networks and therefore behaves identically to a single lattice under failures.

After removing a fraction of $1 - p$ nodes from one of the networks, there can arise random fluctuations such that the effective fraction of surviving nodes p in one region can be smaller than the overall average. Therefore, small clusters in this region may become isolated from the giant component and fail even when the entire lattice is still connected. This leads to a hole that propagates spatially outward as described in the previous section.

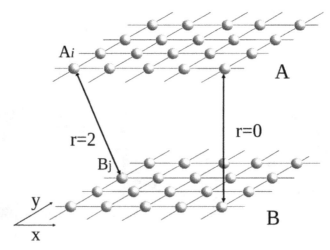

Figure 5.12. Interdependent lattices. Here, each node A_i in lattice A depends on a node B_j in lattice B via a dependency link, with the constraint that $|x_i - x_j| \leqslant r$ and $|y_i - y_j| \leqslant r$. Network A is shifted vertically for clarity. Reprinted with permission from [27], copyright 2012 by the American Physical Society.

5.5.1 Theoretical model of spatial failure propagation

In order to systematically study and understand the conditions for propagation of a local hole, we can consider the artificial case of propagation of a flat interface. To do so, after constructing the interdependent system in figure 5.12, we remove all nodes within distance r from one edge of lattice A. The only difference from our original system is that after random removal of a certain fraction of nodes, $1 - p$, we also eliminate the nodes in lattice A with coordinates distance $y_i \leqslant r$ to create an artificial flat damaged interface. Simulations show that the flat damaged interface freely propagates and that the interdependent lattice system totally collapses if $p < p_c^f(r)$, where $p_c^f(r)$ is approximately a linear function of r with $p_c^f(0) = p_c = 0.592\,7$, $p_c^f(r_f) = 1$, and $r_f \cong 38$. For $r > r_f$, the interface of the strip freely propagates through the system even when the lattice is completely intact, $p = 1$. This happens because the removed nodes of lattice A in the strip eliminate half of the nodes in lattice B with $y_j \leqslant r$. Thus, the effective concentration of nodes in lattice B linearly changes from p at distance r from the interface to $p/2$ at the edge of the interface. This is analogous to percolation in diffusion fronts, which was studied by Sapoval et al [31]. There is thus a certain distance from the interface $r_c = r(2p_c - p)/p$ that corresponds to the critical threshold of conventional percolation. If r_c is much larger than the typical cluster size in the range between p_c and $p/2$, all the nodes in lattice B will be disconnected and hence the interface will propagate freely. The interface will stop propagating if $r_c = \xi(p/2)$, i.e., at the connectedness correlation length [14, 21] when $p/2$ is less than p_c. We can evaluate the critical concentration p_c^f from the equation $\xi(p_c^f/2) = r(2p_c - p_c^f)/p_c^f$, which yields $r_f = \xi(1/2)/(2p_c - 1) = 41$ for the case of $p = 1$, where $\xi(1/2) = 7.6$ is obtained by numerical simulations of conventional percolation on a single lattice. This predicted value of r_f agrees well with simulations ($r_f \cong 38$). The propagation of the flat interface close to $p_c^f(r)$ is also similar to invasion percolation [14, 21], which is a fractal process with a vanishing number of active sites, and the average interface velocity approaches zero at $p_c^f(r)$, a characteristic of second-order phase transitions. Thus, the system completely collapses when (i) a flat interface exists and (ii) $p < p_c^f$. The conditions for flat interface propagation, $p_c^f(r)$, were obtained for the artificial model where the flat interface is initially created [27]. However, when the system is initiated by random failures, a flat interface may be created through random fluctuations on the lattice.

5.5.2 Cascades propagation due to random failures

What can we learn from the flat interface behavior for our original system with only initial random failures? When r is large, the system begins to locally disintegrate and, at $p < p_c^f$, a local cascade of failures is initiated. As soon as a hole of size r is formed, an interface appears in a low p regime, and freely propagates through the system— because p is already below the critical point p_c^f of the interface propagation. As a result, the interface will completely wipe out the remaining giant component (see figure 5.11). Thus, for large r, the transition is first order, meaning the system

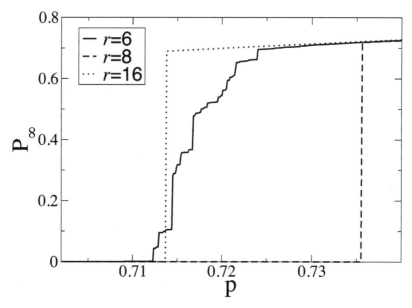

Figure 5.13. The fraction of nodes in the giant component as a function of p, the fraction of non-removed nodes in the initial attack. We perform the simulations of decreasing p by gradually removing additional nodes. For $r = 6$ the decrease of giant component occurs in multiple steps, characteristic of a second-order transition. For $r = 8$ and $r = 16$, the giant component may completely collapse at p_c by removal of even a single additional node, characteristic of a first-order transition. Reprinted with permission from [27], copyright 2012 by the American Physical Society.

experiences a complete breakdown or nothing, similar to spontaneous nucleation. At these conditions, the removal of even a single additional node may cause the disintegration of the entire system (figure 5.13).

The dynamics of the system becomes completely different for small r. In this case, when p_c^f is small, the characteristic size of the holes ξ_h in the percolation cluster is sufficiently large and there are many holes of size $\xi_h(p_c^f) > r$. Thus, the flat interface is formed before it begins to propagate. Once p approaches p_c^f from above, the interface begins to propagate simultaneously from all large holes in the system. It can spontaneously stop at any stage of the cascade, leaving any number of sites in the mutual giant component (figure 5.13). The average number of sites in the giant component will approach zero as p approaches p_c^f, subject to strong finite-size effects as in conventional second-order percolation. So for small r, the transition is second order, and $p_c^\mu(r) = p_c^f$ linearly increases with p (figure 5.14(a)).

Figure 5.14(a) describes how p_c changes non-monotonically with r, experiencing a sharp maximum at $r = r_{max}$. For $r < r_{max}$ the percolation phase transition is continuous of second order, while for $r > r_{max}$ it is abrupt and of a first-order nature. Figure 5.14(b) shows that at $r = r_{max}$, $\xi_h(p_c^f(r)) = r \approx 8$, and a flat interface will not spontaneously form. Thus p must be below $p_c^f(r)$ in order for a hole of size r to appear in the system. Once a single hole of that size appears, the flat interface will

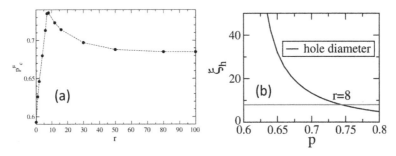

Figure 5.14. (a) The critical p_c as a function of dependency link length r. The critical p_c of mutual percolation increases for small dependency length, reaches a sharp maxima, and then gradually decreases to a finite value. The percolation transition is of second order for small dependency lengths and changes to first-order transition after the maximal p_c. (b) Diameter of the naturally occurring hole size ξ_h as a function of p. The hole size $\xi_h \approx 8$ at a value of $p_c = 0.744$, which agrees with the simulations. Reprinted with permission from [27], copyright 2012 by the American Physical Society.

freely propagate below its critical threshold wiping out the entire coupled network system, in a first-order transition. Note that $p_c^f(r_{max}) \approx 0.738 > p_c^\mu = 0.682\,7$. Thus, as r increases, $p_c^\mu(r)$ gradually decreases (figure 5.14(a)). This gradual decrease is caused by two factors. When r increases in the vicinity of just below r_{max}, smaller and smaller p is needed in order to create holes of size r. When p approaches p_c^μ, the system begins to undergo local cascades of failures if the average density in the region of size r falls below p_c^μ. The average over r^2 nodes of this region can deviate from the mean p on the order of a standard deviation $\sqrt{p(1-p)}/r$, thus making the disintegration possible if $p = p_c^\mu(r) \approx p_c^\mu + C/r$, where C is a constant. Note that $p_c^\mu(r)$ has a tendency to increase with the system size. The larger the system, the more likely a sufficiently large hole or a sufficiently large fluctuation in local density will lead to a local cascade of failures.

5.6 Effect of connectivity link length, the ζ-model

The effect of spatiality on the robustness of a pair of interdependent networks embedded in 2D space, can also be modeled by connectivity links in each layer having a variable length while the dependency links are between nodes at the same location ($r = 0$). This system can be regarded as a multiplex where a single set of nodes have two different sets of links between them [29]. The model is motivated by empirical measurements of real-world networks, where exponentially distributed link lengths with characteristic length ζ are found, as demonstrated in figure 5.15(a). By changing ζ, one can modulate the strength of the spatial embedding. When $\zeta \to \infty$, all link lengths are equally likely, the spatiality does not affect the topology and the system is like an infinite dimensional system. However, when $\zeta \to 0$ only short links are allowed, and the topology is overwhelmingly determined by the spatial embedding. It was found in [29] that, though longer links strengthen a single-layer network, they make a multi-layer network more vulnerable. Furthermore, similar to the r-model in figure 5.14(a), when ζ is longer than a certain critical value, ζ_c, abrupt, discontinuous transitions take

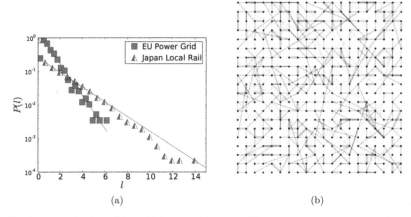

(a) (b)

Figure 5.15. The model of spatial multiplexes. (a) Real-world networks have been found to have an exponential distribution in the length of their links, thus having a characteristic link length. This is shown for both the EU power grid and the Japan train network. (b) An example of a spatial multiplex generated via the model. Note that there are two sets of links colored in green and blue, respectively. For a node to be functional it must be in the giant component of both the green and blue links. Image from [29], copyright EPLA 2016.

place, while for $\zeta < \zeta_c$ the transition is continuous, indicating that the risk of abrupt collapse can be eliminated if the typical link length is shorter than ζ_c, see figure 5.15(b). Below we present the ζ-model of [29] in more detail.

The spatial multiplex ζ-model

The ζ-model consists of a multiplex with two layers, each having the same number of nodes, a characteristic link length ζ and an average degree $\langle k \rangle$. To model connectivity links of characteristic length in each layer, we construct both layers as follows. We begin by assigning each node an (x, y) coordinate with integers $x, y \in [0, 1, \ldots, L)$. To construct the links in each layer, we select a source node at random with coordinates (x_0, y_0) and draw a length l with probability $P(l) \sim e^{-l/\zeta}$. We choose the permitted link length $(\Delta x, \Delta y)$ which is closest to fulfilling $l = \sqrt{\Delta x^2 + \Delta y^2}$, select one of the eight length-preserving permutations $(\Delta x \leftrightarrow -\Delta x, \Delta y \leftrightarrow -\Delta y, \Delta x \leftrightarrow \Delta y)$ uniformly at random and make a link to node (x_1, y_1) with $x_1 = x_0 + \Delta x$, $y_1 = y_0 + \Delta y$. This process is executed independently in each layer and is continued until the desired number of links $(N\langle k \rangle/2)$ is obtained. However, because they are constructed independently, the links in each layer are different and this disorder enables the critical behavior which we describe below.

When a fraction of $1 - p$ nodes fail in the network, cascades can emerge as is common in interdependent networks. As long as ζ is short, the cascades remain confined to small areas and do not trigger global collective failures. Because the cascade damage is limited, the mutual giant component size decreases continuously as the removal fraction increases, and the system undergoes a second-order percolation transition. If we consider a system with a larger ζ, above a critical

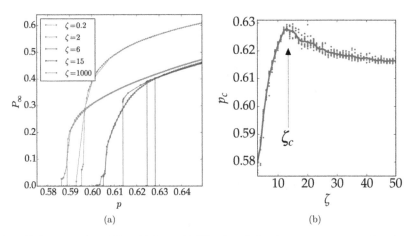

Figure 5.16. Robustness of spatial multiplexes. (a) The size of the giant component as a function of p for different values of ζ in the ζ-model. For $\zeta > \zeta_c$ the transition is seen to be abrupt, due to *nucleation* of the damage, while below it is continuous. (b) The value of the critical transition, p_c as a function of ζ. Where p_c reaches a peak, the transition changes from being second order (below) to first order (above). Image from [29], copyright EPLA 2016.

length ζ_c, then the initial failure holes can propagate, which leads to abrupt (first-order) transitions as shown in figure 5.16(a). This form of cascading failures is similar to that discussed earlier for the interdependent lattice networks when controlling the lengths of dependency links.

Just as for the case of the interdependent lattices, systems with intermediate spatial embedding ($\zeta \approx \zeta_c$) are more susceptible to cascading failures rather than those with greater or lower embedding as evidenced by the peak in the value of p_c and the transition from continuous to abrupt transition, figure 5.16(b).

5.7 Localized attacks

Spatially embedded interdependent networks have been studied in the previous sections under *random* attack, where a new kind of abrupt collapse was found. However, failures in spatially embedded systems are often not random but rather geographically localized to some region. We refer to such failures as 'localized attacks'. These localized attacks can be caused by natural disasters (e.g., the 2011 Tōhoku earthquake and tsunami) or malicious attacks (e.g., weapons of mass destruction). The robustness of a spatial complex system with dependencies under attack of this type has been considered in a series of papers [33–35], which we discuss in this section.

The key message from these papers is that spatially localized attacks on interdependent spatial networks can be far more damaging than random attacks. Specifically, there can exist a finite critical initial attack size above which the initial hole can spread to the entire system (figure 5.17(a), top). Notably, this hole need not be a fraction of the system, and in the limit of very large systems can even be a zero-fraction of the system as a whole. In other words, a localized attack can be far more damaging than a random attack of the same magnitude, i.e., the same number of initial failures (figure 5.17 bottom).

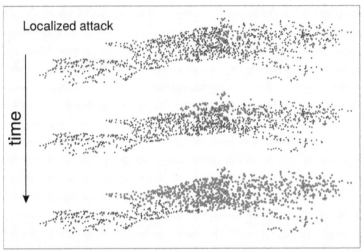

Figure 5.17. Temporal snapshots of damage propagation in systems with dependencies. Comparison between a *random* attack and a *localized* attack of the same size (37 nodes removed–less than 3% of the system) on a network with the same structural layout as the European power grid [32] with spatially constrained dependencies ($r \approx 500km$) between different nodes. The random attack does not cause substantial further damage while the localized attack (of the same number of nodes) triggers a cascade that overwhelms the entire system. (Number of nodes $N = 1254$, $\langle k \rangle = 2.88$). Reproduced from [33], CC BY 4.0.

Localized attacks have also been considered on random networks, though these results are not reviewed here since the nature of the resulting cascade is not spatial [36, 37].

5.7.1 Localized attacks on spatial networks with short-range dependency links

The first model of such localized attacks was presented in Berezin *et al* [33], which describes the effects of local attacks on an interdependent network system similar to that of section 5.5.

Specifically, the work in [33] uncovered a 'metastable' phase, in which there exists a critical damage size with radius r_h^c, above which localized damage will spread and destroy the entire system and below which the damage will remain in a small region (see figure 5.18(a) and (c)). This critical size is determined solely by system properties (such as degree of connectivity and typical dependency distance) and thus, in marked contrast to random failures, the critical radius does not scale with system size and constitutes a zero-fraction of the system in the limit of large systems ($N \to \infty$) (figure 5.18(d)).

We recall that based on universality principles, all single network models embedded in a space of the same dimension, have the same percolation critical

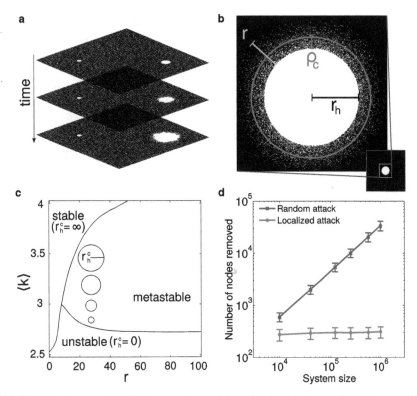

Figure 5.18. The effect of a localized attack on a system with dependencies. (a) Propagation of a localized attack in a system of two interdependent diluted lattices with spatially constrained dependency links between the lattices (only one lattice is shown here). The hole on the right is above the critical size r_h^c and spreads throughout the whole system while the hole on the left is below r_h^c and does not grow. (b) A localized circular failure of radius r_h in a lattice with dependency links of length up to r. Outside the hole, the survival probability of a node increases with the distance ρ from the edge. The parameter ρ_c denotes the distance from the edge of the hole at which the occupation probability is equal to the percolation threshold of a lattice without dependencies $p_c \approx 0.592\,7$ [14, 21]. (c) Phase diagram of two interdependent diluted lattices. Depending on the average degree $\langle k \rangle$ and dependency length r, the system is either stable, unstable or metastable. The circles illustrate the change (when $\langle k \rangle$ increases) of the critical attack size (r_h^c) that leads to system collapse in the metastable region. (d) As the system size increases, the minimal number of nodes which cause the system to collapse increases linearly for random attacks but stays constant (≈ 300) for localized attacks. This figure was obtained for a system of interdependent lattices diluted to $\langle k \rangle \approx 2.9$ and $r = 15$ (in the metastable phase-see (c)), with 1000 runs for each data point. Reproduced from [33], CC BY 4.0.

behavior [14, 21]. Therefore, any 2D network belongs to the same universality class as regular lattices. For tractability, the theory presented in this section is based on 2D lattices. However, the effects of localized attacks on systems with dependencies are the same for any system embedded in 2D space, as illustrated with the European power grid [35] in figure 5.17 and for synthetic power grids [38] in [33].

Berezin *et al* [33] modeled spatially embedded systems via square lattices diluted to degree $2.5 \leqslant \langle k \rangle \leqslant 4$. The dependencies between nodes are constrained to be less than a distance r (in lattice units). See [33] for details of system construction.

The localized geographical attack involves the removal of all nodes within a radius r_h from a random location in the system (see figure 5.18(b)). This triggers a cascade as in the other models of interdependent networks discussed previously.

It was found that the $(\langle k \rangle, r)$ plane can be divided into three distinct phases as seen in figure 5.18(c). In the stable phase, for any finite r_h the damage will remain localized and the system is resilient. In the unstable phase, the system spontaneously collapses even with $r_h = 0$ (no attack). In this phase, low $\langle k \rangle$ along with the dependencies leads to the emergence of holes which propagate (see figure 5.11) and destroy the system. Between these phases, the system is metastable. If a hole smaller than r_h^c is created, the system remains resilient. However, if a hole of size $\geq r_h^c$ is removed, it triggers a failure cascade, which destroys the entire system. This cascade is characterized by the spread of damage from the initial localized attack throughout the system (figure 5.18(a)). This metastability is analogous to the well known supercooling property of water in which water can be cooled well below its freezing point and remain in the liquid state until a disturbance triggers crystallization of a critical size (nucleation) and it grows and turns the water into ice [39].

If a system in the metastable phase experiences random attacks, the number of nodes that must fail in order that the system will collapse scales linearly with the system size (see figure 5.18(d)). Therefore, as $N \to \infty$, the number of nodes that must be removed scales as $O(N)$. However, if the attack is localized, the number of nodes required remains constant (figure 5.18(d)) and even a removal of a zero-fraction of nodes can trigger a cascade which destroys the entire system. Thus, increasing the size of the system does not increase its robustness with respect to localized attacks.

Predicting the value of r_h^c for a given system is an important question which we discuss below both theoretically and numerically. It was found in [33] that r_h^c is entirely determined by the average degree $\langle k \rangle$ and the typical dependency link length r. These are intensive system quantities and therefore r_h^c does not increase with system size (figure 5.18(d)). Figures 5.19(c) and (d) show how the critical damage size changes with regard to $\langle k \rangle$ and r, respectively, for a system of size $L \times L = 1000 \times 1000$. In figure 5.19(c) we can see that the metastable region covers a wider range of $\langle k \rangle$ values when r increases. In the metastable phase, for every r, r_h^c increases with $\langle k \rangle$ and jumps dramatically to the system size at a particular $\langle k \rangle$ value which represents the end of the metastable phase and the beginning of the stable phase. Furthermore, we see that this jump occurs at larger $\langle k \rangle$ values for larger r values (figure 5.19(c)). In figure 5.19(d), we see that above a certain minimum value, r_h^c has an approximately linear dependence on r in the metastable region. This is due to the fact that a larger r means that a given node's dependency link can be located farther away. Thus, the secondary damage from the localized attack is more dispersed and a larger attack size is required to initiate a cascade. Furthermore, it is found that the critical damage size takes a minimal value and the system is most susceptible to small local attacks when r is near the stable phase. Extensive numerical simulations of r_h^c over a high resolution grid of parameters $\langle k \rangle$ and r is shown in figure 5.19(a) and the theoretical prediction is given in figure 5.19(b). The theoretical arguments of the effect of $\langle k \rangle$ and r on r_h^c are presented below.

Since the metastable region spreads over a wide range of realistic values of r and $\langle k \rangle$, it is worth understanding how this transition takes place and how analytic

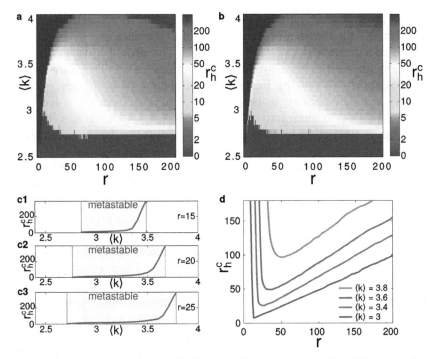

Figure 5.19. Dependence of the critical attack size r_h^c on the average degree $\langle k \rangle$ and the system dependency length r. The value of r_h^c as a function of the dependency length r and average degree $\langle k \rangle$ is represented as a log-scaled colormap for (a) simulation results and (b) analytic results. (c) c1,c2,c3, critical attack size r_h^c as a function of average degree $\langle k \rangle$ for three r values, determined via simulations. The curves represent moving along vertical lines from bottom to top in (a). The marked region represents the metastable region of $\langle k \rangle$ for each r. The area to the left of the shaded region is unstable and to the right is stable. (d) Critical attack size r_h^c as a function of system dependency length r for several $\langle k \rangle$ values, determined via simulations. The minimum of each curve represents the dependency length for which the system is most vulnerable to localized attacks. Reproduced from [33] CC BY 4.0.

calculations can predict the value of $r_h^c(r, \langle k \rangle)$. To do so, one first considers in detail the chain of events triggered by the geographically localized damage. When a hole of radius r_h is formed in the system, it can directly disable nodes up to a distance r from its edge due to the existence of dependency links of length $\leqslant r$ (see figure 5.18(b)). The probability that a given node is dependent on one of the removed nodes is highest at the edge of the hole and monotonously decreases with the distance from the edge, until it equals zero at distance r. To calculate this decrease, we need to calculate the probability that a node i depends on a node which was removed in the localized attack (figure 5.18(b)). This probability is determined by the area of intersection of two circles: the localized attack (with radius r_h) and the circle of maximal dependence (with radius r and center i). Assuming ρ is the distance from the edge of the hole, the gradient of occupation probability following an attack can be evaluated as

$$p(\rho, r, r_h, \langle k \rangle) = p_s(\langle k \rangle) \frac{I(r_h, r, \rho)}{\pi r^2},\tag{5.25}$$

where $p_s(\langle k \rangle)$ is the occupation concentration before the attack and $I(r_h, r, \rho)$ is the standard formula for the area of intersection of two circles of radius r and r_h with centers located a distance $\rho + r_h$ from each other. This probability describes a lattice concentration gradient in the form of an annulus of width r surrounding the removed hole, see figure 5.18(b). For a given set of system parameters $(r, r_h, \langle k \rangle)$ we can set $p(\rho)$ on the LHS of equation (5.25) to p_c of the lattice and solve for ρ. If a solution in the region of interest $(0 < \rho < r)$ exists, it corresponds to a distance ρ_c at which the lattice concentration will be equal to its critical value, p_c. The existence of such a point is a necessary but not a sufficient condition for the hole to propagate. Below ρ_c, the network forms clusters with a characteristic size $\xi_<(p)$, which diverges at p_c, where $\xi_<(p)$ is the connectedness correlation length for $p < p_c$ [14, 40]. Hence the sufficient condition for damage propagation is that the critical region $0 < \rho < \rho_c$ be wide enough for clusters of size $\xi_<(p)$ to form and break away.

The value of $\xi_<(p)$ is determined by the underlying topology and can thus be calculated from the percolation problem on a lattice without dependencies using an appropriate estimation for ρ in the $0 < \rho < \rho_c$ region. From equation (5.25), $p(\rho)$ increases monotonically over this region and an accurate evaluation solution for $\xi_<$ would require treating the full gradient percolation problem [31]. In Berezin *et al* [33], for simplicity it is assumed that $p = \bar{p}$ which is the average of $p(\rho)$ over the region of interest. Additionally, the removal of the hole causes secondary damage due to dependencies in the annulus and the concentration of the gradient is decreased by a factor of $g(r)$ which is calculated numerically and found to vary monotonically from 0.85 to 0.89 as a function of r. We can thereby estimate $\bar{p} = \int_0^{\rho_c} p(\rho)d\rho$. It is possible to evaluate $\xi_<$ following [14] as follows:

$$\xi_<^2 = \frac{1}{N_p} \sum_{(i,j)} |\mathbf{r}_i - \mathbf{r}_j|^2 \tag{5.26}$$

where (i, j) refers to nodes i and j which are in the same connected component, $\mathbf{r}_i$ is the coordinate and, N_p is the total number of such pairs of nodes. In order for the hole to propagate, the clusters which are of typical size $\xi_<$, need to be smaller than ρ_c. Therefore, the critical hole size (r_h^c) for any system is obtained from the self-consistent solution of

$$\xi_< = \rho_c, \tag{5.27}$$

where both sides are functions of r, r_h and p_s. Using these considerations, one can predict r_h^c for every set of (k, r) parameters as shown in figure 5.19(b). These theoretical results are in close agreement with the numerical simulations (figure 5.19(d)) for the value of r_h^c as well as its lack of scaling with system size (figure 5.18(d)).

Note that all parameters in the above scenario are local: nodes can have dependency links only up to length r, the connectivity links are tied to an underlying lattice structure with characteristic length of one unit in the model or are limited by length-cost in the real-world system and the attack is restricted to a hole of finite radius r_h. However, as shown above in figure 5.19(a) and (b), for a wide range of system parameters, this leads to a small finite damage that can yield a catastrophic cascade which destroys the entire system.

It is instructive to compare this process to a single spatially embedded network without dependencies. If a hole of any finite size is created in a lattice or other spatially embedded infinite network, it will have no effect on the overall system robustness. Only the trivial case of r_h approaching the system size L leads to system collapse. A similar argument holds with respect to dependency links which are not restricted in length. If a hole of size r_h (mass of order $\approx r_h^2$) is formed in one network, it will lead to random removal of a fraction r_h^2/N in the other network. Therefore, in the limit of large systems, the numerator remains constant while the denominator tends to infinity and we find that here too the localized attack will have negligible impact. Only when the dependency links are of limited length does this unique catastrophic damage spreading phenomenon arise.

Surprisingly, the localization of dependency opens the door for the spreading phenomenon which amplifies the local damage and leads to total system collapse. When a hole of radius r_h is removed from the system, the nodes that depend on them must be within a distance r of the hole. Thus the secondary damage is highly concentrated around the edge of the hole, leading to the creation of a damage front which propagates outwards, step by step. This is why the amount of damage caused per node removed is substantially higher when the damage is localized as compared with random removal (figure 5.18(d)). If $r \to \infty$ or $r \to 0$, this weakness would not exist because the secondary damage would spread everywhere uniformly or remain in place. Paradoxically, the highly localized topology of embedded interdependent networks enables relatively small localized attacks to cause catastrophic global damage.

Furthermore, it has been suggested [41] that the dependency model can be connected to the classical model of overload failures based on betweenness centrality [42, 43]. Essentially if the overload failures propagate at a nearly constant speed, this suggests a characteristic dependency distance between failures at one time and those at the next time. Similarly, since the speed of failure propagation varies with the tolerance parameter of the nodes, different lengths of dependency links can be mapped to different tolerances. Such a mapping is particularly useful for modelling since betweenness calculations require instense computations, whereas the model of interdependence is more efficient allowing larger systems to be studied. A further similarity to the overload model was found by Perez *et al* [44]. The authors found that similar to interdependent networks, there exists a localized critical radius above which cascades spread and the whole system collapses.

5.7.2 Localized attacks on spatial multiplexes

Later work studied localized attacks on the ζ-model of section 5.6 [29]. Recall that the model is a multiplex with exponential link-lengths distribution of connectivity links in each of the two layers, where ζ determines the connectivity link characteristic length and thereby the strength of the embedding in a manner analogous to r for the case of dependency link lengths. In contrast, the dependency links are local, meaning that a node in one lattice depends on a node in the other lattice in the same spatial location. In figure 5.20, we demonstrate the localized attack on the spatial multiplex model.

For localized attacks [34] on the spatial multiplex model, it was also found that for a broad range of parameters the system is metastable similar to figure 5.18(c) (where r is replaced by ζ), meaning that a localized attack larger than a critical size induces a cascade of failures that propagates from its center and encompasses the whole system, whereas a smaller localized attack does not spread [34]. Here we review both theory and simulations that predict the critical size of the initial local damage for the system to collapse. When the localized attack is above the critical size—the cascade initially takes place randomly within a disc of radius $\approx r_h$, and then it propagates spatially until consuming the entire system. This theory also identifies a new scaling exponent describing the critical nucleation (of damage) size.

In analyzing the damage spreading from localized attack on spatial multiplexes, different $\langle k \rangle$, ζ and r_h should be considered. Simulations showed that for a radius of attack below r_h^c the damage remains localized while above r_h^c the damage propagates radially and destroys the entire system. When calculating the critical attack size r_h^c for different $\langle k \rangle$ and ζ, as for the dependency model, there are the same three regions (similar to figure 5.21): stable (in red), unstable (in blue), metastable (between the above-mentioned regions).

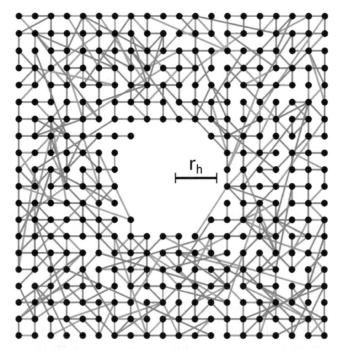

Figure 5.20. Demonstration of a spatially embedded multiplex network immediately after localized attack of radius r_h. The nodes are regular locations in 2D lattice while the links in each layer (purple and orange) have lengths that are exponentially distributed (equation (1.25)) with characteristic length $\zeta = 3$ and are connected at random. Reproduced from [34] CC BY 4.0. Copyright 2017 The Authors. Published by IOP Publishing Ltd on behalf of the Institute of Physics and Deutsche Physikalische Gesellschaft.

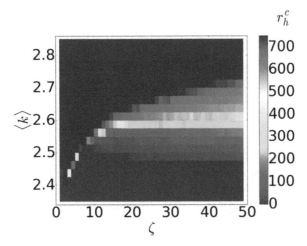

Figure 5.21. Phase diagram for localized attack on spatial multiplexes. This is in analogy with figure 5.18(c) where here only r is replaced with ζ. The color bar shows the size of r_h^c and in this figure $L = 1500$ with each point averaged over 5 runs. Reproduced from [34] CC BY 4.0. Copyright 2017 The Authors. Published by IOP Publishing Ltd on behalf of the Institute of Physics and Deutsche Physikalische Gesellschaft.

To understand the cascade analytically, one can consider the network as being composed of regions of size $\approx \zeta$ that are tiled on a 2D lattice, where each contains a random network. The localized attack of size r_h can then be approximated as a random attack of size πr_h^2 in an interdependent random network with $\sim \zeta^2$ nodes. Recall from chapter 3 that for interdependent random networks $p_c = k_c/\langle k \rangle$, where $k_c \approx 2.4554$ for $n = 2$.

Thus, critical attack size r_h^c near k_c can be predicted as follows:

$$\frac{\pi (r_h^c)^2}{\pi (a\zeta)^2} \cong 1 - \frac{k_c}{\langle k \rangle}, \tag{5.28}$$

from which,

$$\frac{r_h^c}{\zeta} \cong a \cdot \sqrt{1 - \frac{k_c}{\langle k \rangle}} \cong \frac{a}{k_c^{1/2}} \cdot \sqrt{\langle k \rangle - k_c}, \tag{5.29}$$

where a is the constant of proportionality for the effective random network (radius) size, which can be determined numerically. The r_h^c found here, is the minimal expected size of a circular hole (inside which all nodes are removed) that can destroy the entire random network within size $a\zeta$. However, since the tiled Erdős and Rényi sub-networks are also interconnected, the collapse propagates toward the surrounding sub-networks and the cascade propagates spatially.

In the limit of $\zeta \to L$, the multiplex can be well approximated as two interdependent random networks, and therefore r_h^c can be found according to:

$$\frac{\pi (r_h^c)^2}{L^2} \cong 1 - \frac{k_c}{\langle k \rangle}, \tag{5.30}$$

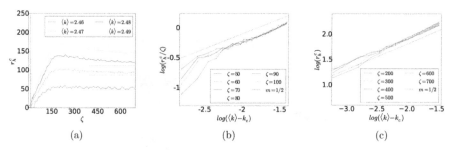

Figure 5.22. Simulations and theory of r_h^c in spatial multiplexes. (a) r_h^c as a function of ζ for four $\langle k \rangle$ values. The dotted lines represent the theory for the limits of ζ from equations (5.28) and (5.30), respectively. Plots of (b) $\log(r_h^c/\zeta)$ and (c) $\log(r_h^c)$ as a function of $\log(\langle k \rangle - k_c)$ for small and large ζ, with the scaling following an exponent of $\frac{1}{2}$ (as predicted in equations (5.29) and (5.31)) highlighted by the dotted line. Here $L = 2000$ and each point is averaged over at least 5 runs. Reproduced from [34] CC BY 4.0. Copyright 2017 The Authors. Published by IOP Publishing Ltd on behalf of the Institute of Physics and Deutsche Physikalische Gesellschaft.

from which,

$$r_h^c \cong \frac{L}{\sqrt{\pi}} \cdot \sqrt{1 - \frac{k_c}{\langle k \rangle}} \cong \frac{L}{\sqrt{\pi k_c}} \cdot \sqrt{\langle k \rangle - k_c}. \tag{5.31}$$

Figure 5.22(a) shows the results of equation (5.28) and equation (5.30) with $a \approx 9$ compared to simulations. More details about a and how its value can vary can be found in Vaknin *et al* [34].

For multiplex networks, near criticality, P_∞ follows the scaling $P_\infty \sim (\langle k \rangle - k_c)^\beta$. For the spatial multiplex ζ-model, it can be determined that r_h^c scales as $(\langle k \rangle - k_c)^{\frac{1}{2}}$, suggesting that $\frac{1}{2}$ is a critical exponent for r_h^c (equations (5.29) and (5.31)). Simulations shown in figures 5.22(b) and (c) support the existence of such a scaling relationship and the value of $\frac{1}{2}$.

In general, statistical physics has struggled to find evidence for universality beyond second-order transitions. This new scaling exponent, related to nucleation type processes, may provide an alternative approach which can be useful more generally outside of the field of networks of networks for understanding universality properties in critical phenomena associated with other first-order transitions involving nucleation processes [45, 46].

Overall, we find that localized attacks on spatial multiplexes of section 5.6 are quite similar to those on the dependency length discussed in the previous subsection. Both models demonstrate the existence of a metastable phase and highlight the significantly increased risks of localized attacks compared to random attacks.

5.7.3 Spatial multiplexes with community structure

A further model where localized attacks have been studied is a multiplex system containing both spatial embedding and community structure, see figure 5.23 [35]. Community structure, where groups of nodes are tightly connected to one another but less connected to nodes in other groups, is common in many networks [47].

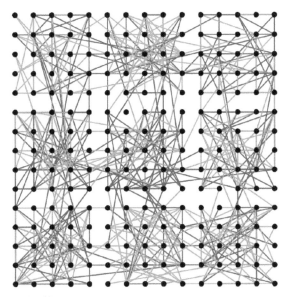

Figure 5.23. A schematic representation of the spatial-community model. The nodes are at the lattice sites of a two-dimensional square lattice of size $L \times L$ with $L = 15$. The system is constructed as $m \times m$ Erdős and Rényi networks. Here $m = 3$ and each community (random network) is of size $\zeta \times \zeta$ with $\zeta = 5$. The green and blue lines represent the links in the first and second layer of the multiplex, and are constructed independently of each other. Reprinted with permission from [35] CC BY 4.0.

In the case of infrastructure systems, this could arise from cities with densely connected infrastructure within the city, but with weaker connections outside of the city.

To model such a scenario, Vaknin *et al* [35] assumed two sets of links between nodes that are again placed at the sites of a square lattice of size $L \times L$. Each set of links begins with the formation of $m \times m$ Erdős and Rényi networks (communities) of size $\zeta \times \zeta$ where $\zeta = L/m$. These ER-type networks (communities) are laid out on a square lattice and nodes in one community can only connect to nodes within the community and to nodes in a neighboring community (see figure 5.23). *Intralinks* are defined as connecting pairs of nodes in the same community, while *interlinks* connect nodes in different, but only neighboring communities. Each node has a degree k_{inter} of interlinks a degree k_{intra} of intralinks, leading to a total node degree of $k_{\text{total}} = k_{\text{inter}} + k_{\text{intra}}$. Finally, the heterogeneity of the system is defined by the interconnectivity parameter

$$\alpha = k_{\text{inter}}/k_{\text{total}}. \tag{5.32}$$

This new model, is similar to the previous model in section 5.6 where all links have a characteristic length ζ, except that it adds heterogeneity due to the community structure with groups of nodes having dense connectivity among them. This heterogeneity is controlled by the parameter α.

The work by Vaknin *et al* [35] considered both analytically and via simulations, localized attacks on this model where nodes within a circular hole of size r_h are removed from the network. Here too, depending on the networks system parameters, there exists a critical radius r_h^c above which the damage spreads radially and the system collapses while below it remains resilient. For a network with certain values of L, ζ and $\langle k_{\text{total}} \rangle$, there are two regimes divided by a critical level of hetereogeneity, α_c. For $\alpha > \alpha_c$ the system is in a metastable regime, where a finite localized attack of a radius larger than r_h^c causes the system to collapse, while for $\alpha < \alpha_c$, the critical attack r_h^c is $\sim 0.5L$, i.e., the entire system must be removed.

This model has certain advantages compared to the previous models since the random structure of the communities enables theoretical analysis and use of certain forms of generating functions, see [35] for details. Furthermore, it reiterates the power of localized attack in yet another model involving both spatial embedding and community structure.

References

[1] Milo R, Shen-Orr S, Itzkovitz S, Kashtan N, Chklovskii D and Alon U 2002 Network motifs: simple building blocks of complex networks *Science* **298** 824–7

[2] Khanin R and Wit E 2006 How scale-free are biological networks *J. Comput. Biol.* **13** 810–8

[3] Cohen R, Erez K, Ben-Avraham D and Havlin S 2000 Resilience of the internet to random breakdown *Phys. Rev. Lett.* **85** 4626–8

[4] Dorogovtsev S N and Mendes J F F 2003 *Evolution of Networks: From Biological Nets to the Internet and WWW* (Oxford: Oxford University Press)

[5] Barthélemy M 2011 Spatial networks *Phys. Rep.* **499** 1–101

[6] Ren Y, Ercsey-Ravasz M, Wang P, González M C and Toroczkai Z 2014 Predicting commuter flows in spatial networks using a radiation model based on temporal ranges *Nat. Commun.* **5** 1–9

[7] Zeng G, Gao J, Shekhtman L, Guo S, Lv W, Wu J, Liu H, Levy O, Li D and Gao Z et al 2020 Multiple metastable network states in urban traffic *Proc. Natl. Acad. Sci.* **117** 17528–34

[8] Helbing D 2001 Traffic and related self-driven many-particle systems *Rev. Mod. Phys.* **73** 1067

[9] Gallos L K, Makse H A and Sigman M 2012 A small world of weak ties provides optimal global integration of self-similar modules in functional brain networks *Proc. Natl. Acad. Sci.* **109** 2825–30

[10] Dehmamy N, Milanlouei S and Barabási A-L 2018 A structural transition in physical networks *Nature* **563** 676–80

[11] Daqing L, Kosmidis K, Bunde A and Havlin S 2011 Dimension of spatially embedded networks *Nat. Phys.* **7** 481–4

[12] Penrose M 2004 *Random geometric graphsOxford Studies in Probability* vol 5 (Oxford: Oxford University Press) ch 5

[13] Bonamassa I, Gross B, Danziger M M and Havlin S 2019 Critical stretching of mean-field regimes in spatial networks *Phys. Rev. Lett.* **123** 088301

[14] Bunde A and Havlin S 1991 *Fractals and Disordered Systems* (New York: Springer)

[15] Bashan A, Berezin Y, Buldyrev S V and Havlin S 2013 The extreme vulnerability of interdependent spatially embedded networks *Nat. Phys.* **9** 667–72

[16] Gao J, Buldyrev S V, Havlin S and Stanley H E 2011 Robustness of a network of networks *Phys. Rev. Lett.* **107** 195701

[17] Bashan A, Parshani R and Havlin S 2011 Percolation in networks composed of connectivity and dependency links *Phys. Rev.* E **83** 051127

[18] Gao J, Buldyrev S V, Stanley H E, Xu X and Havlin S 2013 Percolation of a general network of networks *Phys. Rev.* E **88** 062816

[19] Parshani R, Buldyrev S V and Havlin S 2011 Critical effect of dependency groups on the function of networks *Proc. Natl. Acad. Sci.* **108** 1007–10

[20] Den Nijs M P M 1979 A relation between the temperature exponents of the eight-vertex and q-state potts model *J. Phys.* A **12** 1857–68

[21] Stauffer D and Aharony A 1994 *Introduction to Percolation Theory* (Boca Raton, FL: CRC Press)

[22] Buldyrev S V, Parshani R, Paul G, Stanley H E and Havlin S 2010 Catastrophic cascade of failures in interdependent networks *Nature* **464** 1025–8

[23] Nienhuis B 1982 Analytical calculation of two leading exponents of the dilute potts model *J. Phys.* A **15** 199–213

[24] Parshani R, Buldyrev S V and Havlin S 2010 Interdependent networks: reducing the coupling strength leads to a change from a first to second order percolation transition *Phys. Rev. Lett.* **105** 048701

[25] Shekhtman L M, Berezin Y, Danziger M M and Havlin S 2014 Robustness of a network formed of spatially embedded networks *Phys. Rev.* E **90** 012809

[26] Gao J, Buldyrev S V, Havlin S and Stanley H E 2012 Robustness of a network formed by n interdependent networks with a one-to-one correspondence of dependent nodes *Phys. Rev.* E **85** 066134

[27] Li W, Bashan A, Buldyrev S V, Stanley H E and Havlin S 2012 Cascading failures in interdependent lattice networks: the critical role of the length of dependency links *Phys. Rev. Lett.* **108** 228702

[28] Waxman B M 1988 Routing of multipoint connections *IEEE J. Sel. Areas Commun* **6** 1617–22

[29] Danziger M M, Shekhtman L M, Berezin Y and Havlin S 2016 The effect of spatiality on multiplex networks *Europhys. Lett.* **115** 36002

[30] Stanley H E 1971 *Introduction to Phase Transitions and Critical Phenomena* (New York: Oxford University Press)

[31] Rosso M, Gouyet J F and Sapoval B 1985 The fractal nature of a diffusion front and the relation to percolation *J. Phys. Lett.* **46** 149–56

[32] Zhou Q and Bialek J 2005 Approximate model of european interconnected system as a benchmark system to study effects of cross-border trades *IEEE Trans. Power Syst.* **20** 782–8

[33] Berezin Y, Bashan A, Danziger M M, Li D and Havlin S 2015 Localized attacks on spatially embedded networks with dependencies *Sci. Rep.* **5** 1–5

[34] Vaknin D, Danziger M M and Havlin S 2017 Spreading of localized attacks in spatial multiplex networks *New J. Phys.* **19** 073037

[35] Vaknin D, Gross B, Buldyrev S V and Havlin S 2020 Spreading of localized attacks on spatial multiplex networks with a community structure *Phys. Rev. Res* **2** 043005

[36] Shao S, Huang X, Stanley H E and Havlin S 2015 Percolation of localized attack on complex networks *New J. Phys.* **17** 023049

[37] Yuan X, Shao S, Stanley H E and Havlin S 2015 How breadth of degree distribution influences network robustness: Comparing localized and random attacks *Phys. Rev.* E **92**

[38] Hines P, Blumsack S, Sanchez E C and Barrows C 2010 The topological and electrical structure of power grids *Proc. of the 43rd Hawaii Int. Conf. on System Sciences*

[39] Debenedetti P G and Stanley H E 2003 Supercooled and glassy water *Phys. today* **56** 40

[40] Coniglio A 1982 Cluster structure near the percolation threshold *J. Phys.* A **15** 3829

[41] Zhao J, Li D, Sanhedrai H, Cohen R and Havlin S 2016 Spatio-temporal propagation of cascading overload failures in spatially embedded networks *Nat. Commun.* **7** 1–6

[42] Motter A E 2004 Cascade control and defense in complex networks *Phys. Rev. Lett.* **93** 098701

[43] Simonsen I, Buzna L, Peters K, Bornholdt S and Helbing D *et al* 2008 Transient dynamics increasing network vulnerability to cascading failures *Phys. Rev. Lett.* **100** 218701

[44] Perez I A, Vaknin D, La Rocca C E, Buldyrev S V, Braunstein L A and Havlin S 2021 Cascading failures in isotropic and anisotropic spatial networks induced by localized attacks and overloads arXiv:2112.11308

[45] McGraw R and Laaksonen A 1996 Scaling properties of the critical nucleus in classical and molecular-based theories of vapor-liquid nucleation *Phys. Rev. Lett.* **76** 2754

[46] Talanquer V 1997 A new phenomenological approach to gas-liquid nucleation based on the scaling properties of the critical nucleus *J. Chem. Phys.* **106** 9957–60

[47] Girvan M and Newman M E J 2002 ommunity structure in social and biological networks *Proc. Natl. Acad. Sci.* **99** 7821–6

[48] Zhou D, Bashan A, Cohen R, Berezin Y, Shnerb N and Havlin S 2014 Simultaneous first- and second-order percolation transitions in interdependent networks *Phys. Rev.* E **90** 12803

Chapter 6

Further features in networks of networks

Besides topology and percolation, networks of networks also show a lot of new features and properties that are significantly different from those of single networks. Examples include global structural properties and dynamical processes, such as synchronization [1–4], robustness [5, 6], cooperation [7], transport [8–10], epidemic spreading [11] and interdependent superconducting networks [12] that change dramatically on a network of networks as opposed to networks in isolation. In this chapter we summarize recent progress in networks of networks in synchronization and dynamics, various network structures, overlap and intersimilarity, and diverse percolation processes.

6.1 Synchronization and dynamics on networks of networks

An important topic in network science has been understanding how the network structure impacts dynamical processes that occur on the networks [13–17]. In the context of networks of networks, a particularly interesting question is how the dynamics on individual networks is impacted by the global network of network structure. In [18] the authors describe how choosing adequate connector links between networks may promote or hinder a particular network's structural and dynamical properties. The different connecting strategies have consequences on the distribution of network centrality, population dynamics, or spreading processes. The importance of designing adequate connection strategies is illustrated with examples of social and biological systems. The structure of many real-world systems is best captured by networks consisting of several interaction layers [19]. Understanding how a multilayered structure of connections affects the synchronization properties of dynamical systems evolving on top of it is a highly relevant endeavor in mathematics and physics. It has potential applications in several real-world systems, such as power grid engineering and neural dynamics. The authors in [19] propose a general framework to assess the stability of the synchronized state in networks with multiple interaction layers, deriving a necessary condition that generalizes the master stability

6-1

function approach. They validate their method by applying it to a network of Rössler oscillators with a double layer of interactions and show that highly rich phenomenology emerges from this. It includes cases where the stability of synchronization can be induced even if both layers would have individually induced unstable synchrony, an effect arising from the multilayer structure of the interactions among the oscillators in the network. Additional work has explored diffusion dynamics [20], finding the overlapping structures of interconnected systems [21] and identifying optimal levels of coupling to enhance information spreading [22]. Other work explored spreading models on multilayer networks to understand epidemics [23]. In reference [24], the authors introduced a framework to intertwine dynamical processes of different nature, each with its own distinct network topology, using a multilayer network approach. As an example of collective phenomena emerging from the interactions of multiple dynamical processes, they study a model where neural dynamics and nutrient transport are bidirectionally coupled in such a way that the allocation of the transport process at one layer depends on the degree of synchronization at the other layer, and vice versa. The framework can be applied to other cases where two or more dynamical processes interact, such as synchronization, opinion formation, information diffusion, or disease-spreading.

Despite advances in structural interdependence, modeling interdependence and other interactions between dynamic systems have proven elusive. Danziger *et al* [25] define a broadly applicable dynamic dependency link and develop a general framework for both interdependent and competitive interactions between general dynamic systems. They apply the framework to studying interdependent and competitive synchronization in multilayer oscillator networks and cooperative/competitive contagions in an epidemic model, as shown in figure 6.1. Using a mean-field theory verified through numerical simulations, they find explosive transitions and rich behavior absent in percolation models, including hysteresis, multi-stability, and chaos. The framework presented there provides a powerful new way to model and

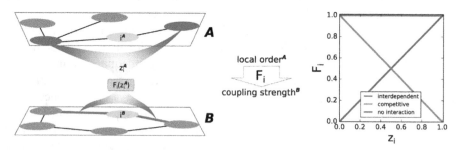

Figure 6.1. Dynamic interdependence and competition. Left panel: the local order z_i^A of node i in network A is determined by the state of its neighbors. This then modifies the effective strengths of the incoming links of node i in network B, according to a function $F_i^{A \rightarrow B}$ of z^A which can reflect cooperative, antagonistic or other interactions. Note that there are typically interactions in the opposite direction as well, i.e. $F_i^{B \rightarrow A}$, which have not been drawn here for the sake of clarity. Right panel: summary of the dynamical interaction strategies considered in the main text. We will adopt linear coupling functions, randomly distributed among nodes, modeling hence interdependence (blue), competition (green), and no interactions (red). Reproduced from [24], copyright 2019 with permission of Springer.

understand many of the interacting complex systems surrounding us. The first physical and controlled realization of interdependent networks that has been studied both experimentally and theoretically is the interdependent superconducting networks [12]. It was found that while each layer shows a continuous superconducting transition, the thermally coupled (interdependent interaction) system shows an abrupt, first order superconducting transition similar to the interdependent percolation system.

Much research has been carried out to explore the structural properties and vulnerability of complex networks. Of particular interest are abrupt dynamic events that cause networks to fail irreversibly. However, in many real-world phenomena, such as brain seizures in neuroscience or sudden market crashes in finance, a significant part of the damaged network is capable of spontaneously becoming active again after an inactive period of time. The process often occurs repeatedly. To model this marked network recovery, Majdandzic *et al* [26] examine the effect of node recoveries and stochastic contiguous spreading and find that they can lead to the spontaneous emergence of macroscopic phase flipping phenomena. As the network is finite and stochastic, for certain parameter values, a large fraction of active nodes switch back and forth between the two network collective modes characterized by high and low network activity. Furthermore, the system exhibits an assertive hysteresis behavior analogous to phase transitions near a critical point. Reference [26] also presents real-world network data showing phase switching behavior in accord with the predictions of the model. Systems composed of many interacting dynamical networks, such as the human body with its biological networks or the global economic network consisting of regional clusters, often exhibit complex collective dynamics. Three fundamental processes that are typically present are failure, damage spread, and recovery. Majdandzic *et al* [27] developed a model for such interdependent systems and found a rich phase diagram that becomes increasingly complex as the number of interacting networks increases. In the simplest example of two interacting networks, they find two critical points, four triple points, ten allowed transitions, and two 'forbidden' transitions, as well as complex hysteresis loops, as shown in figure 6.2. Remarkably, the triple points play a dominant role in constructing an optimal repairing strategy in damaged interacting systems. To test their model, they analyzed an example of real interacting financial networks and found evidence of rapid dynamical transitions between well-defined states, in agreement with the model predictions.

6.2 Different network structures in networks of networks

6.2.1 Clustering

Huang *et al* [28] developed an analytical method for studying how clustering within the networks of a system of interdependent networks affects the system's robustness. They find that clustering significantly increases the vulnerability of the system, which is represented by the increased value of the percolation threshold p_c in interdependent networks. Shao *et al* [29] generalized the study of clustering of a fully coupled pair of networks and applied it to a partially interdependent network of networks

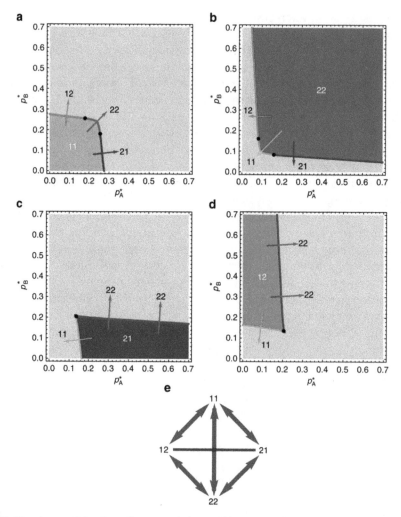

Figure 6.2. Four layers of the phase diagram and the transitions connecting them. (a) Region of 11 state, in green. Possible transitions are $11 \to 12$ (orange line), $11 \to 22$ (blue line) and $11 \to 21$ (purple line). This layer of the phase diagram has two triple points, marked as black points. (b) Region of 22 state (blue), with two triple points and three transitions. (c) Region of 21 state (purple), with two transition lines (to 11 and 22 state) that merge in a critical point. (d) Region of 12 state (orange), with two transition lines (to 11 and 22 state) that merge in a critical point. (e) Illustration showing states (11, 12, 21 and 22) with allowed (blue arrows) and forbidden (red line) transitions. Reproduced from [27] CC BY 4.0.

with clustering within the network components. They showed, both analytically and via simulations, how clustering within networks affects the percolation properties of interdependent networks, including the percolation threshold, the size of the giant component, and the critical coupling point at which the first-order phase transition changes to a second-order phase transition as the coupling between the networks is reduced.

6.2.2 Node correlations

Zhou *et al* [30] investigated the effects of topology on failure propagation for a model system consisting of two interdependent networks. They found that the internal node degree–degree correlations in each of the two interdependent networks significantly changes the critical threshold of failures that triggers the total disruption of the coupled network system. Specifically, they find that the assortativity (i.e., the likelihood of nodes with similar degree to be connected) within a single network reduces the robustness of the entire system. Reis *et al* studied the cascading failures of correlated networks of networks and developed a theory based on a recursive set of equations [77]. They tested these predictions with two different systems of brain connectivity based on functional magnetic resonance imaging (fMRI) data. They showed that if interconnections are provided by network hubs, and the connections between networks are moderately convergent, the system of networks is stable and robust to failure [77].

6.2.3 Directed networks

Liu *et al* [31] developed a general theoretical framework for analyzing the breakdown of interdependent directed networks with, or without, in-degree and out-degree correlations, and apply it to real-world international trade networks. Surprisingly, they found that the robustness of interdependent heterogeneous networks increases, whereas that of interdependent homogeneous networks with strong coupling strengths decreases with in-degree and out-degree correlations. They further extended the approach to networks of networks (NON) and developed an analytical framework for examining the robustness of networks formed from directed networks of different topologies, as shown in figure 6.3. They use it to predict the phase transitions that occur during node failures and to generate the phase diagrams of a number of different systems, including tree-like and random regular (RR) networks of directed Erdős–Rényi (ER) networks and scale-free networks.

6.2.4 Community structure

Additional network models that have been considered in the study of robustness of NON are those that incorporate community structure within each network. Shekhtman *et al* [32] focused on the robustness of interdependent networks in the case of initial attacks on the so-called 'interconnected nodes' that link between communities [33]. The authors also assumed that nodes within a community were dependent on other nodes within the same community in the other network. This could be the case for example of cities where each city has its own infrastructure system with many connections within the city though few outside and the infrastructures within each city depend on each other. The authors found that, depending on the model parameters, the system can undergo two transitions as it first separates the communities from each other and then after more attacks, each community collapses. Later work [34] extended this to a case of hierarchical networks, where there exist communities within each community. In that case, the system could have even more than two transitions as each layer of the hierarchy could separate as more failures were induced.

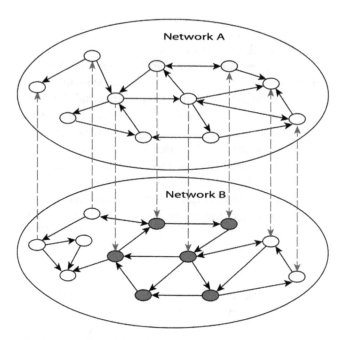

Figure 6.3. Schematic demonstration of interdependent directed networks and the final giant strongly connected component (GSCC). Directed networks A and B are coupled by directed dependency links (dotted lines) with a no-feedback condition. A dotted directed line from node *i* in one network to node *j* in the other network indicates that a failure of node *i* will cause node *j* to fail. The yellow nodes (network A) and red nodes (network B) indicate the final GSCC at the completion of cascading failure. Reproduced from [31], copyright 2016 The Authors. Published by the National Academy of Sciences.

6.3 Overlap and intersimilarity in networks of networks

Multiplexes may display an increased fragility concerning the single layers that constitute them [35]. The similarity represented by the overlap of the links in different layers is an essential factor in determining their robustness. Parshani *et al* [36] studied the effect on the the resilience of two coupled real-world networks, the world wide airline network and the port networks. Cellai *et al* [37, 38] and Hu *et al* [39] show analytically and via simulations that the overlap among layers, also called intersimilarity, can significantly improve the robustness of interdependent multiplex systems and change the critical behavior of the percolation phase transition in a complex way. Therefore, these studies represent an important step for characterizing the robustness properties of real multiplexes, and it is also likely to impact the dynamic processes occurring on multiplex systems. Bianconi [40] also characterized microcanonical and canonical multiplex ensembles satisfying respectively hard and soft constraints and discussed how to construct multiplexes in these ensembles. Furthermore, Bianconi [40] provided the expression for the entropy of these ensembles that can be useful to address different inference problems involving multiplexes. The above studies present a scenario for studying multiplex ensembles and characterize null models of multiplexes including a significant global or local overlap of the links in the different layers. The theoretical analysis can be extended to more complex situations, such as to directed and weighted networks, and the application of the entropy of multiplexes for extracting information from multiplex data sets.

6.4 Different percolation processes in networks of networks

6.4.1 Bond percolation

Beside site percolation studies, Hackett *et al* [41] presented an analytical approach for bond percolation on multiplex networks and use it to determine the expected size of the giant connected component and the value of the critical bond occupation probability in these networks. They advocate the relevance of these tools to the modeling of multilayer robustness and contribute to the debate on whether any benefit is to be yielded from studying a full multiplex structure as opposed to its monoplex projection, especially in the seemingly irrelevant case of a bond occupation probability that does not depend on the layer. Furthermore, Chen *et al* [42] extended this work to the general case of network of networks. The authors found that, for interdependent ER networks, in contrast to site percolation, for bond percolation p_c varies nonlinearly with the inverse of average degree. They also found, for the case of bond percolation where initial link failures occur in all layers, that the critical percolation threshold is the same as that of site percolation, but the behavior of the giant component above p_c is different.

6.4.2 Reinforced nodes

Percolation theory assumes that only the largest connected component is functional. However, in reality, some components that are not connected to the largest component can also function through alternative support. Thus, Yuan *et al* [43] generalized percolation theory by assuming a fraction of reinforced nodes that can function and support their components, although they are disconnected from the largest connected component, as shown in figure 6.4. They studied the resilience of interdependent networks in the presence of reinforced nodes. They found that a small fraction of reinforced nodes significantly increase the resilience and prevent cascading failures and the abrupt collapse. Including reinforced nodes implies actually reducing centralization (decentralization) of the system, i.e., in order to function there is no need to be connected to the giant component. A recent study by Kfir-Cohen *et al* [44] found how to optimize the resilience of a modular network via reinforced nodes.

6.4.3 Combining *k*-core and interdependent percolation

Another study [45] considered *k*-core percolation, which can also induce cascading failures, and analyzed how a combined model of interdependent networks and *k*-core percolation may lead to substantial failures from both cascading processes. Panduranga *et al* [45] studied the complete phase diagram of the percolation

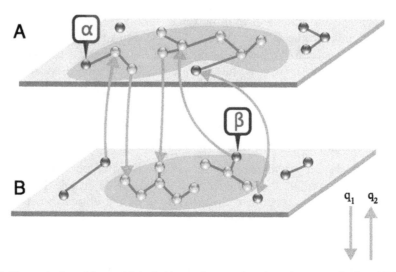

Figure 6.4. Demonstration of the model studied here, where two interdependent networks A and B have gone through cascading failures and reached a steady state. The yellow arrows represent a fraction $q_{A(B)}$ of nodes from network A(B) depending on nodes from network B(A) for critical support. Reinforced nodes α and β (purple circles) are nodes that survive and also support their clusters, even if the clusters are not connected to the largest component. These nodes have, for example, their own power support or alternative communication routes that can support themselves and their surrounding nodes. Some regular nodes (green circles) survive the cascading failures, whereas some other regular nodes (red circles) fail. Note that the clusters of circles in the shaded purple areas constitute the functioning component studied in our model. Reproduced from [43], copyright 2017 The Authors. Published by the National Academy of Sciences.

transition as the average local k-core threshold is tuned and the coupling between networks is varied. They found that the phase diagram of the combined processes is very rich and includes novel features that do not appear in the models studying each of the processes separately [35, 46]. Furthermore, at certain fixed interdependencies, the percolation transition changes from first order to second order, to two-stage and to first order as the k-core threshold is increased.

6.5 Multimodal transportation

Transportation dynamics on networks can be, in general, interpreted as the flow of elements from origin nodes to destination nodes [47]. Multimodal transportation can be mathematically abstracted as transportation dynamics on a multiplex structure. Note that routings on the multilayer transportation system are substantially different concerning routings on single-layer transportation networks. In the multilayer case, each system's location (e.g., geographical location) has various replicas representing each system's entry point using the different transportation media. Whether flow of people, fluids, or electrical currents, these systems can be characterized by specifying the topology of the underlying network [8], a source-sink distribution, and a dynamic (figure 6.5). For example, to redistribute the traffic flow on a low-speed transportation network (e.g., railway network), we can

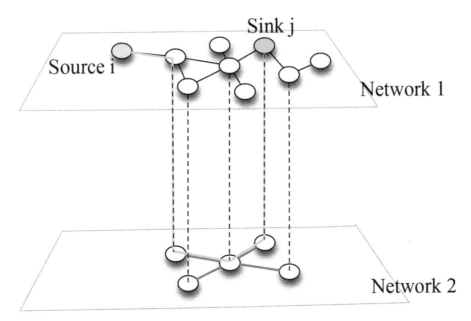

Figure 6.5. A system made of two coupled networks where the nodes of network 2 form a subset of the nodes of network 1. Edges of network 1 are shown in black, edges of network 2 are shown in red (gray offline), and nodes in common to both networks are considered to be coupled (shown by dashed lines). Highlighted in green (gray offline), we represent a path between two nodes, the 'source' i and the 'sink' j. Reprinted with permission from [8], copyright 2012 by the American Physical Society.

build a new high-speed network (e.g., airline network) in the active regions or between the high-flow stations [48]. Until recently, some researchers have studied multimodal transportation dynamics, such as enhancing the traffic capacity of multilayer networks to alleviate traffic congestion. For example, Sole-Ribalta *et al* [47] developed a standardized transportation model on multilayer networks, showing that the structure of multiplex networks induces congestion because of the unbalance of shortest paths between layers. Morris and Barthelemy [8] analyzed the two-layered traffic networks, showing that network utility relies subtly on the interplay between the coupling and randomness in the source-sink distribution. Du *et al* [49] explored the influence of transfer costs on the transportation system's capacity, showing that an optimized allocation of transfer costs is achievable by adopting a particle swarm optimization algorithm to increase the total capacity of the infrastructure. Unlike monolayer networks, the structures of multilayer networks bring new challenges when designing effective congestion alleviation strategies. On the one hand, the topology of multilayer networks can relieve the traffic congestion of one layer, but it may cause congestion on the other layer simultaneously [47]. Although establishing high-speed transportation networks can improve the traffic capacity of low-speed networks, we would be confronted with another problem: how to redistribute the traffic flow reasonably. Previous investigations about traffic congestion on multilayer networks mainly focused on the differences between layers [8], or the local structure of nodes within the same layer [50], without considering both of them. Consequently, Gao *et al* [48] considered the role of nodes' local structures on the microlevel and the different transporting speeds of layers in the macrolevel, and developed an effective traffic-flow assignment strategy on multilayer networks.

6.6 Games on networks of networks

Evolutionary game theory focuses on how individuals choose to cooperate in order to achieve a particular desired outcome [51]. A classic example is the prisoner's dilemma where two criminal conspirators must decide whether to inform on one another, and if both stay silent they each benefit, yet each individual has an incentive to inform on his partner to improve his personal outcome [52]. Research on networks has considered evolutionary games on networks and how the topology could impact optimal strategies and other aspects [7, 53–56]. Researchers of game theory on networks have also expanded such works to multilayer networks [57], finding in particular that degree assortativity can improve cooperation in certain circumstances [58] though biases in payoffs in the different layers are still crucial [59].

6.7 Controllability of a network of networks

One fundamental goal of our effort for understanding complex networks is to control the complex systems [60]. Due to the large scales and complexities, controlling complex networks still remains a significant challenge. One pioneer work about network control is to understand the structural control of complex networks [60], triggering another breakthrough in the research of complex networks [61–65]. In recent years, network control has been extended to understand the functionality of brain [66, 67], global risks [68], airline delay [69]. It is necessary to take into account temporal information of the connections when the interaction events are not evenly distributed over time, but have nontrivial temporal correlations. Pósfai *et al* [70] and Pan *et al* [71] applied the controllability theory to temporal networks. Due to the wide applications of multiplex networks, the structural controllability theory has been applied to multiplex networks [72–76]. Pósfai *et al* [70] focus on the problem of the controlling two-layer multiplex and multi-time-scale networks with one-to-one interlayer coupling. In figure 6.6, we illustrate the concept of two-layered network control. They investigate practically, the relevant case when the control signal is applied to the nodes of one layer. By identifying the underlying mechanisms that connect time-scale difference and controllability for a simplified model, they provide crucial insight into clarifying how our ability to control real interacting complex systems is affected by a variety of sources of complexity.

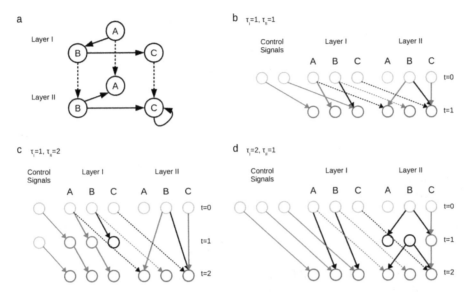

Figure 6.6. Structural controllability of two-layer multiplex networks. (a) A two-layer network. (b-c) To determine N_i, we construct the dynamic graph representing the time evolution of the system from $t_0 = 0$ to $t_1 = \max(\tau_{\mathrm{I}}, \tau_{\mathrm{II}})$. The system is controllable only if all nodes at t_1 (blue) are connected to nodes at t_0 or nodes representing control signals (green) via disjoint paths (red). (b) In the case of no time-scale separation ($\tau_{\mathrm{I}} = \tau_{\mathrm{II}} = 1$), each disjoint control path consists of a single link, yielding $N_i = 2$. (c) If Layer I updates twice as frequently as Layer II ($\tau_{\mathrm{I}} = 1$, $\tau_{\mathrm{II}} = 2$), we are allowed to inject control signals at time steps $t = 0$ and 1, reducing the number of inputs to $N_i = 1$. (d) On the other hand, if Layer II is faster ($\tau_{\mathrm{I}} = 2$, $\tau_{\mathrm{II}} = 1$), Layer II needs to support longer control paths, yielding $N_i = 3$. Reprinted with permission from [76], copyright 2016 by the American Physical Society.

6.8 Interdependent superconducting networks

Network theory, although originated and motivated by physics problems, such as percolation theory, have been mainly applied in many other disciplines, rarely in physical systems. Very recently, it has been shown that the concept of interdependent networks can be applied to develop interdependent physics systems showing novel phase transition features. A system that was studied theoretically and experimentally is the interdependent superconducting networks, showing that while each layer when measured separately, has a second order (continuous) superconductor–conductor phase transition with some temperature, when both layers are coupled via thermal interactions, the coupled system exhibits an abrupt first order transition [12].

References

[1] Um J, Minnhagen P and Kim B J 2011 Synchronization in interdependent networks *Chaos* **21** 025106

[2] Della Rossa F, Pecora L, Blaha K, Shirin A, Klickstein I and Sorrentino F 2020 Symmetries and cluster synchronization in multilayer networks *Nat. Commun.* **11** 1–17

[3] Zhang H, Zhang W and Gao J 2019 Synchronization of interconnected heterogeneous networks: the role of network sizes *Sci. Rep.* **9** 1–12

[4] Zhuang J, Cao J, Tang L, Xia Y and Perc M 2018 Synchronization analysis for stochastic delayed multilayer network with additive couplings *IEEE Trans. Syst. Man Cyber. Syst* **50** 4807–16

[5] Gao J, Buldyrev S V, Havlin S and Stanley H E 2011 Robustness of a network of networks *Phys. Rev. Lett.* **107** 195701

[6] Gao J, Buldyrev S V, Stanley H E and Havlin S 2012 Networks formed from interdependent networks *Nat. Phys.* **8** 40–8

[7] Gómez-Gardenes J, Reinares I, Arenas A and Mario Floría L 2012 Evolution of cooperation in multiplex networks *Sci. Rep.* **2** 620

[8] Morris R G and Barthelemy M 2012 Transport on coupled spatial networks *Phys. Rev. Lett.* **109** 128703

[9] Lazaridis F, Gross B, Maragakis M, Argyrakis P, Bonamassa I, Havlin S and Cohen R 2018 Spontaneous repulsion in the $A + B \rightarrow 0$ reaction on coupled networks *Phys. Rev. E* **97** 040301

[10] Danziger M M, Bashan A and Havlin S 2015 Interdependent resistor networks with process-based dependency *New J. Phys.* **17** 043046

[11] Granell C, Gómez S and Arenas A 2013 Dynamical interplay between awareness and epidemic spreading in multiplex networks *Phys. Rev. Lett.* **111** 128701

[12] Bonamassa I, Gross B, Laav M, Volotsenko I, Frydman A and Havlin S 2022 Interdependent superconducting networks arXiv:2207.01669

[13] Barzel B and Barabási A 2013 Universality in network dynamics *Nat. Phys.* **9** 673–81

[14] Cornelius S P, Kath W L and Motter A E 2013 Realistic control of network dynamics *Nat. Commun.* **4** 1942

[15] Hens C, Harush U, Haber S, Cohen R and Barzel B 2019 Spatiotemporal signal propagation in complex networks *Nat. Phys.* **15** 403–12

[16] Harush U and Barzel B 2017 Dynamic patterns of information flow in complex networks *Nat. Commun.* **8** 1–11

[17] Nishikawa T, Sun J and Motter A E 2017 Sensitive dependence of optimal network dynamics on network structure *Phys. Rev. X* **7** 041044

[18] del Genio C I, Gómez-Gardenes J, Bonamassa I and Boccaletti S 2016 Synchronization in networks with multiple interaction layers *Sci. Adv.* **2** e1601679

[19] Buldú J M, Sevilla-Escoboza R, Aguirre J, Papo D and Gutiérrez R 2016 Interconnecting networks: the role of connector links *Interconnected Networks* (Berlin: Springer) pp 61–77

[20] Gomez S, Diaz-Guilera A, Gomez-Gardeñes J, Perez-Vicente C J, Moreno Y and Arenas A 2013 Diffusion dynamics on multiplex networks *Phys. Rev. Lett.* **110** 028701

[21] De Domenico M, Lancichinetti A, Arenas A and Rosvall M 2015 Identifying modular flows on multilayer networks reveals highly overlapping organization in interconnected systems *Phys. Rev. X* **5** 011027

[22] Tejedor A, Longjas A, Foufoula-Georgiou E, Georgiou T T and Moreno Y 2018 Diffusion dynamics and optimal coupling in multiplex networks with directed layers *Phys. Rev. X* **8** 031071

[23] Sahneh F D, Scoglio C and Van Mieghem P 2013 Generalized epidemic mean-field model for spreading processes over multilayer complex networks *IEEE/ACM Trans. Netw* **21** 1609–20

[24] Nicosia V, Sebastian Skardal P, Arenas A and Latora V 2017 Collective phenomena emerging from the interactions between dynamical processes in multiplex networks *Phys. Rev. Lett.* **118** 138302

[25] Danziger M M, Bonamassa I, Boccaletti S and Havlin S 2019 Dynamic interdependence and competition in multilayer networks *Nat. Phys.* **15** 178

[26] Majdandzic A, Podobnik B, Buldyrev S V, Kenett D Y, Havlin S and Stanley H E 2014 Spontaneous recovery in dynamical networks *Nat. Phys.* **10** 34–8

[27] Majdandzic A, Braunstein L A, Curme C, Vodenska I, Levy-Carciente S, Stanley H E and Havlin S 2016 Multiple tipping points and optimal repairing in interacting networks *Nat. Commun.* **7** 1–10

[28] Huang X, Shao S, Wang H, Buldyrev S V, Stanley H E and Havlin S 2013 The robustness of interdependent clustered networks *Europhys. Lett.* **101** 18002

[29] Shao S, Huang X, Stanley H E and Havlin S 2014 Robustness of a partially interdependent network formed of clustered networks *Phys. Rev. E* **89** 032812

[30] Zhou D, Stanley H E, D'Agostino G and Scala A 2012 Assortativity decreases the robustness of interdependent networks *Phys. Rev. E* **86** 066103

[31] Liu X, Eugene Stanley H and Gao J 2016 Breakdown of interdependent directed networks *Proc. Natl. Acad. Sci.* **113** 1138–43

[32] Shekhtman L M, Shai S and Havlin S 2015 Resilience of networks formed of interdependent modular networks *New J. Phys.* **17** 123007

[33] Shai S, Kenett D Y, Kenett Y N, Faust M, Dobson S and Havlin S 2015 Critical tipping point distinguishing two types of transitions in modular network structures *Phys. Rev. E* **92** 062805

[34] Shekhtman L M and Havlin S 2018 Percolation of hierarchical networks and networks of networks *Phys. Rev. E* **98** 052305

[35] Buldyrev S V, Parshani R, Paul G, Eugene Stanley H and Havlin S 2010 Catastrophic cascade of failures in interdependent networks *Nature* **464** 1025–8

[36] Parshani R, Rozenblat C, Ietri D, Ducruet C and Havlin S 2010 Inter-similarity between coupled networks *Europhys. Lett.* **92** 68002

[37] Cellai D, López E, Zhou J, Gleeson J P and Bianconi G 2013 Percolation in multiplex networks with overlap *Phys. Rev. E* **88** 052811

[38] Cellai D, Dorogovtsev S N and Bianconi G 2016 Message passing theory for percolation models on multiplex networks with link overlap *Phys. Rev. E* **94** 032301

[39] Hu Y, Zhou D, Zhang R, Han Z, Rozenblat C and Havlin S 2013 Percolation of interdependent networks with intersimilarity *Phys. Rev. E* **88** 052805

[40] Bianconi G 2013 Statistical mechanics of multiplex networks: entropy and overlap *Phys. Rev. E* **87** 062806

[41] Hackett A, Cellai D, Gómez S, Arenas A and Gleeson J P 2016 Bond percolation on multiplex networks *Phys. Rev. X* **6** 021002

[42] Chen S, Gao Y, Liu X, Gao J and Havlin S 2020 Robustness of interdependent networks based on bond percolation *Europhys. Lett.* **130** 38003

[43] Yuan X, Hu Y, Stanley H E and Havlin S 2017 Eradicating catastrophic collapse in interdependent networks via reinforced nodes *Proc. Natl. Acad. Sci* **114** 3311–5

[44] Kfir-Cohen Y, Vaknin D and Havlin S 2021 Optimization of robustness based on reinforced nodes in a modular network *Europhys. Lett.* **137** 41003

[45] Panduranga N K, Gao J, Yuan X, Eugene Stanley H and Havlin S 2017 Generalized model for k-core percolation and interdependent networks *Phys. Rev.* E **96** 032317

[46] Baxter G J, Dorogovtsev S N, Goltsev A V and Mendes J F F 2011 Heterogeneous k-core versus bootstrap percolation on complex networks *Phys. Rev.* E **83** 051134

[47] Solé-Ribalta A, Gómez S and Arenas A 2016 Congestion induced by the structure of multiplex networks *Phys. Rev. Lett.* **116** 108701

[48] Gao L, Shu P, Tang M, Wang W and Gao H 2019 Effective traffic-flow assignment strategy on multilayer networks *Phys. Rev.* E **100** 012310

[49] Du W-B, Zhou X-L, Jusup M and Wang Z 2016 Physics of transportation: towards optimal capacity using the multilayer network framework *Sci. Rep.* **6** 1–8

[50] Tan F, Wu J, Xia Y and Tse Chi K 2014 Traffic congestion in interconnected complex networks *Phys. Rev.* E **89** 062813

[51] Nowak M A and May R M 1992 Evolutionary games and spatial chaos *Nature* **359** 826–9

[52] Masuda N and Aihara K 2003 Spatial Prisoner's dilemma optimally played in small-world networks *Phys. Lett.* A **313** 55–61

[53] Szolnoki A, Perc M and Danku Z 2008 Towards effective payoffs in the Prisoner's dilemma game on scale-free networks *Physica* A **387** 2075–82

[54] Gómez-Gardenes J, Campillo M, Floría L M and Moreno Y 2007 Dynamical organization of cooperation in complex topologies *Phys. Rev. Lett.* **98** 108103

[55] Santos F C, Pacheco J M and Lenaerts T 2006 Evolutionary dynamics of social dilemmas in structured heterogeneous populations *Proc. Natl. Acad. Sci.* **103** 3490–4

[56] Gómez-Gardenes J, Gracia-Lázaro C, Floria L M and Moreno Y 2012 and Yamir Moreno. Evolutionary dynamics on interdependent populations *Phys. Rev.* E **86** 056113

[57] Wang Z, Wang L, Szolnoki A and Perc M 2015 Evolutionary games on multilayer networks: a colloquium *Eur. Phys. J.* B **88** 1–15

[58] Duh M, Gosak M, Slavinec M and Perc M 2019 Assortativity provides a narrow margin for enhanced cooperation on multilayer networks *New J. Phys.* **21** 123016

[59] Wang Z, Szolnoki A and Perc M 2012 Evolution of public cooperation on interdependent networks: the impact of biased utility functions *Europhys. Lett.* **97** 48001

[60] Liu Y-Y, Slotine J-J and Barabási A-L 2011 Controllability of complex networks *Nature* **473** 167–73

[61] Gao J, Liu Y-Y, R M D'souza and Barabási A-L 2014 Target control of complex networks *Nat. Commun.* **5** 1–8

[62] Jia T, Liu Y-Y, Csóka E, Pósfai M, Slotine J-J and Barabási A-L 2013 Emergence of bimodality in controlling complex networks *Nat. Commun.* **4** 1–6

[63] Yan G, Ren J, Lai Y-C, Lai C-H and Li B 2012 Controlling complex networks: how much energy is needed? *Phys. Rev. Lett.* **108** 218703

[64] Liu X and Pan L 2014 Detection of driver metabolites in the human liver metabolic network using structural controllability analysis *BMC Syst. Biol.* **8** 1–17

[65] Liu X, Pan L, Stanley H E and Gao J 2017 Controllability of giant connected components in a directed network *Phys. Rev.* E **95** 042318

[66] Yan G, Vértes P E, Towlson E K, Chew Y L, Walker D S, Schafer W R and Barabási A-L 2017 Network control principles predict neuron function in the caenorhabditis elegans connectome *Nature* **550** 519–23

[67] Towlson E K, Vértes P E, Yan G, Chew Y L, Walker D S, Schafer W R and Barabási A-L 2018 *Caenorhabditis elegans* and the network control framework—FAQS *Philos. Trans. R. Soc.* B **373** 20170372

[68] Brissette C, Niu X, Jiang C, Gao J, Korniss G and Szymanski B K 2021 Heuristic assessment of choices for risk network control *Sci. Rep.* **11** 1–8

[69] Niu X, Jiang C, Gao J, Korniss G and Szymanski B K 2021 From data to complex network control of airline flight delays *Sci. Rep.* **11** 1–10

[70] Pósfai M and Hövel P 2014 Structural controllability of temporal networks *New J. Phys.* **16** 123055

[71] Pan Y and Li X 2014 Structural controllability and controlling centrality of temporal networks *PloS One* **9** e94998

[72] Nie S, Wang X and Wang B 2015 Effect of degree correlation on exact controllability of multiplex networks *Physica* A **436** 98–102

[73] Yuan Z, Zhao C, Wang W-X, Di Z and Lai Y C 2014 Exact controllability of multiplex networks *New J. Phys.* **16** 103036

[74] Rajaei R, Bagheri A, Ramezani A, Cornelius S P and Gao J 2018 Designing pinning network controllability for interdependent dynamical networks *2018 Annual American Control Conference (ACC)* (Piscataway, NJ: IEEE) 3478–83

[75] Menichetti G, Dall'Asta L and Bianconi G 2016 Control of multilayer networks *Sci Rep.* **6** 1–8

[76] Pósfai M, Gao J, Cornelius S P, Barabási A-L and D'Souza R M 2016 Controllability of multiplex, multi-time-scale networks *Phys. Rev.* E **94** 032316

[77] Reis S D S *et al* 2014 Avoiding catastrophic failure in correlated networks of networks *Nat. Phys.* **10** 762–7

CPSIA information can be obtained
at www.ICGtesting.com
Printed in the USA
BVHW010448271022
649776BV00003B/15